ONE UP

Sarah Ford

ONE UP

A WOMAN IN ACTION
WITH THE SAS

HarperCollins*Publishers*

HarperCollins*Publishers*
77–85 Fulham Palace Road,
Hammersmith, London W6 8JB

Published by HarperCollins*Publishers* 1997

Copyright © Sarah Ford 1997

The author asserts the moral right to
be identified as the author of this work

A catalogue record for this book is
available from the British Library

ISBN 0 00 255819 X

Set in Janson by
Rowland Phototypesetting Ltd,
Bury St Edmunds, Suffolk

Printed and bound in Great Britain by
Caledonian International Book Manufacturing Ltd, Glasgow

For my mother,
whose strength of character has
made me who I am

CONTENTS

List of Illustrations   ix

Acknowledgements   xi

Prologue: All Senses Alert   1

1   Our Mam   19

2   Getting Out   38

3   An Obsessive Regime   51

4   Maximum Disruption   84

5   Covert Attraction   109

6   Across the Water   139

7   'Zero Sierra Roger'   176

8   On Permanent Standby   203

9   Final Flight   223

Epilogue: Close Protection   253

Glossary   271

ILLUSTRATIONS

My brother Dean and me, aged three and two.

Dean and me plotting to catch birds in the back yard of Ashton Street.

Us four girls with our prized possessions.

First school photograph. I'm ten and deeply protective of the little 'uns.

With five kids, every day was wash day for our Mam.

So proud! Immaculate in my Wrens uniform five weeks after leaving home, October 1983.

Training at HMS *Daedalus* to become an AEM.

Aged twenty. A skinhead was to replace my quiff within a few weeks.

Protecting my scooter from the frost while sharing a hovel with Dean and Tel at HMS *Heron*, Yeovil.

Receiving my N.I. Medal from the boss of 45 Commando RM, whilst practising my cheesy Rupert grin.

'Don't worry, lads. I'll get supper ready.' Me on one of the many pre-Det training sessions.

Across the water in summer 1990. South Det geeks posing in front of our Gazelle.

'Right lads, listen up!' Teaching the admin staff basic firearms techniques.

Luke and me at a regimental dinner in 1990, before things began to fall apart.

After signing out my sexy legs I was propping up South Det bar waiting for a lift to Belfast.

Congratulating Taff on numerous hours of flying time. I was with him for most of them!

The South Det lads and me down at Ballykinler range keeping our skills up to scratch.

The horror of our lucky escape. More operators are killed across the water in road traffic accidents than by enemy action.

Practising debussing skills with my HK53.

Knackered! After I'd worked around the clock on surveillance serials, my basha didn't offer too many home comforts.

My watercolour painting of weary troops returning from war.

Posing up the Mourne Mountains on a much-needed day away from the compound.

Jock after running me ragged across the mountains.

Me and Joe during the ill-fated skiing trip to Bavaria.

My partner Jed enjoying a day off at one of Ulster's beautiful tourist spots, Strangford Lough.

Tooled up with my 9mm Browning, HK53, Op Gracie and a bag of maps after a routine aerial surveillance job.

Official Det memorabilia, quoting St Luke.

ACKNOWLEDGEMENTS

I owe a huge debt of gratitude to Jane, for coaxing out my story over countless hours. She turned facts into feelings, got to grips with the complex technical jargon of Special Forces, and put herself through late nights and long days to make this project a reality. Thank you to Jack, who researched and supplied additional military material and checked the manuscript for accuracy. I am also grateful to my agent a go-getter with unsurpassed negotiating skills, and to Richard, for his encouragement and suggestions.

Additionally, I would like to extend a personal thank-you to John (you know who you are) for being a genuine friend and suggesting I tell my story, and also to my dear friends Jill and Graham for their much appreciated help and support.

Owing to the sensitivity of the contents of this book, the manuscript was submitted to the Ministry of Defence prior to publication. At their request some changes were made to the text – including altering the names of individuals and places – in order to protect the work of the unit, who play a key role in the fight against terrorism.

It is not the critic who counts, not the man who points out how the strong man stumbled, or where the doer of the deed could have done better.

The credit belongs to the man who is actually in the arena, whose face is marred by dust and sweat and blood, who strives valiantly, who errs and comes short again and again, because there is no effort without error and shortcoming, who does actually strive to do the deeds, who knows the great enthusiasms and spends himself in a worthy cause, who at best, knows in the end the triumph of high achievement, and at worst, if he fails, at least fails while daring greatly.

His place shall never be with those cold and timid souls who knew neither victory nor defeat.

THEODORE ROOSEVELT

ALL SENSES ALERT

WE WERE KILLING TIME in the romper room, sorting out our holsters and flicking through mail. There was a litter of mugs and week-old coffee rings on the central table, and the musty smell of stale cigarette smoke. It was 9 a.m., but it might as well have been midnight – the blinds were down, and the only available light came from a flickering fluorescent tube. I reached into my locker and slid out my 9mm Browning Hi-Power pistol from amongst the usual stuff: earpiece, spare ammunition, Tampax and trusty nailfile – I was always tearing my fingers to shreds. Next to the row of lockers was a weapons rack. Normally I'd reach into my slot for my Heckler & Koch 53 like everyone else, but today I was only taking the Browning. I loaded up the magazines, one in the gun and two spares in my mag pouches. They each held thirteen rounds, but I only ever put in twelve. By not filling the magazine to capacity I was cutting down on the slight risk of a stoppage caused by the overloaded spring. Having a stoppage during a contact would not be a good day out.

We always loaded our weapons in the romper room. The green army have a designated loading/unloading bay, so if they have an ND (negligent discharge) the bullet embeds itself in a sand bunker, rather than slicing through the cardboard-thin walls and perhaps slotting an operator. But Special Forces have their own way of doing things.

The romper room was on the second floor of a gloomy Porta-kabin which was twenty feet high, sixty feet long and as narrow as a railway carriage. Beneath us, the bleeps (electricians) hung out doing their work, fitting radios into the vehicles. On our floor were the (intelligence) ops room, boss's office, DSM's office, briefing room and int room. The Portakabin was one of eleven units, including several brick accommodation blocks, housed inside a vast barn-like building on the edge of a security forces base in County Antrim. It was a rough, tough environment, with few concessions to comfort. I lived in a basha, my own small Portakabin, just outside the building. It had no interior decoration, just an old blanket slung across the window to stop randy colleagues snooping and to repel the twin irritations of petrol fumes and heli noise. For eight months this had been my home, one that I shared with the Troop (22 SAS) and my colleagues in 14 Int, known as the Walts (short for Walter Mittys). The Troop are across the water to deal with the terrorist threat. We exist to prepare the groundwork.

This was no fastball. Paul, the ops officer, had told us the previous night about a planned RV (rendezvous) between two known members of the Provisional IRA. An SB tout (Special Branch terrorist informer) had given us the information, and the writing was on the wall – literally. A plastic dry-marker board had been penned in the night before with the surveillance team names for Operation Spear: Jed, Kurt, Greg, Jack, Connor, Sarah.

Jed, also known as Alf (alien life-form), was my partner. An ex-Royal Engineer from London, he was one of the best operators in the province, as well as a great laugh, and I'd learned a lot from him. We'd gelled from the start, and he was well aware of the benefits of having a woman on the team. I'd been lucky to get partnered with him; some of the other guys were closet or even overtly sexist. Jed had a brain like a computer and knew every player (suspected terrorist), their associates, and even their car make, model and registration number. He was six foot tall, heavy-set with short black hair – not bad-looking, really – and always rattled through everything he had to say, usually faster than his brain could operate. He was famed for being a messy eater; there were always bits of food hanging off him.

I would be taking Op Remus, the video car, into the target area of Dungannon/Coalisland. After the operation the video footage would add to our library of terrorist activity. The TOG (time on the ground) was set for 1030 hours. We'd had a quick briefing the night before, so we knew the score.

Paul interrupted our friendly banter. 'Right. Basically, lads, this is what's happening. From intelligence received we know that Baldy Quinn will be meeting up with Seamus McAmee at lunchtime. As you know, they're both known players, but not usually associated. We don't know where the meeting will be held, so we're going to cover both options.'

'Ah, fucking business as usual then,' said Jed with a laugh. Everyone grunted. We'd been here before.

'Sarah, can you cover Baldy with Op Remus?' I already knew from last night's briefing that this would be my task, but it was still phrased as a question. We were always asked to do tasks, rather than told. It was just the way it was. The guys on the ground make decisions, not the people in the ops room.

'Yes, it's sorted and ready to go. Did we get the spare tapes?'

He nodded. 'They're in the ops room.'

Driving the video car into the estates and parking it so the camera can record suspected terrorists' movements was one of the tasks I was given frequently, especially in the bad-arse areas. Being a female gave me an advantage over the lads in that role. I could act a bit dizzy and get away with it. It wouldn't look out of the ordinary for a woman to shunt a car back and forth or to park badly, half on the kerb. If you see a woman faffing with a car you just think, 'Stupid old trout.' She'd be fulfilling expectations. A bloke, however, would swiftly be spotted as a bit of a dickhead if he dithered about getting the video car into position. And across the water it's all about blending into the environment as naturally as possible. All you want to be is the nondescript woman at whom no one looks twice. That's why I'd dyed my hair blonde but kept my roots black. All the women on the estates had abortionate hair-dye jobs, so I blended in a treat with my council-estate fashion sense. At least, that's what I told the lads when the colour was growing out.

One of the bleeps swung through the door and chucked the tapes at me. Paul was still filling us in, informal as ever. 'Jed, you go with

Sarah to Dungannon. Connor, have you sussed out a good OP [observation post] position?'

'Well, as good as we're going to get on that estate. I'm going up by the football ground. I'll have a clear view of Baldy's front door, but without my round-the-corner eyes I can't see his back yard.'

'OK. Kurt, Greg and Jack, can you cover the options in Coalisland?'

'No probs, mate,' said Kurt. 'I know a good spot, but I ain't telling any of you bastards where it is.'

Most lay-ups were common knowledge, but sometimes you'd find your own sneaky little place which you wouldn't want to share. Frequently it's a wind-up, though. Greg quickly grabbed the chance to give Kurt a well-deserved slagging.

'Hope it's better than your lay-up position in Cookstown last month. If you get compromised and have to dye your hair again you'll be in the same league as Baldy Quinn, and suing the MoD for your alopecia.'

Too true! Twenty-two-year-old John – aka Baldy – Quinn was halfway through a protracted legal action against the ministry. He claimed his bare scalp had been caused by the stress of constant police questioning. Everyone knew he was a player – in fact Baldy was the officer in charge of the IRA's ASU (active service unit) in Cappagh – but the law dictated he had to be caught actually committing a terrorist act. In the meantime he was quite happy to clog up the courts with his bogus personal injury claims. Anyone, even an unconvicted terrorist, has the right to due process, but it's annoying to see them exploiting the courts in this way. Unfortunately, it isn't uncommon.

After the brief we donned our personal radios. I had a choice of rigs. In bad weather I'd wear a jacket with the comms equipment concealed inside. It was well used; the province attracts 90 per cent of the UK's rainfall. But on that rare mild day I'd stick out like a nun in a whorehouse if I went foxtrot (on foot) in winter wear. The boys had an easier time of it. Rain or shine, they could stick their radio on their inner thigh under baggy jeans, or wear a vest inside their T-shirt and stash the comms equipment in there, next to their chest. They had a natural flat patch to stow things, but I was restricted to a six-inch space between my boobs and waist. At the end of the day, if all you're wearing is jeans and T-shirt, it's a lot more practical to conceal the radio in a handbag.

I'd spent a productive morning down at the local market at Nutts Corner, where the majority of stallholders were Indians with incongruous Northern Irish accents, and haggled over a cheap black imitation-leather number. Back in the barn I'd spent a concentration-soaked morning threading the mike and the antennae up through the strap. In the main compartment I stowed the slimline radio and next to it, in the zippered side pocket, I'd stuck down the pressle (transmitting button) with a Velcro tab. The pressle is slightly smaller than a matchbox. You press it and your whispers are picked up by the microphone in the handbag strap. Whenever I wanted to transmit I'd simply lay my hand on the bag. It was very neat, and I was delighted with my customised handiwork.

I swung the bag over my left shoulder so I could keep my firing hand free. It meant that all I had to conceal on my body was the pistol. I picked up an IWB (inside the waistband) holster and threaded it through my belt so it sat inside my jeans, fastened the belt tightly and slid in the pistol. Next, I picked out my small flesh-coloured earpiece from a leather pouch in my locker. On top of it is a tiny cap which flips up, and inside is the battery. It makes a constant hiss which drives you nuts after a while. You end up having to change ears if you're out on a job for long.

I was wearing jeans, not too scruffy, not too posh. They were appropriately geeky, with the name of an Asian clothing manufac-turer no one had ever heard of emblazoned on them. I had a pair of brown boots which were very High Street, and a T-shirt with some long-faded design.

We all bundled downstairs to the vehicles. I'd already done my comms checks and tested the video equipment inside Remus to make sure it was operating smoothly. I'd also given the vehicle, a grey – in both senses of the word – Cavalier, the once-over. Oil, water, tyres, lights, and engine cut-out switch were working fine.

It had an average amount of road dirt on it. Not squeaky clean, but you didn't want cobwebs hanging off it either. After you'd washed it you'd put a bit of dirt back on by doing a few handbrake turns in the compound. It didn't have any dents or distinguishing features.

We were keen to get out on the ground, but you didn't want to be the first out of the barn; it meant you had to open the compound gate. Far better to hang back and let someone else do it for you.

Out on the main camp it was a bright, late-summer day. I stuck my foot to the floor and spun the wheels. That was part of the daily ritual: operators never just brake when we can skid to a halt, never just turn a corner when we can pull a handbrake turn. Caught up in such a masculine environment, these *faux* heroics felt utterly commonplace.

'Zero Sierra out on green,' I said as I turned right out of the camp and onto a quiet country lane. Our comms were secure, but code is quicker to interpret and cuts down on air-time – consequently every road, operator, vehicle, building etc. has a code-word. Sierra was my call-sign, Zero was the ops room. You minimise what you say on the net so you don't clog it up . I could hear the team telling the ops officer back in the camp where they were heading. The ops officer would acknowledge by saying 'Zero roger.' The ops room needed to know where we were at any given moment. Their job was a bit like air traffic control. 'Sierra towards blue,' I said as I turned right. While driving I was switched on to vehicle comms. Personal comms are only used when you go foxtrot.

At blue one-four the other three peeled off towards Coalisland. Jed, Connor and I continued along the motorway and came off at the next junction – blue one-five – heading towards Dungannon. When we arrived, Connor turned left towards the football ground.

As Jed and I approached the target estate I pulled over into a layby. Washing was gusting on a line in a cramped back garden over the adjacent fence. Somehow I just couldn't picture myself bogged down in the weekly wash. I could already feel the delicious sensation of adrenaline building up as Jed did a gentle drive-through of the area and past my insertion point. I needed to know if the option was OK, and he was acting as my eyes, seeing if it was clear.

After a bit Jed came up on the net. 'Sierra Oscar?'

I responded, all senses alert. 'Send.'

Normally I'd have expected to hear him say, 'Sierra Oscar all clear, on you go.' But on this occasion he came back, 'No problem with option one, apart from a shopping trolley half on kerb, half on road.'

'Sierra roger, how does that affect the field of view?'

'Oscar, park three feet further forward than expected.'

'Roger that, mobile towards target,' I said as I pulled into the road, excited to be on the move and about to make something happen. You get so claustrophobic in the A-frame.

This was an estate we all knew well. We'd inserted so often that we were familiar with all the options, but the moment Jed was out I was straight in, pressing my foot down to give some swift acceleration. You can't afford to hang about in these situations. You're going to look a bit of a prat if an articulated lorry has arrived since the recce drive-through. As I drove into the estate I could hear the boys in Coalisland giving their location. Connor came up with 'Zero India, I have the trigger.' This meant he was in position, with a clear view of Baldy's house.

I cruised through the Catholic estate at twenty miles an hour, keeping an eye out for children. It looked a typical grubby sixties council-housing estate, just like the ones you can find anywhere in Britain – only worse. People stood around gossiping on their front doorsteps, little kids played football, older ones sucked on cigarettes. It was a depressing, cold environment, with no greenery to relieve the concrete monotony. The atmosphere was particularly oppressive. It was not so much the bricks and mortar that were different from the estates back home in the north-east, it was the feeling of the people. The majority were on benefit and had nothing better to do with their days than to hang around street corners. A Walker's crisp packet eddied across the road and under the car. I passed some blokes working on a vehicle without wheels. It wasn't raining, but it felt as if it should have been.

I drove along my prepared route through the maze of snaking streets. As I turned into Baldy's road I could see the abandoned wire supermarket trolley straddling the kerb thirty metres from his house, just where I'd planned to put my rear wheels. It's the small things that temporarily disrupt these meticulously planned ops.

'Sierra approaching target.' I pulled gently into position and reversed, stopping at a thirty-degree angle to the kerb, with the trolley alongside my rear passenger door. All the while I was telling my face to look lightly flustered. Of course, there's a play-off between understating it and overdoing it.

Jed had parked 150 metres from the estate. The plan was for me to join him, but first I had to go foxtrot out of the estate, leaving the car with its hidden video in position. I could sense someone peering at me from a doorway at 11 o'clock, but I resisted the temptation to look up. Instead I did the cursory faffing with my hair in the rear-view mirror. Women the world over do that, so it's part of fitting in, but it also gave me the chance to get a decco at Baldy's tatty front door. I flicked on the engine cut-out switch installed by the bleeps to immobilise the vehicle. The last thing we wanted was for some estate kid to hot-rod it and make off with all our precious recording equipment. I picked up my handbag and turned on my personal comms.

'Zero Sierra going foxtrot,' I said quietly. The net went silent to let me get away from the car. It was another vulnerable moment, and I knew that, with everyone else in their positions, Zero was awaiting my next transmission. I was leaving behind the security of a discreetly armoured car: the Cavalier's bodywork hid sheets of bulletproof Kevlar which had been inserted like a sandwich filling between the external bodywork and interior panels.

Now I was on my own. I grabbed my red and white plastic carrier bag from Wellworths, a local supermarket. I'd padded it out with a spare jumper, a packet of Old Holborn – I used to roll my own – and a box of tissues to hide the maps underneath. The area we were covering was massive, and although we knew some parts by heart we always carried all our maps just in case the targets moved elsewhere. You get attached to the familiarity of your own set of maps and the way they fold shut. Finally I picked up a large bag of disposable nappies from the back seat. The estate was full of young mothers whose kids were always running around with snotty noses and shitty nappies on, so I'd decided to use my bumper pack as cover to blend in with the environment. This was another definite advantage I had over the blokes. The whole name of the game is fitting in, attracting as little attention as possible. Sometimes I carried a toddler's plastic trike. I often thought it would be dead handy to have a kid in the barn to take out on ops to look even more natural. With a highly trained SAS decoy baby, no one would spot you for an operator.

The consequences of being compromised were always in the back of your mind at moments like this. If the IRA didn't slot you immediately, you faced the prospect of hours of torture. They were well known for their 'punishment squads', which they used on their own men who had fucked up in some way. Pinning the lad to a wall, they would drill his kneecap, or shatter it with a small-calibre bullet. Anyone they believed to have touted faced death: they would hood him, remove his shoes, shoot him through the head and dump him on waste land. If they suspected treachery but couldn't prove it, they might try an interrogation: tying up the tout's ankles with his shoelaces before dunking his head in a bathtub of water, or hanging him upside down before beating his shins and thighs with iron bars. They also liked to smash in their chests with planks covered in nails which had been half hammered in. If the IRA could deal out such punishment to their own men, they would certainly have found our company endlessly stimulating. On 14 December 1977, Corporal Paul Harman was lifted in the Turf Lodge, a bad-arse area of Belfast. His body was found the next day. Geneva Convention? I think not.

I locked the car and headed towards my preplanned route down a back alley on the opposite pavement. Your route through the estate must look realistic at all times. It's no good parking thirty metres from your alley then walking straight along the road towards it. It doesn't look natural.

Holding the nappies and carrier in my left hand I kept my right hand free, and started chewing the gum that had been lodged in my mouth since I left the barn. I'd become a master of ventriloquism, always chewing gum or smoking so that I could whisper into my mike at the same time. If things got really hairy and I was unable to speak because I was in a crowd, there was always the option of using the tone button to transmit in beeps, like Morse code.

'Zero, Sierra towards Oscar,' I said. Oscar was Jed's call-sign. He knew my exit route and had pulled over outside the estate to await me.

'Zero roger.'

'Oscar roger.'

My senses were on overdrive. I was looking hard, listening hard, getting the feel for the area, while trying to look vacant and switched off. This estate was riddled with players. You'd get some indication if you'd been spotted; everyone would stare at you. But that wouldn't help, because they're all eyeballing you constantly anyway. That's just what they do for a living. I could see people in doorways, just standing and watching the street. It would be easy to think, 'Fuck, they're looking at me,' and get paranoid. But you have to remain indifferent. You don't want them to know *you* know they're looking at you. You can't afford to increase your pace. You can't slow down. You have to gauge a normal speed and stick to it, come what may. It's easier if it's raining. Then you just put up your hood, slouch your shoulders and move along nice and quickly. But, just my luck, today was dazzling bright sunshine. It normally pisses down over the water.

By now I was halfway down the next alleyway. Anyone watching me would have assumed I was making my way to a friend's house. In fact I was embarking on a complicated route down alleys and cut-throughs. Because every turning has to look natural, I had memorised a map of the area. Operators have been shot in the past for making one false move; hesitating, waiting too long in a doorway or parking once too often in the same spot.

I came out of the alley and crossed a paved square where some kids were messing around noisily on bikes. They all had dirty knees, and even the waist-high ones were effing and blinding as they half-heartedly slugged their battered footballs. Mums who didn't have time to care, and dads who weren't around to care. It was the law of the jungle here, and everyone had eyes in the backs of their heads. I walked on.

Although I wasn't looking directly at my surroundings, I could sense things. Doors opened and slammed shut, children shouted, a football bounced across my path. As I passed an end-of-terrace house the chipped front door flew open and a frizzy-haired blonde wearing a lilac housecoat fell into the street, snarling like a cat at the man in the leather jacket who had pushed her. As he glowered at her and brandished his meaty fist, she spat magnificently at him. I looked up fleetingly. I didn't want to attract their attention, but an onlooker might have found it curious if I hadn't registered vague interest in this domestic meltdown.

I swiftly retuned my ears to the background noise. I could hear vehicles moving around various parts of the estate, and car doors slamming a street away. I adjusted my grip on the bag of nappies for reassurance. 'I'm a young mother looking after her child,' I kept telling myself. I turned into the next street and headed for a bend. Not far to go now. My hand was sweaty on the plastic. Another row of houses, another sea of faces. Any one of them could latch on to you or ask their mates who you were. Although most people on these estates knew everyone else, no one was likely to actually approach you unless you drew attention to yourself.

A few streets later I crossed a patch of withered grass, stepped over the kerb and started walking out of the estate. The folksy sound of The Chieftains blared from an open window, followed by Wham! from next door. My younger sister Melissa used to be into Wham!, but I preferred The Chieftains. The road curved gently, and I could now see Jed's blue Orion.

He'd been watching in his rear-view for me. 'Zero, Sierra approaching Oscar.' It was easier for him to inform the ops room than for me.

'Zero roger.'

As I opened the passenger door I felt the tension ebbing out of my body. Jed gave me a beaming smile, but I couldn't really relax; worse was to come. At lift-off I'd face a return walk to the video car. Oh, for a nice quiet office job! Jed wasted no time in winding me up about the bag of nappies.

'How was the trouts and rug-rats group today, then? Not too shitty, I hope?'

He got a slap for that one. Then it was straight back to work. 'Oscar mobile around general area,' said Jed as we moved away.

Kurt came onto the net from Coalisland. 'Zero Papa, curtains open, negative activity at Alpha Two,' he said. McAmee was still lying low.

'Zero roger.'

Jed and I drove a few minutes south to the peaceful waters of Ballysaggart Lough, where we sat back and waited for something to happen. Connor had eyes-on, so there was no need for us to be in the estate. But we still had to be near enough to provide back-up should he need it. Jed stretched out and started making lip-smacking noises while patting his stomach. I ignored him, so he started fidgeting and prodding me in the ribs, pretending to search for grub. Innocently I said, 'Yes, can I help you?'

'Well, seeing as a shag's out of the question, where's the scoff?'

'We haven't got any, fat boy. Anyway, you can't be hungry after that huge breakfast you demolished this morning.'

'I'm a growing lad,' he said indignantly. 'Come on, where's the Wagon Wheels?' He started frisking me again and tickling my tummy. He got a swift backhand to the ribs.

'If you're a good boy and keep quiet for a whole minute, I might give you something.'

He threw himself back in his seat and made an exaggerated mouth-closing gesture before shutting his eyes and putting his hands over his ears. He looked like the three wise monkeys all rolled into one. Then he looked at me with hungry puppy eyes.

'All right, I give in,' I said with a laugh. 'They're in the carrier bag, but don't scoff them all.'

Jed and I were a good double-act. Any onlooker would think we were young lovers. A lot of courting went on in cars in Northern Ireland. Jed shoved two Wagon Wheels down his throat, spraying his chin and shirt with crumbs.

Connor came up over the net with 'Standby, standby.' Baldy Quinn was opening his front door. Good. Some activity at last. We all acknowledged the movement in quick succession.

'Zero roger.'

'Sierra roger.'

'Papa roger.'

'Hotel roger.'

'Golf roger.'

Baldy was an ugly bastard with a permanent scowl. He was of average build, and would have been last in line for a Nobel Peace Prize. Connor watched and reported as he stood on his front door-step with a mug of tea. Just standing and staring, but for all we knew he was waiting for Seamus McAmee or a pick-up. He scratched his balls and disappeared round the back of the house.

Then Kurt sparked up from Coalisland. 'Standby, that's Bravo Two mobile in on red.' Seamus McAmee had driven past him. This was very good news indeed. I felt that old excitement rising. Kurt followed up with the VRN (vehicle registration number), car model, and driver and passenger description. 'Seamus McAmee is passenger, with unknown male driving.' Like Baldy, Seamus was no oil painting.

Jack came over the net. 'Stop, stop, stop. That's Charlie One static outside newsagents'.' Seamus had got out of the Fiesta and gone into the shop. When he re-emerged with a paper and pulled out, there was no need for Kurt or Jack to move straight away. Greg was laying up and covering the options further on. Soon there was a steady stream of information spilling onto the net about both targets' movements.

We now knew there was a possible meeting taking place. We'd got one target up and about, and the other mobile. It was dead on 11.30 a.m., so it looked as if the lunchtime tip might be accurate. Could this lead us to the bomb factory we'd been searching for for the past two months?

Connor saw Quinn come back through the garden gate, round the front of his house and go inside. Meanwhile, Bravo Two was driving along green from Coalisland to Dungannon. The team followed.

The red Fiesta revved into the estate. The team pulled off Bravo Two as he entered, and split up to stake out the area. This was very good. It was happening as planned. I felt a thrill of excitement. So many times surveillance is about waiting for nothing, but this was going down.

McAmee and his driver pulled up outside Quinn's house.

'Zero India, that's Bravo Two at boot of Charlie One removing a small holdall and a long object wrapped in a black bin liner.'

McAmee had got out of the car, walked around to the boot and lugged out a heavy-looking holdall and a slender object about four feet long wrapped up in a bin bag.

'Zero roger.'

My pulse quickened. Like the other operators, I was reading between the lines. It obviously looked the size and shape of a rifle, but Connor could report only what he saw. You can't afford to make assumptions in this game.

Bravo Two did a furtive look-around, then he and the unknown driver walked fairly briskly up Baldy's path. All three then went into the house and the front door closed.

The tension was building over the net. Here were two known players, who didn't normally associate, together inside the house with a heavy holdall and a long object in a bin liner. We waited it out. I reached over to the back seat for the flask, and had a much-needed swig of sugary lukewarm coffee. I wasn't going to give any to Jed until he said please.

Greg pulled up next to us, and I wound down the window.

'All right, mate? Do you want some coffee?'

'Yeah, cheers.' Jed whinged a bit as the aroma wafted towards him.

'So, what do you think he's got in the bin liner?' said Greg.

I took a swig. 'Difficult to say, really. It could be an obvious, but you never know.'

Connor spoke up. 'Zero India, movement of curtains at Alpha One.' This was interesting. Was Baldy expecting someone else, or was there a dicker keeping watch? Then the front door opened, and all three men came out and walked round to the back of the house, lugging the heavy holdall and the bin liner.

'Zero India, that's all three Bravos with bag and long object to rear of Alpha One and unsighted.'

As we waited, the ops officer came back with the result of the numberplate check.

'Zero roger that, reference Charlie One. The Fiesta belongs to Mairead McAmee, cousin of Seamus. No connections.' She was an innocent bystander.

Five minutes later McAmee and Baldy emerged empty-handed, and went back in the front door. It was a bummer that Connor couldn't see what the hell they were up to.

'Zero India, Bravo One and Two at the front of Alpha One and now gone complete.'

A minute later McAmee and Baldy re-emerged from the house wearing overalls, and slipped round the back. Suddenly Connor cursed. 'Zero India, I no longer have the trigger.' A removal van had parked behind McAmee's car, blocking Connor's view of the house.

Now we really were unsighted. Bloody brilliant. We'd got some activity, with two known players around the back, but now Connor had lost the trigger, and the video car's view was also obscured. A walk-past had become unavoidable. It was my shout. We got the affirmative and Jed went mobile. The other call-signs moved in closer. Without a trigger, we needed a tighter stake-out.

Jed drove me to the entrance of the estate. I knew every square inch of this area. Intelligence stored and shared from previous operations, all wired up on the hard disc of my memory.

'Zero Sierra going foxtrot towards Remus.' Just before I got out I leaned over, kissed Jed full on the lips and tousled his hair. Anyone watching needed to be convinced we'd just been out for a snog and a drive together. In fact, looking at Jed's cute little face, that didn't seem like such a bad idea. I needed some leave!

Adrenaline pumping, I walked back through the estate, approaching Remus from the same side alley. A stray dog loped past with its tail at full-mast, clearly on a crucial mission. As I walked up Baldy's street my heart was beating as loudly as my footfalls, and the bag of nappies swung in time with my steps. Suddenly I was solo, vulnerable and very tense. I was in here by myself, on Baldy's side of the street, and anything could have been going on. But this was what the months of training had prepared me for.

My plan was to walk past the house, and have a quick look down the shared alleyway as I drew level with it. Then I'd head round the back of the opposite terrace, which would eventually bring me back to Remus on the opposite side of the street. Over the net I mumbled as quietly as possible, 'Zero Sierra approaching target.' I was dying for a wee, and I could sense my heart rate quickening. Baldy's house was four doors away ... three ... then two. As I came level with his fence I flicked my head to the right for a second or so as my feet pushed me on, trying to make the movement look as natural as possible.

In that fleeting moment I had a clear view down the alleyway past a tangle of half-dead ivy, broken bricks and discarded Coke cans. At the end was a patch of overgrown lawn where Baldy and McAmee were hunched over a bag of cement. The unidentified man was on his hands and knees mixing in a blue bucket. A four-foot spirit level was propped up against the wall. Then I saw a brick barbecue, half-built, next to a flowerbed.

I couldn't fucking believe it. I was now well past the alley, and desperate to let out a tension-relieving snigger, but I couldn't allow my face to register any change. It was still silent on the net. The rest of the team were waiting in a state of extreme anticipation to hear what I'd seen. They would be charged up in case there was a contact. I couldn't afford to jeopardise myself by speaking so close to Alpha One.

I waited until I was round the back of the houses and it was safe to come up on the net. 'Zero Sierra, that's three Bravos building a barbie.' A note of sarcasm slid into my voice.

But I wasn't out of the woods yet. The targets weren't tense or twitchy, but I had to keep third-party awareness. I couldn't risk a compromise at this stage in the game. Chances were that because they were not engaged in terrorist activity there was no dicker keeping a lookout. But you never knew who was watching you.

Approaching the car was another vulnerable moment. I had to shift the trolley, which was blocking me in from behind, but at least I didn't have to drop my keys and go through that routine. When I was out in Belfast on an admin or shopping run I would always fumble in my bag until my keys clattered onto the pavement, giving me a few seconds to do a covert check under the car for an explosive device, which could range in size from a cigarette packet to a shoebox.

Because I'd been able to walk back to Remus without being compromised, I was fairly certain that no one suspected the car, but you can never afford to feel totally secure: if they've seen you leave they might suspect where you've been. That's why inserting the car has to be done correctly in the first place, so you don't attract interest.

I got in, flicked off the engine cut-off switch, locked the doors, turned my personal comms off and switched to vehicle comms. 'Sierra complete and mobile.' I felt cocooned inside its protective exterior once again. As I drove out of the estate, I was relaxed enough to give a full description of what I'd seen. Then the inevitable jokes began. Kurt was in there first.

'So, what time's bangers at Baldy's, then?'

As I pulled out towards spot four-one I checked my watch. It was 12.30. It had been another typical day on the job. So much for the source. Quite often we were just covering our options, but however dull a job might seem, you could never let yourself relax for a moment. It could have been a weapons move with a CTR (close target reconnaissance) to follow.

We all headed down to the lough to meet up and have a chinwag and a whinge, and to wonder what time we could lift off. You can't get too het up about failures. Not everything in life is as it seems.

*   *   *

It was August 1990, and I'd been a member of 14 Intelligence Company for eight months. 14 Intelligence, or the Det, is a small, select part of Special Forces which has always operated in a fog of official secrecy. The unit was set up in 1974 when half of B Squadron, 22 SAS, was combined with a bunch of Intelligence Corps surveillance specialists and some volunteers from the infantry. 14 Int was the cover name they had used in the late 1970s, and it had stuck. Our job was to conduct covert surveillance operations in the most hostile parts of Northern Ireland. Alongside its operational techniques, developed by the SAS and military intelligence over many years, there is one aspect peculiar to the Det within the British Special Forces community. It recruits women on a basis of equality with men. I was a member of Britain's most secret élite force.

ONE

OUR MAM

WHEN OUR MAM was eight months pregnant with her second child, her husband Eric stuck a fork in the back of her head. Then he kicked her down the stairs. She rolled down two flights before she stopped, and woke up on a drip in Redcar Hospital.

While she was in hospital recovering, my older brother Dean, who was just a toddler, went to his maternal grandma's in Eston. But Eric wasn't having any of it. He adored his son, and went to pick him up. Granddad met Eric on the doorstep and battered him around the head until the police arrived. When our Mam came out of hospital she got Dean back and life went back to normal. A month later, on 13 November 1965, my Auntie Pauline helped deliver me in my parents' cold flat in the seaside retirement town of Marske-by-the-Sea, Cleveland. Even before my birth I'd met violence. The pattern had been set, but so had the fact that I'd survived.

I was twelve days old when our Mam and Eric moved to Skelton, Eric's home town. Eric was an apprentice fitter, tall and well built, with receding fair hair. When he wasn't at the factory he was down the pub. If he was on night shift he would lock the house and take the key with him. Our Mam thought this was normal; after all, Granddad, who'd been a miner, used to lock Grandma in the larder when he was going out drinking, and beat her up when he got back.

When our Mam went out dancing as a girl, Granddad would wait on the step, peering at his watch. If she wasn't back on time she got a battering. That was just the way it was. Granddad didn't want his six children running wild, and he believed firmly in paternal discipline. It was like a religion in their house. Our Mam left home at sixteen and worked as a cleaner and maid at a boys' boarding school in Ripon. She had jet-black hair and brown eyes, and a strong, well-built frame. At nineteen she met and married Eric. The drunken beatings started shortly after Dean's birth, so our Mam went back to Grandma's. Eric came to get her on the night of her twenty-first birthday, and by way of many happy returns he beat her up. But she still went back with him.

When Dean was three and I was two, our Mam decided she'd had enough. One lunchtime before Eric left for the 2–10 p.m. shift he'd smashed a couple of milk bottles over her head. They had been lined up like soldiers on her sideboard in the front room ready to go on the doorstep. Our Mam wasn't having any more, so she put us in the double pushchair, collected some nappies, a change of clothes for each of us and a few personal treasures, including her framed photographs of her Mam and her Grandma. She popped them into plastic carrier bags which she hung on the handles of the pushchair. Then she put dummies in our mouths and carefully pinned a spare one to each of our tops. It was a humid afternoon in July, but she resolutely pushed us to a telephone box in Redcar, seven miles away. By the time we arrived three hours later we both had wet nappies and were whingeing, but our Mam never complained. She phoned Grandma's next-door neighbour, who had a telephone, and she got a message to Granddad to come and get us.

We stayed in Grandma's three-bedroom Victorian house for a long time. There were ten of us there, including our Mam's five brothers and sisters. The heating came from open fires, and there was no hot running water, just a tin bath in the kitchen and an outside toilet.

Grandma knew someone who rented out council houses near her home in Eston, a suburb of Middlesbrough which must rate as the British equivalent of the South Bronx. A crime-ridden, econ-omically deprived hell hole. Our new home was a two-up, two-down with no sink, no back window and no hot tap. We didn't have a cooker, so our Mam was forced to cook over the two-bar electric fire. This was fairly typical. I was seventeen before I discovered what a mortgage was; I assumed everyone lived in a council house.

We thought we would live there happily ever after, but within months Eric had started visiting again. Our Mam felt sorry for him, so we moved back to Skelton with him. Things went well for a while, but then it was back to normal, in fact worse than before, so we moved into lodgings in Marske. Eric was enraged. Our Mam ended up in Redcar Hospital again, this time with broken ribs, a bust nose and extensive bruising. That episode led to court, and Eric was fined and put under an injunction to stay away from us.

When the house went under a demolition order our Mam accepted a council house in Middlesbrough, but she couldn't settle there so we moved again. First we took a house in North Ormesby, Middlesbrough, and shortly after that we moved to 13 Ashton Street, which was nearby. That house is my earliest memory. There was no central heating or hot water, and the toilet was in the back yard, but we were happy there. For once we put down some tentative roots. Our Mam supplemented her benefit with cleaning jobs in the King's pub, among other places. She made some friends, and so did we. Money was a source of constant stress. It was a continual struggle to find enough to feed our hungry mouths. Sometimes, in desperation, she was forced to fry a flour and water mix to fill us up. On other occasions, it was tatty-peeling soup.

By the time I was five, Eric had gone for good. He'd come back fleetingly to get our Mam pregnant with Melissa, who was born when I was three, but a year later he was out of the picture. Our Mam got involved with Bruce, a builder who was passive where Eric was violent. Bruce was a bit of a singer, who did turns in local pubs and clubs, and he fathered my sisters Katherine, born a year after Melissa, and Jane. I vividly remember Jane's birth, a year after that. I went downstairs one morning to find our Mam holding a baby, who she introduced as our newest sister. She walked over to the chest of drawers and made the baby a little nest of blankets in the top drawer, and that was her cot until she grew too big to fit inside.

Our Mam took all sorts of jobs to buy us the things we needed.

There was an endless list: shoes, clothes, haircuts, school outings. She saved for months to buy a second-hand fridge and a twin-tub of which she was dead proud. With five children under six it must have been a godsend. In the back yard was a mangle. Sometimes Dean would feed the hem of my dress into it and wind me in. Bathtime was Sunday evening; in order of age we'd hop into the tin tub in front of the kitchen fire filled with scalding pots of water off the stove. The youngest ones always came out dirtier than they'd got in.

I was always getting into trouble. The first time I stole anything I was six. I knew exactly what to do as I lodged myself between two shoppers and stuffed a packet of chocolate digestive biscuits up my jumper, then tagged behind them as they walked out. I filled my face on the way home to try and get rid of the evidence, and handed out a biscuit to every child I met. I vividly remember walking into the house, my face purple with embarrassment and my arms folded over my cardigan. Our Mam asked what was up my jumper. Shamefaced, I admitted, 'A packet of biscuits I've nicked, but I can't eat them all.'

She looked back down at the terry-towelling nappies she was hand-washing in the big square ceramic sink. 'Well, put them in the biscuit tin then and go upstairs and play with Jane,' she said matter-of-factly. So stealing was OK if you were poor.

One day I was with some friends in the King's when we discovered their baby sister playing with hundreds of pounds she'd found rolled into bundles under the couch. It must have been their parents' bar-takings which they kept stashed under there. We excitedly scooped up all the money and went down to Noble's Café to eat everything we fancied, then we went to the cake shop and bought fresh cakes. We felt like millionaires. In our family we always had day-old bread and cake, and broken biscuits. Having no idea of the value of money, we hid some of what was left up a drainpipe, and the rest under a brick by the British Legion Club at the end of our street. But my brother kept back five pounds to buy our Mam a box of After Eights, which he took to school. That afternoon the headmaster escorted Dean and his goods home for safekeeping. Our Mam smiled sweetly and confirmed that yes, indeed, she knew all about the chocolates, but the second Mr Harris disappeared down the street she walloped us from one end of the house to the other. She battered us and dragged us screaming to the police station, telling us we would be locked up for ever if we didn't admit where we'd got the money. We were almost inside the station when we broke down, confessed that there was more money hidden, and took her to where it was stashed. She'd never seen so much money in her life, but like an honest fool she scooped it all up and took it back to its owners. They hadn't even noticed it was missing, and didn't reward her with so much as a cup of tea.

Beatings were routine in our house, that was just part of life. My mother usually used her hands. She only hit me with a belt once, when she flipped over nothing in particular. I remember crouching under the kitchen table among a jungle of chair legs as she waved the leather belt about, and wondering, 'What do I have to say to get out of this?' I later learned she'd had a nervous breakdown and had been on Valium for much of my childhood.

But on the whole, life was very happy. I revelled in my urban tomboy existence, playing in derelict buildings and on patches of waste ground. One Christmas when I was seven our Mam told me to go and amuse myself for half an hour. When I came back a bright yellow Chipper bike was standing on the hearth. Christ knows where she got the money. I looked after it carefully. I took the chain off to regrease it, kept the frame clean so it didn't corrode, and made sure the tyres were free of foreign bodies. The bike was well out of fashion by the time Jane finally got it as a hand-me-down. On my eighth birthday our Mam put a request on the radio for me, and we all danced to 'Raindrops Keep Falling on my Head'. She might have been hard pushed to cope, but she did so much for us. She also had a sense of humour despite all the hard work. One day she was cooking us a tin of treacle pudding, and let it boil dry while she chatted to her friend Sandra. There was an almighty 'Kaboom!' as it exploded, and runny treacle sponge ended up all over the kitchen ceiling. This struck her as deliciously funny, and she said with a touch of pride, 'My ceilings are as clean as any plates. We can eat it off there.' When the rent man came we sometimes hid behind the couch so he couldn't see us through the window. It was fun when our Mam crouched down with us too. When we were really desperate she would break into the gas meter to get out the 50p pieces so we could feed them back in again.

Dean and I were forever trying to catch the pigeons and sparrows which landed in the back yard. We made a trap from an overturned vegetable box propped up on a twig. There was a string leading upstairs, and grubs lying on the ground under the box. We spent hours keeping absolutely still for that magical moment when the bird would flutter under the box and we would pull the string and catch it. We never did – birds were much more switched on than we realised. Had we caught one, I suppose we would probably have tried to kill it, although I don't know how we would have gone about it. But I wasn't completely merciless. One day I found a tiny bird, the size of a walnut, which had just hatched. I got the top off a bottle of Domestos, ripped off a handkerchief-sized piece of a sheet and gently laid the bird into its new nest, all snug and soft. I made him a little cover and tried to save him. When he died I let everyone know how upset I was.

The goldfish we won at a fair didn't survive either, but that was my fault. We used to scoop it out of its bowl with a big silver spoon and watch it thrash around. When it went still we'd dunk it back into its bowl and watch in wonder as it sprang back to life. But one day, as it flopped about on the spoon, my hand wobbled and the fish plopped onto the floor, slithering about all over the place. It didn't spring back to life that time, but we put it back into the bowl anyway and told our Mam it had died of natural causes. Then we flushed it down the toilet.

We played mainly out the front. There wasn't enough room in the concrete back yard which housed the mangle. Old Mrs Wood would keep an eye on us. She wore voluminous skirts and blouses and had her hair up in a bun. She always used to say, 'Keep on the flags, don't go on the road.' It was her mantra. Our Melissa had been playing with little Julie from next door the year before when Julie was run over by a car and killed.

But even the back alleys weren't safe. When Katherine was four she was playing with some friends under the washing blowing on the lines when a middle-aged man took her hand and started to lead her away. Fortunately a friend of ours sitting on his back doorstep with his leg in a cast saw it all. He shouted at the man, and his daughter ran to our house and told our Mam. She flew out of the house at a hundred miles an hour and grabbed Katherine by her tiny wrist. As the man was scarpering she got a look at his face and recognised him from the British Legion Club. She went and told the doorman what had happened, but he just laughed and said, 'Oh, yeah, love, we know who you mean.' Our Mam was fuming. In those days women were barred from entering the club so she couldn't deal with him. Instead she went down to the nick. 'If I get my hands on that dirty bastard I'll kill him,' she said. The policeman laughed and said, 'Don't take things into your own hands, love.' Our Mam had to wait until the evening for her revenge. She stormed back up the British Legion Club, pushed past the doorman and ran cursing at the old lecher, kicked him ferociously in the bollocks and told everyone what he'd done. He half-hobbled out of the bar. Our Mam followed him, picked up a heavy stick she'd stashed outside and chased after him. 'If you ever show your face again I'll break your fucking legs!' she screamed down the road.

Dean and I started daring each other to nick more and more stuff. There was a pie man who used to deliver to the butchers at the end of the street. In return for helping him unload the pallets of freshly baked steak-and-kidney and pork pies he'd give us one each. He never caught on to the fact that every time his back was turned we were stuffing our pockets full of them. Once I nicked a whole forty-eight-packet box of crisps from a van with a roll-up back flap delivering to the shop.

We also discovered a free source of sweeties. On the way to school there was a shop with a mechanical dispenser. You put in a penny and it fed you a handful of brightly coloured chews, but we found that a button would also turn the mechanism. We gathered up all the buttons we could find, telling our Mam it was for a school project, so she kindly gave us what spare ones she had.

I loved school, especially the big dinners and the apparatus in gym classes, which was like a mini-assault course. I was always eager to get onto the equipment, and one day I tore out of class so fast that I slipped and cut my head open on the side of a desk. Blood poured from the wound on my forehead,and the teachers called an ambulance. I still have the livid pink scar today. I played football with the boys in the schoolyard, and no one ever batted an eyelid.

Sometimes when our Mam was working I had to nip out of school and collect Melissa from the nursery, take her the half-mile home, feed her and dash back to school without being seen. By the time I was eight, Dean and I were babysitting some nights when our Mam went to work. We started smoking on one of those evenings. First we rolled up a piece of paper, then we stuck it in the fire and started sucking on it. We nearly killed ourselves with the smoke. After that we would raid my mother's baccy tin where she left the stumps of her roll-ups for recycling. Sometimes she'd send us out into the street to pick up dog-ends for her to make roll-ups, and other times we'd rifle through the bins outside the pub, hoping to find rich pickings.

Our Mam told Dean and me the facts of life one night after she'd been drinking. 'Do you know where babies come from?' she asked.

'Out of your belly button,' I said solemnly.

Dean laughed. 'Don't be silly,' he said. 'They come out of your mouth.' We both looked to our Mam for clarification.

'They come out of where you have a wee,' she informed us concisely. That was the sum total of my sex education.

I shared a room with Melissa, Katherine and Dean. Our Mam slept with Jane in her bed. One night I was lying in bed unable to sleep when I heard shouting in our Mam's room. I slipped out of bed and padded across the landing. The door into her room was open, and the net curtains were lit up by the moonlight and billowing in the breeze. Strangely, the sash window was all the way up. Our Mam was lying sobbing on the bed. I tiptoed to the window and peered out, sensing something bad. On the pavement under the window lay the motionless body of a man. Our Mam said, 'Run

26

round to the police station, Sarah, there's a good girl.' With a dreadful feeling in my tummy and tears streaming down my face I ran barefoot down the stairs and off along the pavement in my nightie, my long blonde hair blowing in the wind. 'Quick, come round,' I shouted. 'My Mam's in a fight and she's sent me.' The policeman scooped me up in his arms, deposited me on the back seat of his squad car and drove me home. Reassured and having done what our Mam had asked me to do, I went up to bed and fell asleep. The next day there was a chalk outline of a person on the ground. It lasted until the rain. I was haunted by the image of what I'd seen. Was he drunk? Did he jump? I wasn't shielded from the realities of life, but it was left to me to draw my own conclusions.

In the kitchen was our one piece of good furniture, a yellow dresser with a flap which pulled down for working on and a sliding glass cupboard where the good crockery and the sugar jar was stored. Dean and I were addicted to sugar sandwiches, a slice of bread and a slick of butter to stick down the sugar. One night when our Mam was out, Dean pulled out the shelf and climbed up onto it to reach the jar. I watched in horror as the dresser began to lurch forward. It came crashing down with a deafening smash as every plate, cup, saucer and bowl that we owned shattered on the lino floor. Dean was trapped underneath, screaming and yelling for air. I tried to shift the dresser, but I couldn't budge it an inch. Then I heard our Mam's key in the lock. She called out, 'Is everything all right?' when she heard the ominous silence. I shouted, 'No, Dean's in the cabinet.' She rushed to the kitchen, and once she'd rescued him and checked he was all right, she gave us both a well-deserved battering. A friend of hers, Glenda, was always joking that she'd paint a red cross on the front of our house if she got the chance.

When a demolition order was placed on Ashton Street, it was time to move on. All around us heavy iron balls on chains were smacking into the houses and reducing them to piles of rubble. You couldn't see down the road for the clouds of choking dust. We were one of the last families to go, just days before my ninth birthday. We moved into a filthy council house in Steel Road. Our

Mam led me upstairs. 'I want to show you something,' she said. At the top of the stairs she opened a door. An inside toilet. Next to it was another room, in which sat a white porcelain bath with hot and cold taps. I had never seen such a thing before.

I used to plead with our Mam to let me go to Grandma's house, the one we'd escaped to after Eric's beatings. Dean was allowed to visit every Sunday because, being his only grandson, Granddad thought the sun shone out of his arse, and I was dead jealous. There was such a loving atmosphere there. We watched wrestling on the telly, and ate jelly and ice cream, and tangerine slices from a tin for tea. Grandma also had a domestic routine on which you could depend. Monday was wash day; Tuesday was for cleaning the front step; Wednesday was sweeping and swilling the back yard; Thursday was windows day; on Fridays she went shopping, usually at North Ormesby market; and every morning she religiously dusted and hoovered. Most amazing of all, she made everyone's bed. In our house we always had to make our own.

We all had nits in our long honey-coloured hair, and our Mam treated us with lotions and clean combs, doing all the right things. One day the school nitty nurse snipped off all the hair at the nape of my neck. When I got home and our Mam saw it she went ballistic. She flew up to school the next day with her carpet scissors and marched into the headmaster's study without knocking. Cowering, he explained that the nitty nurse wasn't due in until later, so our Mam waited fuming in the corridor. When the nurse arrived, our Mam got hold of her head and chopped off handfuls of her hair. Our Mam always stood up for us.

One day our Mam asked us what we all wanted to be when we grew up. I said an astronaut, Dean said a fireman. Jane, who was five, said, 'I want to be a Mammy like you.' True to her word, she was pregnant at eighteen and soon being routinely beaten by her boyfriend.

In 1978, when I was twelve, I joined the local branch of the Sea Cadets. I was given a uniform, which I adored: flat black shoes, black tights and skirt, a doubled-breasted jacket and a white shirt and hat. I scrubbed the hat with toothpaste to keep it white and polished my shoes. I even put a bow in my hair to hold it back neatly. I was very proud, very smart, and loved the discipline. Some people turned up looking like scram bags. I couldn't understand this; it just seemed normal to turn out well presented. We had parade night twice a week and band practice on Sundays. I played the bugle. Most of the cadets were like us, and didn't have much, but it was the highlight of our week. I got a badge for drill and loved all the marching around. I learned rope work and could soon tie a sheepshank and a reef knot.

I started entering swimming galas, and won medals for back-stroke. I went canoeing in Redcar and out on the boats at Hartle-pool. It was on those weekends away, with packed lunches, outdoor activity and fresh air, that I got my first taste of life beyond North Ormesby.

But there was still the odd lapse. We were issued with collecting tins for Poppy Day, and people wanted to give so readily that we were handing out our hats. I knew I was supposed to put the money into the tin, but instead I stole it. To this day this makes me feel guilty; now, when I spot people collecting I always give them lots of money to make up for my wicked behaviour.

It was no wonder I loved the Sea Cadets so much. I came from a domestic environment where self-discipline was as automatic as a reflex. Our Mam always made sure we were as smart as soldiers, and although we might not have had the smartest kit, what we did have was clean, pressed and well looked after. Everything in the house was always in apple-pie order; even the dustbins in the yard were neatly lined up. Every day our Mam would do a room inspec-tion to check that everything she had laboriously washed and pressed was laid out correctly. Every week there would be forty white cotton socks to be washed. So she would know which belonged to who, she colour-coded each sock with a little cotton loop. Mine were blue. Despite our unruly behaviour when she was out, we always made sure that when our Mam came home every-thing was perfect, so she wouldn't have cause to worry.

The first time I got really drunk was with Granddad Sammy. He wasn't really our granddad, but he was a lovely old boy who was a long-standing friend of our Mam's. One afternoon when I was twelve she decided it was time he took me out to get me drunk. We walked down to the Red Lion, and he bought me half a lager. No one blinked an eye – this was a community where everyone knew everyone else, and which was united against the police. Anyway, I was with Granddad Sammy, and no one was going to argue with him. We chatted about whippets and pigeons and how school was going. Then he asked if I wanted another beer. When one of our Mam's friends spotted us, she shouted, 'There's Val's bairn. What's she having then?' After two pints I wasn't just wobbling, I collapsed. Granddad Sammy carried me home in a fireman's lift, and our Mam laughed as he propped me up gently on the couch.

Our Mam was deeply distrustful of men, so there weren't many 'uncles'. She'd been on her own too long, and had developed her own set ways of doing things. She was very strong and independent, and wasn't going to have a man dictate terms to her after what she'd been through.

I soon started going on the piss regularly with our Mam. She couldn't wait for me to grow up. I'd drop into the Green Man in my Sea Cadet uniform and I'd sip shandies with her friends, who wore rollers in their hair. You could tell they'd popped in for a lunchtime drink and stayed all day.

One day the Sea Cadets were given a slide show and a talk about life in the Women's Royal Navy Service. With eyes like saucers we watched tanned and energetic-looking people in summer uniforms and plimsolls sipping Pimms and lemonade in Hong Kong, or windsurfing in Gibraltar. My imagination was captured. I saw escape, adventure, independence and happiness. From the age of thirteen I was going to join the WRNS. There was no question of not being accepted; that didn't enter the equation. I had made up my mind.

I was so determined to get away from home that I started running away when I was fourteen. Our Mam and I were going through the usual teenager–mother relationship thing, and wanted to kill each other the whole time. I wanted to be out with my friends later and more often than our Mam allowed, and I was fed up with always having to help with the chores. So one night, after yet another argument, I took my £20 Christmas and birthday money which I'd hoarded, put on my coat and set off. I walked and walked, ending up in the middle of a thick forest on the North Yorkshire moors. I didn't know where I was, and I was getting scared, so I knocked on the door of a cottage and said, 'Please call the police, I want to go home, I'm lost.' At three in the morning they dropped me back. Our Mam hadn't even noticed I was missing, which made me feel even more unwanted and worthless. On the next occasion I rather more sensibly chose to run away to Grandma's.

When I was fifteen I tried to slash my wrists with a piece of glass from a broken milk bottle I'd fished out of the bin. I suppose I was craving attention – I certainly didn't want to die. I'd got as far as producing a few scratches and some tiny flecks of blood when Katherine wandered in to get her Kermit the frog puppet. She stopped and stared. 'What are you doing?' she said in a tiny voice. Then she saw the blood. 'Don't do it,' she implored. 'Come and play with me and Jane.'.

I looked up with a scowl. 'Go away. Leave me alone, Katherine. And don't tell our Mam.'

She stared at me and nodded slowly. With a sob, she ran out. I thought about what I was doing, and realised there was no point in it. I'd only get blood on the carpet and have to clean it up.

Our Mam started going a bit funny shortly after that. One night I'd been down the pub with her and her mates after Sea Cadets, listening to 'Crystal Chandeliers' and other old Dean Martin and Ned Miller numbers on the jukebox. We stopped at the chippy on the way home for a treat. Anything you bought from a shop, as opposed to made yourself, was special. Melissa and I were sitting on the couch stuffing chips down our throats when I said something inconsequential that annoyed our Mam. She flipped, chucking her plate at me. We didn't have a carpet, just the concrete floor, and the plate smashed into pieces. They skidded across the floor towards me, and one of them hit me on the right foot, taking off a thick slice of flesh and skin. Our Mam was going crazy, and I was trying to disguise the blood seeping all over the floor in case she went even more mental. Melissa was rooted to the spot, terrified, like a rabbit in headlights. I hobbled to the kitchen and pulled off my tights. There was blood pissing out everywhere. Our Mam was still going nuts, so Melissa and I decided to phone Grandma, 'Something's happened. Our Mam's flipped,' I said quietly. Immediately Grandma jumped in a taxi and took over. 'Bloody hell, Valerie, what's going on?' she said, before phoning an ambulance. By this point I must have lost pints of blood. Mam's GP had also turned up, and he started shoving tablets down her throat.

Ten days later I had six stitches taken out of my foot. The following day our Mam threw the telly at me. It landed squarely on my foot, opening the wound. As the picture tube went, it made a popping sound. When she heard it our Mam ran upstairs with the words, 'You'd better get that telly fixed before I come downstairs.' I looked at the flex: it was hopeless – our Mam had wrenched the fitting out of the wall. When she came down and asked if I'd fixed it yet, I had to admit that unfortunately I hadn't. Despite everything, I always loved our Mam to bits. She was under huge pressure bringing up the five of us, and they didn't spot mental illnesses as easily then as they do now. She was probably too busy, or just too tired, to get to the doctor.

Dean and I fell out big style when I was fourteen and he was fifteen. He had started thieving and glue-sniffing, and I could see the worry he was causing our Mam. He's in his early thirties now, and he's still at it. He started being sent to detention centres, then borstals, and finally the lock-up itself. He was really good at breaking into things. He should have been a fireman. We thought he was in with the wrong crowd, but it turned out he *was* the wrong crowd. I hated the fact that he was bringing badness into our house.

All this fuelled our Mam's opinion that men were bad news and to be avoided. 'I haven't got a man here because all men are bastards,' she would say. 'They beat you up, they take advantage. Never get married.' She would back this up by showing me the thick welts of scar tissue on her arms, the slashes on her face, and the marks on her head where the milk bottles had shattered.

'Don't worry, Mam, I'm not ever getting married. I'm staying with you,' I promised. But seeing the bad side of life made me more determined to do better. I had to take control.

This was not to say I didn't get into trouble. One night the Sea Cadets had a dance. There was a girl there doing a poofy dance, and my friends dared me to go over and take the piss. She was a New Romantic and wearing frills, while I was into Adam Ant facial warpaint. We had a small scuffle on the floor, and she stomped home to put on her boots and bring back her mates. The second fight, on the ground outside, was an altogether more violent affair. She bit my right bicep badly, but that didn't bother me because I won the fight, belting her on the head with my fist.

Every night I'd get on with my homework. I was Captain Sensible, trying to do as well as I could in every subject. But our Mam didn't understand why it was important. She preferred me to stick to my chores. At school I refused to study home economics and opted for engineering drawing instead, which I reckoned would be more useful for my chosen career as a mechanic in the WRNS.

Money was always a problem. All our clothes came from jumble sales, but you didn't whinge about that. All that would do would be to make our Mam feel shitty, which was the last thing you wanted. One Christmas we didn't have any money for presents, so we got toys off the welfare. There was an Action Man who only had one eye, jigsaws with pieces missing and puppets with broken strings. When a French exchange was arranged at school we were given letters to take home to ask permission. It was obvious to me that there was no way our Mam could afford it, so I just signed her name under the 'no thank you' part and handed it back.

Our school uniforms all came off benefit. Mine consisted of an A-line below-the-knee grey skirt and a white nylon shirt with red stripes. It was disgusting. Everyone knew that the people who had those kind of clothes were on benefit. Queuing for free school lunches wasn't very nice either, as you had to form a special line and everybody knew. Once I had a fight in the dinner queue with a boy in the class above me; it was either over the free dinners or the uniform. I ended up punching him and pulling his hair out. But normally I didn't get into fights. I left that to Dean. I was doing engineering drawing one day when we heard a scuffle outside the classroom. The teacher opened the door and we watched as my brother lamped the headmaster. Mr Hoddle crumpled into a heap, which everyone thought was dead funny, but I was worried about how Dean was going to explain that one away to our Mam. I also felt sorry for the headmaster, who was old and only had one leg. Dean was suspended for a couple of weeks and ended up not taking any exams at all. Our Mam was angry and frustrated, and blamed herself, as parents do. But being Dean's sister had one advantage. Steel Road was going downhill fast, there were burglaries and cars being set alight every week, but strangely we didn't get turned over once.

Homework was still a problem. Mr Walker, my engineering drawing teacher, saw my potential and wrote to our Mam when he saw my work was suffering. He tried to convince her to give me more time to do homework. Our Mam was resolute – I could have more time for homework, but I would still have to do my bit in the house.

I was always a skinny kid, built like a racing snake. I didn't have an ounce of fat. I was fifteen before I started getting any shape to me at all. Three months later I went to the toilet and discovered blood. I went to our Mam's cupboard and fished out a Dr White with loops from her sanitary drawer, then went and bought some Tampax. I never bothered telling her my periods had started, and she never asked.

When O-levels came round our Mam really thought I was a novelty as I sat there earnestly revising. When her friends came round she was dead proud, showing me off as if I was a circus performer. To me it was simply a means to an end. All I wanted was my independence: a decent car, a decent job and a place of my own. That was the sum total of my aspirations. I was the first girl at Mellbrook School to get an O-level in engineering drawing, and I was overjoyed with my total of seven, which was some going in our parts. I remember saying, 'Mam, I've passed seven O-levels.' She simply said, 'Well done. Now pass those plates and lay the table.'

I applied for the WRNS when I was sixteen, but I wasn't allowed to join until I was seventeen and a half. I could barely wait; it would mean getting away from Middlesbrough. Although going into the Wrens offered an escape, I felt very guilty about leaving our Mam, even though we were still driving each other nuts. Once, during a particularly fraught encounter, I was so angry with her that I raised my fist. I thought I was going to drop dead just from the dark look in her eyes, and limply lowered my hand as she said, 'Just you dare, my lass. It'll be your last.' It was hard to keep my rage suppressed, holding everything deep inside while trying to please her.

I went to technical college to study general engineering while I awaited the day when the Wrens would have me, and worked part-time in a garage to make money. I got £15 cash in hand every Friday. I was fascinated by the principle by which a four-stroke engine works – suck, squeeze, bang and blow. It seemed so marvellous that this mechanical rule could operate a plane or a car. I liked learning things, and no doubt I bored everyone with inane questions like, 'Do you know how much Jaguar tyres cost?' or 'Bet you don't know how much engine oil is lost between oil changes on a Ford Capri.' I was in overalls, with the blokes, and I felt like I was doing a real man's job. The lads didn't treat me any differently, although in those days you'd have expected it. Maybe it was because I met them on their own ground. I never liked to feel inferior; I'd rather have broken my back than admit I couldn't lift a component.

At nights I called out the numbers in a bingo hall in Redcar, and soon I'd saved up the £80 to buy my first scooter, a much-coveted Lambretta GP150. I was so proud of my acquisition that I spent hours at the garage stripping it down and doing it up. One afternoon I painted every inch of the bodywork bright yellow, including the fuel tank and carburettor, not realising that the heat would make the paint flake off them. I loved taking part in rallies from Scarborough to Skegness, flying along the country lanes, exhilarated by my liberation.

At weekends I would doll myself up in jumble-sale twinsets with tight-fitting tops, or jeans and Fred Perry shirts. My hair went through several mod evolutions. I had a flat top for quite a while, with a quiff like James Dean, then a skinhead.

I was seventeen when I met Davey Friar. He was my first real boyfriend, and a good ten years older than me. We used to spend a lot of time in his tatty bedroom in Stainsby. With the lights turned low we listened to Tangerine Dream and practised sex. In the Sea Cadets I'd hung around with a boy called Steve, but we hadn't done anything physical. Steve's older brother, James, was nineteen. I fancied him rather more, and one night, three weeks before my sixteenth birthday, he and I had done it. It had been pretty horrible, although James seemed to enjoy it. But Davey Friar was old enough to know what he was up to, and he became my sex instructor.

One of my friends, Sue, was always at the clinic getting pregnancy tests. So often, in fact, that one day the nurse asked her, 'Do you want to become pregnant?' Sue adamantly shook her head, but shortly afterwards she was, along with many other girls of our age. I was determined not to fall into that trap. I had a vision of the future, and was determined to make something of myself.

By now Dean was more or less permanently inside, and when our Mam told him my scooter had been nicked he used his underworld contacts to see to it that the bloke got a good kicking, after which I was sent round to collect the money for it.

The Sea Cadets didn't treat me as an oddity when I said I wanted to be a mechanic, but I was gutted to discover there was no role for vehicle mechanics in the Wrens: becoming an AEM (Aircraft Engineering Mechanic) was the next best option. The Lieutenant sent me down to the local careers office where I got an information pack and a form to fill in. I went up to Hartlepool for interviews and IQ tests. I was bright enough to pass, and obviously did well because I didn't end up as a chef or a steward. My medical was to be held in Newcastle. I borrowed a pinstripe suit from my friend Jackie, and felt very girl-about-town as I caught the train. I failed the medical because of tonsillitis, but two weeks later I passed with flying colours. Now all I needed was my joining-up papers, proof that I had dedicated the next nine years of my life to the military.

They would arrive as soon as there was a vacancy for a trainee aircraft mechanic.

Two weeks later the envelope with a Portsmouth postmark turned up. I was elated, but there was no one at home to tell, so I ran next door and told the neighbours, Tony and Sandra. They offered me a can of beer to celebrate. I had been waiting for this moment for four years, perhaps for my whole life.

TWO

GETTING OUT

I LEFT STEEL ROAD in September 1983. It was a bright, crisp morning and the milk float was whirring up the street from house to house, bottles clinking, as our Mam and the little 'uns lined up in their nighties on the front doorstep. I'd booked a taxi to take me to Middlesbrough station, and the driver waited patiently, his engine ticking over, as I kissed Melissa, Katherine and Jane good-bye. 'I'll see you at your passing-out in five weeks,' said our Mam simply as she clamped her strong hand on my shoulder. We took it as a given that we'd meet up then; I never once considered that I wouldn't pass.

I heaved my borrowed suitcase into the back of the taxi and as we drove down the street the waving figures in their billowing nightdresses got smaller and smaller. I felt independent, free, eager to make something of myself.

As I waited on the platform for the train taking me towards my new life, I noticed that the zip at the top of my hessian shoulderbag was slightly open. Inside I could see a white envelope. It contained a card from our Mam. On the front was a picture of a little smiling cat in a dustbin. Inside in capital letters she'd written: 'Wishing you Good Luck in your chosen career. Very Best Wishes Sarah, lots of love and thanks for being my friend, Mam.' There were fourteen kisses. My lip wavered and I realised I was starting to cry. I didn't do that often. Tears quietly welled up and rolled down my cheeks. I felt so guilty and so disloyal. Here I was, happy to be getting away from someone who was thanking me for being her friend.

When I arrived at HMS *Raleigh* in Plymouth for five weeks'

basic training, I looked at the other recruits with embarrassment. They were all wearing skirts and dresses, balancing on high-heeled shoes and brushing their long flowing hair. In contrast, I looked as though I should have been going to Borstal. I was dressed in a green bomber jacket over a scooter T-shirt which I'd hacked the arms off, drainpipe jeans and a pair of red desert wellies. My hair was cropped in a severe skinhead. Nobody spoke to me for three days. They must have thought I was some sort of thug.

My first visit to the galley was an overwhelming experience. I was dazzled by the vast quantity and breathtaking variety of food on offer. There was a salad bar, a selection of cold meats, an array of hot dishes, a chilled cabinet filled with desserts, and a drinks machine. I had never had such a choice in my life. As I tucked into a plastic tray loaded up with lasagne, chips and salad, I was beginning the inevitable journey to wobbly 'Wren's bottom'. When I'd had my medical I'd weighed only eight stone, and the doctor had commented that I would benefit from putting on a few pounds. Shouldn't be too much of a problem here, I thought.

Two weeks after joining up I got my first wage packet of £116 and felt like a millionaire. After I'd sent Grandma the £20 I owed her, plus a fiver for interest, I opened my first bank account to deposit the rest.

There were rounds to inspect our mess every morning at 8 a.m. sharp. The officer would expect to bounce a 10p piece off your bed, which you were supposed to have made as tight as the skin on a snare drum. I reckoned it would make more sense to sleep on the floor to beat this, but the Petty Officer in charge of our squad soon rustled me. Smoking was banned, so I'd run a boiling hot bath and smoke amidst the steam. Much of the routine was mindlessly regimented. We had to sweep leaves off the courtyard in October despite the swirling wind that whipped up every pile we made. We endlessly had to clean windows with scrunched-up newspapers and paint the stones lining the training ground with white emulsion.

I wasn't terrifically impressed by my peers. Throughout the training there was a lot of pathetic whimpering going on. I would watch in confusion as girls sobbed down the phone to their mothers and boyfriends. Why were they being so feeble? It seemed very silly to me. I never cried the whole way through training, and I could see no reason for tears.

Our Mam did come to my passing-out parade, which took her fourteen hours by bus from Middlesbrough. I didn't see her in the stand until we'd done our final march-past. As we were dismissed we threw our hats into the air. I saw her watching me with a look of pride on her weatherbeaten face. I briskly pushed through the jostling parents, and saw her standing there clutching her black handbag, in her blue knee-length skirt, floral blouse and cardigan. I was overcome with emotion. Our Mam had come all that way for no other reason than to support me. It was wonderful. As a child I'd never doubted that she loved me; it was just that she sometimes had a funny way of showing it, i.e. by chucking things at me. By coming all the way to Plymouth she'd done something especially for me, and I was able to show her that I'd made some-thing of myself. It was all too much, and the tears finally came. She punched me on the arm. 'What you doing that for?' she asked, embarrassed, her arms wrapping around me. 'If I had my time again I'd be like you, Sarah,' she whispered. It was a defining moment. Here we were, surrounded by all these other relatives with their pet dogs and their Mercedes, but we had none of these things, only each other. And we regarded each other as adults.

I was posted to HMS *Daedalus* at Lee-on-Solent near Portsmouth for six months to learn my chosen trade of AEM. I couldn't believe I was being paid to be taught. After learning the theory of flight, we studied each system in the aircraft individually, from the pneu-matics to the hydraulics of the undercarriage and the method by which the panels were riveted together.

I also had a new boyfriend. Tel was based at Yeovil as an AEM and was on a course at *Daedalus*, and we would spend the weekends in a local B&B. I was on duty one night when he came to visit me. I urgently needed an excuse to get off camp, so I went to the Petty

Officer in charge of duty personnel and told him matter-of-factly, 'I'm not enjoying what I'm doing and I'm considering leaving. My mother has come to try to talk me out of it. Could I have the night off to see her?' Of course he agreed, and I spent the night with Tel. In the morning I was suddenly much more enthusiastic about staying.

During Christmas leave in 1983 I went up to London and struggled through the crowds on the day Harrods was bombed. All the tube stations were blocked as a result of the commotion. Up until that day the IRA's activities had had no relevance to my life. I was confused that terrorists thought they could get anything out of bombing a shop full of innocent people.

I was posted to HMS *Heron*, Royal Naval Air Station Yeovil, HQ of the Fleet Air Arm. The job was shite. I'd expected a wonderful life dashing about seeing foreign countries and drinking Pimms and lemonade; instead I was stuck in grubby men's overalls staring up at the underbellies of Wessex and Sea King helicopters wearing steaming bats (flat-footed, rock-hard boots). I'd been lured in by images of Hong Kong and Malibu. No one had told me the most glamorous place I was going to get to was Prestwick.

It was monotony of the highest order. To complete simple tasks you had to negotiate obstacle courses of red tape. We had to stand to semi-attention before working twenty-four about (a twenty-four-hour shift). I'd hang around in a smoke-filled Portakabin awaiting my aircraft. Then I'd pick up the chocks, two slabs of cheese-wedge-shaped wood. The fifty-tonne heli would hover deafeningly above me, seeking my permission to touch down. I soon started to question the sense of this marshalling. These pilots had been on spectacular missions, most recently in the Falklands. Why couldn't they land by themselves? But no, I had to gesture them down, as they burned and turned above me. Then we'd do a bit of routine thumbs-up before I put the chocks fore and aft. Once I'd done that the pilot would make a neck-slashing movement meaning 'Can I cut rotors?' I'd respond by spinning my hand above my head, then mimicking his gesture, 'Yes, you can cut rotors.' It was like something out of a bad B-movie.

After the janners (Somerset locals working on the base) had helped to refuel I'd check over the heli bodywork for signs of damage, then, using a pole with a clamp on it, spin the five rotor blades until they laid side by side down the length of the helicopter. A tractor would then pull it into the hangar, and I'd examine the service record to see what needed doing to it that day. Some tasks were done daily, others weekly, and some every few hundred or thousand hours' flying time. I hated being bogged down in so much procedural detail.

In February 1984 I got a phone call from our Mam to say that my Granddad had died. I promised to go up to Middlesbrough for the funeral the following day. That night there was a party planned at a friend's house. I wasn't going to go, but my friend Lena persuaded me it would be better than sitting mournfully in the mess by myself. We were all very drunk when Cara, a happy-go-lucky fellow AEM in her early twenties, got a lift back to camp on a motorbike. When we piled out of a taxi at the gate two hours later the security chief told us Cara had been killed and the motorcyclist was critically ill. They were heading north up the A37, a notorious accident black-spot, when they'd lost control on the ice. I spent the evening in a state of shock.

Next day, after my Granddad's funeral, we were solemnly drinking cups of tea and eating Spam sandwiches in Grandma's house when I heard someone whisper, 'She'll be able to have a life now he's out of the way.' The sentiment echoed my thoughts. She'd been a skivvy all her life; maybe now she could do something for herself.

In late 1984 Tel and I moved into a cottage in a small village ten miles west of camp. The only heating was a coal fire in the front room, so it was always freezing. I'd bought a new scooter, a GP200. It was orange, covered in sixteen wing mirrors, and I loved it so much I'd park it in front of the settee at nights.

Two months later we drove to Middlesbrough to collect Dean, who was coming to live with us. He'd never been the world's best brother, but we got on just well enough for me to care about him. I had a meeting with a local probation officer, said I'd be responsible for him, and found him a job in a meat processing plant. He and Tel got on brills. We were always skint, and couldn't afford coal, so they would nip over to the building site opposite and nick wooden pallets for burning instead.

Over Christmas Tel and I were on security duties at camp. In the Wrens' duty cabin there was an open metal cupboard, inside which were two complete sets of DPM (disrupted pattern material) rig. After a week I decided to borrow them, and gave one set to Dean because he was freezing his arse off on a building site. My feet were cold, so I wore the other pair of boots. When I took sick leave after Christmas I asked Tel to return the kit, but he forgot. I ended up in navy court for that one. I pleaded guilty on the advice of my Divisional Officer, got one year's loss of good conduct, was fined and given two weeks' nines (on report). I was pissed off with my DO. He might have had stripes on his shoulder, but his advice had been crap. I decided that respect was earned, not assumed. The job didn't really seem the same after that.

After January leave I came back to find the cottage had been trashed. Tel and Dean had thrown a party without telling me. Nestling in among the empty beer cans and fag ends I found the antique silver butter-knife Grandma had given me when I'd joined up. It was in two pieces. I absolutely flipped, and did a Mam on them. 'How can you care so little about me to do this?' I yelled. Tel and Dean just laughed at me. 'Fuck you both!' I screamed, foaming at the mouth. 'You can piss off home and you can bugger off for good, too.' I was maturing much quicker than either of them, and this was the last straw. Tel and I split up and Dean returned to Middlesbrough.

I moved back to camp and started going out with Stan, a good-looking smoothie, but it didn't last long. My hair was growing out of a flat top, which was very James Dean, and one day I announced that I was going to cut it. 'If you cut your hair I'll finish with you,' Stan said. So I went straight out and got a skinhead. Later that day I marched up to him and said, 'I take it we're finished then?' I wasn't going to have a man dictate terms to me. I owed it to our Mam not to get sucked into that trap.

In March 1985 I decided to move out of camp again, this time with two girlfriends. We rented a three-bedroom semi, six miles outside camp, on the edge of a farmyard. This house was seriously cold in winter. There were gaps under every door and window, and again the only heating was an open fire. All I ever ate was cereal. Clare stuck to meatballs, and Donna preferred beans. One day I was in the bath when Donna ran in. 'There's a cow in the front room,' she shouted.

'I'd lay off the metal polish if I was you,' I said. But I hopped out and went to have a look. There *was* a cow. We tried to shoo it outside, but with neither of us being country girls, we were talking to it as if it was a dog. 'Come on, boy,' I coaxed, clicking my tongue. After five fruitless minutes while the severely underwhelmed cow simply stared at us, I nipped up to the farmhouse and came back with the farmer who shifted it for us.

The following month, on leave, I decided that I was going to pass my driving test. I took five lessons and passed the day before I was due back on base. That night, after the test I borrowed our Mam's silver Chevette, reassuring her that I'd be fine, and nervously drove 380 miles through the night, map-reading my way back to Yeovil. I was well pleased with myself.

Yeovil was a life of hard working, hard drinking and hard playing. There was always a big group of us hanging around together. One friend, Big George, made home brew out of a mixture of gin, tonic, Bacardi and Coke. It tasted gopping.

By way of contrast, I started writing poems at this time. Loads of words about people I loved, anarchic issues and soldiers were always spinning in my head. Getting them on paper was a way of silencing those verbose demons.

The job was disciplined, but it was the only life I knew. I'd never been a Wild Child – no Mandy Smith, me! – but after a few months I'd had enough, and began popping into the regulating office every few days to pester the Chief Drafting Officer. 'Got any drafts going anywhere? Whatever it is, wherever it is, just send me and I'll do it,' I pleaded.

So it was that in February 1986 I ended up in Northwood,

London, as a driver, ferrying senior military personnel and VIPs. The job was OK, but Northwood was a dump. I'd left a shite job in a nice place to go to a nice job in a shite place. It was the world's shortest draft – it only lasted three months.

During my time at Northwood I went on a skiing holiday in Aviemore with some mates. We drove up in a twelve-seater Sherpa van. I'd never been skiing before, but by day four I was dangling off the towbar of a drag lift pulling me to the top of a black run. I was two hundred metres up the slope when my mate fell off and started scrabbling her way over to the loose snow at the edge. I fell hard onto the packed icy snow. I began slipping back down the steep drag path, rapidly gaining speed and screaming, 'Stop the lift!' The skiers being peacefully pulled up the slope realised with horror that this careening flash of baby blue was going to smash into them. As I collided with each shouting body my position changed. I ended up on my front, pointing downhill like a human toboggan. I tore someone's cartilage and gave a young girl a cut that needed twelve stitches. One expert skier was able to open his legs and I shot between them. At the bottom of the drag lift I was a bloodied heap. I had a broken nose and a cut lip, and a ski had sliced through my suit, burning my groin. I checked my zippered pocket to see if my fags were still there. It hadn't been a good day out, but at least I could still have a smoke. A week later my chest was still an ugly mass of bruising. I decided I'd better stick to summer sports.

One day back at camp in May 1986 I saw a signal from Navy communications: 'Any Wrens wishing to volunteer as augmentees for a tour of duty in Northern Ireland with 45 Commando Marines please contact...' I didn't want to go back to fixing boring helis, so I applied. I didn't think I had much of a chance, but I got the draft along with five other Wrens. Accepting such a posting means you might be filling a role that isn't your trade, but I didn't care. I was going to Northern Ireland to do a job with the Marines, and that was enough to make it worthwhile. It had to be better than what I was doing.

Then I discovered that I'd got the shittiest job going, as an

45

officers' mess steward. Stewards are there as servants to the Ruperts, and in the military it doesn't get any lower.

I went up to 45 Commando in Arbroath, Tayside, and was met at the gate by a big black Marine sergeant who showed me the way to the Wrens' quarters. There were three companies there: X-Ray, Yankee and Zulu. I later discovered that the Marines' sick sense of humour meant that all the black blokes automatically went into Zulu Company.

I was washing up, learning how to juggle silver cutlery and make Ruperts' beds – clearly they weren't switched on enough to make their own. I couldn't believe people would actually join the Navy expressly to do a job like this. You might as well stay at home and look after your Mam and Dad. I didn't find the job demeaning, because I didn't see the Ruperts as better than me. But I got a good grounding in etiquette. I learned how to set a table and what a fish-knife was. I also did a short stint as a wine waiter, but my style didn't go down too well. The first night I appeared at the mess door with a bottle of red in my left hand, and a bottle of white in my right. 'Hands up who wants red and who wants white,' I shouted at the Ruperts dining around a mahogany table the size of a tennis court. I was kept in the kitchen after that.

There were eight Wrens and a thousand Marines in Arbroath. The whole unit was starting its Northern Ireland training, so we had lectures in terrorist recognition, which included potted biogs of active players. There was also 'Doc Jolly's horror show', a series of slides introducing us to the devastating effects of bombs and bullets. Many of the bodies were pulped beyond recognition. We saw slides of decapitated corpses being scooped up and put into body bags. There was an old lady with a chair leg through her thigh, and one poor bastard had a piece of wood through his chest which looked like a stake through his heart. That got the vampire jokes going. It wasn't a very nice show, but I wasn't gagging. When I was little there had always been something going on on the medical front.

One night, after a group of Marines had finished their basic training they were made to stand on the roof of the accommodation

block for a game of human Space Invaders, as an initiation ceremony. They had to march back and forth in rows making beeping
noises while the older blokes lobbed bricks at them and kept a tally
of who scored the most points. It was funny to watch, but I did
feel for these young lads being humiliated after their tough training.

After a month in Arbroath we went to a training camp in the
south of England, where units heading across the water were given
NITAT (Northern Ireland Training and Advisory Team) training.
A mock village had been built inside the camp to look like a typical
rough Republican area. There were council houses, pubs, shops,
clubs and derelict buildings. The lads were taught FIBUA (fighting
in built-up areas), to give them simulated hands-on experience of
crowd control on the streets of Northern Ireland. We were there
to act as civ pop (civilian population). The lads would drive out in
an APV (armoured personnel vehicle) or patrol in a four-man brick
while we acted as an angry crowd, antagonising them by giving
them verbal abuse. Exciting mob fights would break out when we
lobbed propellant canisters at them. It was great fun, but some of
the Marines went over the top and there were a few broken bones
among the civ pop. One bloke in a patrol was set on fire by an
instructor who threw a petrol bomb. He didn't use his shield correctly, the flames licked underneath and he was badly burned.

In June 1986, after final preparations in Scotland, I flew from
Edinburgh across to Belfast on my first commercial flight. I was
the first to go over from our batch of augmentees. The advance
party of Marines were already there, setting up the admin and
accommodation arrangements, and the Ruperts couldn't manage
to brew their own cups of tea. I was stationed at Musgrave Park
Hospital, a military compound which was home to the REMFs
(rear echelon motherfuckers), including the padre, travel planners,
transport section and admin staff. For nearly five months I looked
after the admin officers, running around like a real Cinderella,
serving and cleaning. But it was worth it. I was over the water,
where the action was. My doing a shitty job meant a Marine could
go on the street and do a real one.

9 August is Internment Day, when the Catholics traditionally

light huge pyres in the middle of roads to commemorate the intro-duction of internment by the Unionist Northern Ireland govern-ment in 1971. This law allowed the RUC to arrest and detain suspected players, irrespective of whether they were Republicans or Loyalists, without charging or trying them. Although internment had worked when it was introduced in the 1930s, forties and fifties, by 1971 the RUC's intelligence was well out of date. By the time they and the squaddies kicked the terrorists' doors down, they were already drinking pints of Guinness down south. Basically it was a fuck-up. Internment was discredited and became a symbol of Unionist stupidity.

The purpose of Internment Day is to create maximum disrup-tion. A friend of mine, Sully, a Sergeant Patrol Commander, let me sneak out with him in his pig (APV) for a look around the area. My hair was pulled up into the helmet so I would look like a bloke. I went top cover and poked my head up through the roof flaps. The atmosphere on the streets was electrifying. I peered through smoking bonfires at people hovering menacingly by piles of bricks, waiting to take out any passing patrol. The air was thick with acrid smoke, and loudspeakers were pumping out Republican music on every street corner. I ducked back just in time as the pounding of bricks rattled against our armoured bodywork. A shouting mob of men and children were lobbing any object that wasn't stuck down at us. I felt exhilarated to be there, but thanked God for the mesh over the windows. The hailstorm of projectiles intensified, but the Marines seemed very calm.

'This is tradition,' my mate explained. 'It's not meant to be incendiary or provocative, but we have to put in a presence.' At that moment the driver saw a burning car blocking the road ahead and lurched sharply to the left in order to clip it. We smacked into it at a fair pace and shunted it out of the way, but the pig barely jolted. The crowd roared with anger. An APV is a massive, heavy vehicle, so moving a car out of the way isn't a hassle, but coming to a halt wasn't an option. That would have made us an easier target for bricks or anything else the mob wanted to chuck at us. Crowds are unpredictable. A small incident can escalate very swiftly into violent mass hysteria, with everyone running on overdrive.

The presence of twenty thousand troops in Northern Ireland meant there were plenty of jobs in trades and services supporting the army. The nature of life in Ulster means that only Protestants did this work. The Provos, with their usual sick logic, had decided that anyone working for the security forces in any way was a 'legitimate target'. Consequently a number of defenceless building contractors, cleaners, milkmen and delivery drivers had been subjected to threats and attacks, and some had even been murdered. For the soldiers the source of greatest concern was the possibility of a base without beer. But, to their credit, Guinness defiantly delivered the goods.

Would-be local employees face an intensive grilling programme before they are allowed to work on the bases. I became friends with some of these women, and they were very good to me. I would sneak them bottles of wine from the officers' mess bar and we'd all sit together drinking and chatting after their shifts. They drank spirits like other people drink tea, and would think nothing of bringing a bottle of vodka in to work, which we'd see off during their shift. When I asked them why they risked working for the security forces their answer was straightforward: 'It puts the bread on the table.' To them it was just a way of life. They were taking a risk, but from their point of a view they were taking a risk by stepping on the road every day.

45 Commando's tour carried on like any other, with the usual excitements. Springfield Road RUC station was bombed twice while I was there, with only one minor casualty. When the bomb sirens went off we had to dash to the courtyard and wait it out. X-Ray company had a success when a young Marine shot and killed James McKernan, a Provo sniper, as he took off from a failed murder attempt still clutching his rifle. The Marine got two crates of beer and a cake as a reward.

I loved being across the water where the action was, and I began to realise there was more to security in Northern Ireland than the boys in uniform on the streets. I wanted a part of it. I wanted to know what was going on, and to understand the structure, to see how intelligence tied in with the bigger picture. In North Howard Street Mill, where my mate Karen was working, there was a door marked 'Int Cell' (Intelligence Cell) with a vast 'No Entry' sign. There was something secret going on in there. Two other Wrens at HQNI in Lisburn, the main operational and administrative headquarters for the whole Province, were required to work in plain clothes. I didn't know what was happening, but it fascinated me. I was lured by the unknown, and made it my mission to find out everything I could about the secret side of the anti-terrorist war.

THREE

AN OBSESSIVE REGIME

I LEFT 45 COMMANDO in the spring of 1987 after a tour of duty in Norway, which was great: lots of beer and parties under the bewitching Northern Lights. I was back at Yeovil, once again cleaning the charmless oily underbellies of aircraft. It was a monotonous eleven-month stint characterised by lengthy and irrelevant paperwork, broken fingernails and the heavy stench of AVGAS.

In the summer of 1987 I changed my name by deed poll from Wilson to Ford, my mother's maiden name. Eric had had nothing to do with bringing me up. He was uninterested in my existence; he didn't even recognise me. Four years earlier I'd gone to court with our Mam, who was chasing him for years of unpaid maintenance. I'd recognised him straight away, but he'd looked at our Mam and muttered, 'Who's that?' She had given him a ferocious look and, bristling with anger, said, 'That's Sarah, your eldest daughter.' I'd felt so small and insignificant. Eric had always been completely irrelevant to who I was, but this had been the last straw. Now I felt no desire to carry his name any longer. I knew our Mam would be chuffed to bits if I changed my name to hers.

After the deed was done I phoned her up and said simply: 'In the future, don't be writing Wilson on my mail. My new name is Ford.' To say our family is not one for great displays of emotion is an understatement, but I knew my decision had given our Mam an inward smile and some quiet happiness. That was enough.

As Wren Ford I went twice to my DO to ask for a job change. I was bored shitless. I did a short spell with the RMP (Royal Military Police) in Aldershot, but it was crap. Very tick-tock and alienated from the rest of the army. We spent our time arresting drunken squaddies and completing yards of paperwork. Then, in a moment of desperation, I even considered becoming an officer. I attended classes at the education centre in Yeovil and had to write essays to justify my position in an imaginary hot-air balloon. It struck me as a lot of nonsense, so instead I sat and quietly wrote poetry all over the page.

In November, along with everyone else in the crew room, I was sickened to hear about the bombing at Enniskillen during the Remembrance Day service. Everyone was horrified (even the Soviet government said it was 'an act of savagery'), and when Gordon Wilson talked about holding his daughter Marie's hand as her life ebbed away under the rubble, I was moved to tears. Fucking bastards. It wasn't about the Cause, it was the senseless massacre of innocents.

After Christmas leave I rescued our Melissa from Middlesbrough and brought her to live with me. She eventually got a job in the NAAFI at Yeovil. A few months later I decided I'd spent long enough going nowhere, doing nothing. My ambitious nature was straining against its short leash, so in May 1988 I went to see my DO, Lieutenant Harry Loon, the first port of call in my bid for Special Duties. Loonytunes was a typical Rupert: very switched on, but couldn't tell you what day Sunday lunch was served. Like most Ruperts, his head was crammed with fascinating, but completely irrelevant information. He could tell you how to split the atom, but ask him the price of a pint of milk and he'd have been stumped.

I rapped on his half-open door and stuck my head around it. His office was nondescript military style: teak-effect desk with peeling veneer, pseudo-plush carpet with more static than a substation. There were Fleet Air Arm pictures on the walls and a brood of smiling children in leather frames on the shelf behind him.

'Can I have a word, sir?'

'Yes, of course. Come in.' He motioned towards a chair. The Fleet Air Arm was more laid-back than other departments of the Navy, so I didn't have to stand to attention. Loony was in his late thirties with severely receding short black hair, big buck teeth and a face like the cartoon character Skeletor.

'Sir, have you heard of 14 Int?'

He smiled, and nodded knowingly. His smug manner said it all: he knew a bit, but not much. Although of course he wasn't about to tell me that.

'Great. Could you tell me how I apply for Special Duties Northern Ireland? It's something I really want to do.'

He leaned back in his chair and placed his hands behind his head like a politician. Pompous git. Did I imagine it, or was he speaking extra slowly? 'Well, you must bear in mind, Wren Ford, that special duties and the Intelligence Corps require a particular sort of individual.' Like an officer, I thought.

'Special in what way, sir?'

'Well, let's put it this way: you could always try for 14 Int, but can I suggest another department which is a bit less demanding?'

Loonytunes didn't know his arse from his elbow on this subject. Like everyone else, he'd no doubt heard rumours about specialist units, although he knew no more than the rest. I soon found out that outside the Special Forces and intelligence community, nobody knew anything about what 14 Int did or how they trained. But Loony would lose face if he admitted this to a mere rating, and a woman at that.

The 'less demanding' department he was referring to was a small sub-unit of 14 Company. I later found out that their training was nowhere near as arduous as the rest of 14 Int, although the job they do is invaluable to the smooth operation of Special Forces, if more backstage. But Loon believed that they were glorified taxi-drivers, which couldn't be further from the truth. While they didn't do surveillance, they were involved in other crucial, sneaky stuff and working in an atmosphere of top secrecy.

Arsehole. I'd show him, I vowed to myself, though to be fair there was no good reason to think that I was suddenly going to turn into Superwren. I was in a shit job, doing as little as possible to get by, and my six-monthly reports reflected this. No wonder Loon felt he had to spell everything out in carefully enunciated words of one syllable, as if I was a moron.

But he was decent enough to direct me to the next stage by

putting me on to the Captain's secretary, a huge bulk of a man in his early forties who answered my questions, as far as he was able. He put my name forward for an interview in October. I was dismayed that I'd have to wait five months, but at least I was on my way.

By now Melissa had moved into NAAFI quarters and I'd started going out with Chris, a Marine who'd just come back from Arctic training in Norway. I'd seen him around the camp, mostly at the bar and the 393 Club, the after-hours drinking den in Ilchester where the Marines were always celebrating something, usually by getting dressed up in women's clothes or fancy dress. On one of those nights I'd had a bet on with my mates that I'd trap before two. I spotted Chris wearing a kilt, sporran and a bushy ginger beard held on with knicker elastic, and decided he was mine. Not that I had a fetish for drunk Scotsmen, but he was having such a good time with the lads that I thought I'd make his night complete and asked him back to my place for breakfast. He accepted. He was a bit of a pin-up, with a gorgeous hunky chest and fair hair, and he was always sending up his Dorset accent. Pretending to be thick, he'd say, 'How many beans make five?' I'd say, 'Five, you daft git.' He'd reply: 'No. Two beans, a bean, a bean-and-a-half and half-a-bean'. He was a good mate, a sensitive lover, and very much one of the lads. He was also a bit of a mummy's boy, taking his washing home every week despite the forty-minute drive each way. Mind you, when I eventually got to see his place I realised why. I'd have spent most of my time there as well. I couldn't believe it. It was one of those places with a semi-circular gravel drive. I'd thought he was a bit more well-to-do than me, but then, so were most people. He never mentioned this grand house in a sleepy Dorset village, with white pillars and steps leading up to the front door. His dad had a sit-down lawnmower. His mum prepared lunch for us, grilled trout with all the trimmings. I'd never tackled a headed fish before, and I thought she'd done it on purpose to embarrass me. I watched Chris make a start before I dared to dissect the aquatic beastie.

We spent a lot of time in the 393 Club, but I was also reading up on the history and current affairs of Northern Ireland; I wanted to absorb as much as I possibly could. I also had a more practical weapon to add to my arsenal of information: the video of the film *Harry's Game*, based on Gerald Seymour's novel, which I used as a training aid. It tells the story of a British agent who infiltrates the Republican community of West Belfast so convincingly that he is fully accepted and able to live amongst them.

I took this to be an accurate portrayal of life inside 14 Int; living among people and fooling them. A convincing Northern Irish accent was clearly going to be a vital tool in my future career, so I would sit reverently in front of the video, remote-control poised, slavishly pressing rewind. It was quite a difficult accent to master. One female character's husband had spent ten years inside the Maze, Britain's top-security prison and home to the most diehard terrorists, so I focused on her phrase 'a tenner in the Kesh'. Fortunately no one discovered my intense homework – not even Chris knew what I was up to. It sounds ridiculous, but I really believed that I had a good chance of fitting in if I worked hard enough. Of course it can't be done; people don't just pop up from nowhere. The members of those small communities have grown up with the Troubles, and are very closely knit. It's also a culture that thrives on gossip. I'd have lasted about ten seconds. About as long as it would have taken me to say, 'Feck you. My da's got a tenner in the Kesh. So wha's you looking at?'

My need to get out of my shitty job and into something worthwhile had become so desperate that I decided I couldn't wait until October. Instead I would try to get on to the earlier intake that was to be held at Yeovil in July. I told no one about my intentions.

I'd spent my summer leave backpacking around Europe on my own, and I came back a day early, on the evening before the interviews were to be held. I cycled up to the camp and slipped into the Portakabin at the main gate to get some info out of the visitors' book. It confirmed that there were about twenty visitors overnighting in the camp. They'd given their destination for the next day as FONAC (Flag Officer Naval Air Command). The last signature on the list was a Wren from Portsmouth. I knew exactly where to find her. I waved my way past the guys on the gate and headed for the transit cabin in the Wrens' quarters. There I introduced myself to the Jenny Wren, who asked if I was on the interview as well.

'Yeah, but I'm just back off leave and I've forgotten what time we've got to report.' Nine o'clock sharp next morning, she told me. 'Got to see what's-his-face, haven't we?' I asked. 'Warrant Officer Wickes,' she said helpfully. She must have thought I was either mega laid-back, or just plain stupid. As if I could have forgotten the most important interview of my life! It was time to bail out. 'Well, must dash, early to bed and all that,' I said as I left, feeling rather pleased with myself. But by the next morning my patina of confidence had disappeared. The chances of being blown out and barred forever for my impertinence seemed a bit higher. But on balance I decided to take the risk. I didn't know what kit, if any, to bring to the interview, so I put on trainers, jeans and a rugby shirt before cycling across to FONAC armed only with my ID card and a lot of neck.

FONAC is a massive three-storey building normally swarming with people, but the day before the end of leave it was as silent as a synagogue at Christmas. Inside the double glass doors I was greeted by a civvy receptionist. 'Hi, I'm here for the interview with Warrant Officer Wickes,' I explained brightly, although my stomach was turning cartwheels. I flashed my ID and scribbled my name. She waved me through the next set of doors. I stood there, not knowing which way to turn, then sidled back to her. Her eyes narrowed as I asked where the interview was being held.

'You *are* on the interview, aren't you?' she demanded, staring at me quizzically.

Time to start waffling. 'Yes, sort of, well, not really, no. I'm on the next interview, but I was hoping to get on this one.'

She bustled off and returned with a dark-haired Warrant Officer in his forties, an Al Pacino lookalike. He seemed a bit perplexed. Feeling rather apprehensive, I explained myself, thrusting my ID card at him. He wanted to know how I'd heard about the earlier interview, so I explained that I'd asked a few questions. He was clearly gobsmacked by my enthusiasm and neck. He led me into his office and started hitting me with questions about Northern Ireland. My answers were as rapid as Uzi sub-machine-gun fire. I didn't falter. Then he asked: 'Why do you want to apply for Special Duties?'

I spoke with passion. I had set myself this goal. I'd never wanted anything as badly before. 'I'm capable of doing it. I've got what it takes, I promise you, sir. I've already worked in Northern Ireland in '86 with 45 CDO, where I met some local women at Musgrave Park. They were such givers, so warm and generous. They had great loyalty to the Crown, they were more British than anyone I'd ever met in England. And all they hope for is peace. They've got dead brothers, dead uncles, dead sons. Maybe I could go out there, do this job and make a small contribution to people like those women. Give them the chance to go to work in the cookhouse on the SF base and not worry about being shot.'

It struck me that I still didn't know what the job entailed, and as I was speaking I wondered if I was hitting the wrong note. Perhaps I shouldn't answer with such emotion. Maybe I should have stuck to the standard answers about it being 'a challenge' and 'wanting to test myself'. But it was too late now.

Wickes spoke sternly. 'Who do you think you are, to presume that you can change other people's lives? Remember, this is not a personal issue.' I froze. Had I blown it? Was he agreeing with me, or criticising me?

He rose to his feet. 'All right, Wren Ford, why don't you go through and join the other interviewees. Do you have your training kit with you?' My devious plan seemed to have paid off. Resourcefulness was obviously admired in this sector. Of course, what I hadn't admitted was that the prospect of a pay rise would be better than a poke in the eye with a rusty nail.

I joined the others in the waiting room. There were twenty or twenty-five in total, but only four of them were girls. The boys were immaculate in their dark interview suits. The girls were wearing skirts and jackets. I reckoned that three of them looked like Ruperts, and the other was the Wren. I self-consciously rubbed my hand through my quiff as I scanned the room. Sitting there was Tel, my ex. 'What are you doing here?' I asked incredulously, but he wasn't in the mood to chat. 'Can't talk now, I'm a bit busy,' he replied, looking as if he had more important people to bother with than me. Then I twigged: he obviously thought I was just delivering a message. He soon got the picture when I walked into the lecture hall with the rest of the crowd. Tel didn't pass the interview – far too cocky and immature, but then, I could have told them that.

There were written tests, including recognition, map reading, general knowledge and the BFT (basic fitness test), a mile and a half in a squad run inside fifteen minutes, followed by an individual return run in under eleven minutes. I'd just been on the piss for two weeks in Europe, so even one press-up would have been a bit of a challenge. Soon my lungs were bursting out of my ribcage, but I made it, earning myself a place on the January 1989 intake. That gave me six months to get my body sorted.

Before we left we were handed a printed sheet with the fitness requirements for Camp One: BFT, CFT (combat fitness test: eight miles cross-country with pack and weapon in ninety minutes) – fine, sixty sit-ups in a minute, sixty press-ups in a minute. I shredded it. I didn't need instruction sheets; I just planned to become as mentally and physically fit as was humanly possible.

That night I was smugly content. I couldn't celebrate with Chris, because he was off on exercise for ten days. Anyway, I hadn't told him what I was up to. I'd have looked a right prat if I'd failed the interview; and anyway, you don't gob off about Northern Ireland.

The next few months were very intense. I devised my own memory recognition tests, forcing myself to become highly observ-ant in normal everyday life. I would make myself remember cars' registration numbers and models after the most fleeting of glances. I would try to recall the nuances of people's mannerisms in shops and on the street, and look for patterns and routines in the daily lives of my friends. I also spent time on 'Kim's game', getting Chris, who was totally supportive, to put various objects under a towel so I could memorise them. We had condoms, KY Jelly, a jockstrap –

you name it. I went to the military section of WH Smith and found a small pocket book called *Rifles, Sub-Machine Guns and Carbines*. It was stuffed with all the spec on a range of guns: country of origin, magazine capacity, cyclic rate of fire. I didn't have much money, but books like this were more important than beer. I wasn't a book buyer, and my previous literary explorations had ranged only as wide as psychic Doris Stokes, Arthur C. Clarke and other science fiction. In my late teens I'd preferred scooter magazines. I'd never been one for women's glossies.

Now I was a freak for the written word. I borrowed books from Yeovil library and sat in the reference room devouring *Jane's Infantry Weapons*, an absolute gun-fest of an encyclopedia. I also took a trip down to Lympstone, the Royal Marines' training camp near Exeter, where they have a weapons museum. I spent all day fully absorbed. The home-made terrorist weapons particularly intrigued me. Crude and semi-effective, they were none the less ingenious, using a simple firing mechanism roughly shaped from metal. The place was really hands on – you could pick each item up and explore it. The old boy running the show, an ex-Marine, was chuffed to bits by my interest. I don't think he had many visitors. I'd had zero interest in guns prior to this, but I knew they would be a major component of the course.

I trained like ten men in and around the camp, running while burdened with forty-pound weights. I cycled, swam and regularly hit the assault course at Lympstone. I put myself through the Royal Marines endurance course, which included pulling yourself along a rope slung across the River Exe and scrambling over a twelve-foot wall. I even went to aerobic classes. When people commented on my permanently sweaty fatigues, I told them I was training to be a PTI (physical training instructor). I was pounding my body over ten-mile runs, and I took my fully-laden bergen, weighing almost sixty pounds, on shorter distances. No matter how hard I trained, or how much I willed myself to go faster, I was simply crap in the legs and lungs departments. I could hike for miles over hills and train for hours in the gym, but getting the BFT down to the required eleven minutes was looking like an impossibility.

In November I was devastated by a bombshell, the first of two. My legs had been giving me serious gyp, but I'd put it down to shin splints. Everyone on the base seemed to be an authority on this explanation for painfully aching legs. Some people thought you should just run them out, and I was one of them. Despite the throbbing pain, I kept going. One particularly grey and overcast day I was out for a run. I had made just a single pathetic mile before the pain turned to nausea. My calves were under such extreme pressure they felt ready to explode. I flopped down on the verge, halfway to Ilchester, and pressed my hands over my legs, which were pumping like red-hot valves. Just beneath the skin's surface all along their length were soft, compact nodules, the size of marbles. I didn't know what was going on. I staggered to the road and hitched a lift back to camp. The agony was constant. Next day I reported to the sick bay. The pain had gone, but I knew I had a serious problem.

I must have sounded desperate to the medic. 'I've really got to sort this out. I'm in preparation for an arduous training course.'

He referred me to a specialist at The Royal Naval Hospital Haslar in Portsmouth, who three days later prodded and poked my calf while I flexed my feet to exercise the different muscle groups. I fervently hoped that he would come up with a simple and effective magic solution. But he had grim news that sent my ambitions into free-fall. Because of my violent training regime I'd developed a condition known as calf compression. My muscle had expanded too quickly for the sheath that contained it. The resulting constriction was preventing my blood from circulating freely. I faced two options. The first was an operation in which the backs of the legs between knee and heel were cut and the sheath was snipped, giving the muscle room to expand. I was only too aware that these were military doctors, not cosmetic surgeons. It was odds on that I would be left with two hideous foot-long scars. Option two was less extreme: rest. This would give the sheath time to expand naturally. Halting training would also cause the muscle to shrink slightly.

There was no contest. If I took it easy, maybe I'd only be out of action for three or four weeks. That would still give me four weeks to get back up to speed for January. If I chose the operation, I'd face three months' rehab.

I kidded myself that this was just a little setback, and ignored the fact that plunging into a physically stressful programme in January could exacerbate the problem. I left the hospital with a completely unrealistic sense of optimism. For the next three weeks I stuck to cycling, swimming and concentrating on my upper-body strength. Everything but running.

The second of the two bombshells hit me at Christmas 1988. I'd missed two periods. The first I'd put down to training; the second was accompanied by waves of evening nausea. The pregnancy test was positive. I'd gone for a simple test while I was home on Christmas leave in Middlesbrough. I'd been on the pill for seven years from the age of sixteen, and had recently changed to the cap. It obviously hadn't worked. In those brisk five minutes my whole life spun like a Catherine wheel. I was facing a completely different reality, one which required me to make the toughest decision I had so far had to make in my life. To have the baby, or to stop it so I could go on with the course? In those days, if you were pregnant you had to leave the forces. That was it, finished. No second chances. It was a tough one. When I was younger I'd wanted six children; I loved them. It was a heart-wrenching decision. Why now?

Chris was brilliantly understanding, and made it clear he would stand by me whatever I decided. I knew that if I had the baby and left the Wrens he would take care of me, but I didn't want to end up stuck in a rut like our Mam. I hoped to have a family when I was financially secure; but not now. I didn't want to rely on Chris. Deep down I knew that he didn't want me to rely on him either. I needed a swift road out of this nightmare. I didn't even consider telling our Mam. I'd always shielded her from the bad things in my life. If I told her, it would become her problem too, because she loved me. Then I'd feel shitty for making her feel bad. I'd still have the original problem, plus the additional guilt. It was easier to stay silent.

I also made a tactical decision not to tell the sick bay about it. Instead, after Christmas leave, I went to the best Rupert I'd ever met. Lieutenant Harris was one of the pilots, a little wrinkled guy with glasses, who was easy to talk to, on the ball and fair-minded. I went straight to the point.

'Look, sir, I've got a bit of a problem and I'm going to ask you to help me out. If you can't help me for whatever reason, can you promise me that this conversation never happened?'

He was very concerned. I was asking him for two favours: time off for the termination, and an indulgence flight to see Chris, who was now back on exercise in Norway. I was at a low point. The pregnancy had been the last straw. Six months' hard training had been for nothing. My legs were fucked and a baby was growing inside me. More than ever I needed the support which I knew Chris would give me. Lieutenant Harris was brilliant. He said he'd sort out the time off, and he did.

I booked myself into a private clinic in Bournemouth and stayed overnight with a friend in Poole. The termination took place early in the morning. I came round from the anaesthetic feeling depressed and alone. I could have done with talking it through with our Mam, who would always make me feel better, but I couldn't burden her with my misery. I was supposed to stay overnight for observation, but that wasn't possible – I was leaving for Norway on a Hercules transport plane at 9.30 that evening. The nursing staff agreed that I could discharge myself if someone came to collect me. I asked my friend to do the honours, and she had to sign a disclaimer in case I bled to death. No sooner was I out of the double swing doors than I gently eased myself into my battered Chevette and drove back to Yeovil.

I spent the night on a tiny square hessian seat rigged up on rails. The Hercules was overloaded with cargo, and the toilet facilities were not the best in the world. There was a bucket reeking of chemical stench shielded by a curtain which wrapped tightly around you when you sat down. The flight was full of matelots and Marines and I was grappling with a thick sanitary pad – the industrial variety. I was bleeding continually and every movement was painful. During the seven-hour flight to northern Norway I had to change the pad twice due to heavy blood loss. I had no option but to put the used pads in a plastic bag and stuff them in my bergen. The plane was cramped, and I couldn't sleep because of the vibration and noise. Here I was, stuck on a transport plane when I should have been in hospital enjoying forty-eight hours with my feet up. I was suffering the most acute stomach ache of my life, but it was overshadowed by my emotional suffering. I felt guilty, confused and worried. I'd stopped my first baby – had I also damaged my chances of conceiving another child in the future? Everything inside my mind was dark and depressing. I was wallowing in self-pity.

Chris was wonderfully supportive for the three days I was able to spend with him. I cried a lot at the great sense of emptiness I felt, and he held me and talked me through the low periods.

As January rolled on, my sense of devastation was acute. The training course for 14 Intelligence Company had begun without me, and I had been thrown back into the world of mind-numbingly dull aircraft work. Angry and frustrated, I kept asking myself, why me? My happiness always correlates with my level of physical fitness. As soon as I could, I started training again in preparation for the July course. My legs seemed OK, if a bit sore at times, but this was more than compensated for by the fact that I was back on track. Sunday was my only day of rest: I'd let myself off lightly with a ten-miler around the countryside before a big scoff and a few beers.

When Chris came back from Norway in March he fully backed my training, even though we both knew that if I passed we faced a separation of many months. As for me, I was totally enveloped by my mission.

I still found time to phone our Mam once a week, and one Wednesday she had bad news. 'You know that local nutter, Mackie, the one that's got a problem with Dean?'

'Yeah, that gormless-looking skinny lad. What's he done, Mam?'

'Well, because Dean's inside and he couldn't get at him directly, he came round and smashed up all my windows last night.' I could feel my anger rising as our Mam told me how she and Katherine had raced downstairs to find glass all over the carpets. They'd been up half the night clearing it up and boarding up the windows in case of a return visit. The following morning they'd heard on the local grapevine that Mackie had been responsible, and later in the day he'd had the gall to walk past with some of his cronies as our Mam was sweeping the front step. He'd started sneering and gloating at her, a sly smile on his cocky face.

'I had a go at him,' she said. 'I told him, "I know it was you, don't think you're going to get away with it. I know where you live." Then he swore at me and started verbally abusing me.'

This had really set our Mam off. 'Dean will come and get you,' she'd screamed. 'Fuck off, you old slag,' he'd replied, then gobbed at her and ran off. Our Mam had chased after him, and even peaceable Katherine had run out of the house waving a broom.

I made my decision. Mackie was going to get it, not from Dean, but from me – although I didn't tell our Mam this. On Saturday I scrounged a lift the 380 miles to Middlesbrough. My arrival was a surprise for our Mam, although I think she knew why I'd come.

That night Katherine and I went round the local pubs in search of the arrogant fucker. We were standing by the bar in the Red Lion when Mackie came over and asked how I was. I caught Katherine's eye. She was urging me to keep calm, and after I'd exchanged a few pleasantries with Mackie she pulled me away before I exploded.

We slunk out, and waited around the corner. Ten minutes later Mackie emerged. I swung my hand out, grabbed his chest and flung him against the wall, firmly holding his windpipe. Three of his mates stood watching, not sure how to react. A few people drifted out of the pub when they heard Mackie kicking up a fuss, but they soon decided to let him sort this out by himself – and so did his mates. At this stage I was only talking to him, but my voice was sharp as a butcher's knife. I had my mother's honour to defend, so I didn't think twice about the fact that he was taller and more muscled than me. I was seething with anger at this poxy man insulting our Mam, and there was no question that I wouldn't take action on her behalf.

'Where did you get the right to go up to my mother and speak to her like that, spit at her and put her windows through? How dare you?' I hissed through gritted teeth. Mackie tried to wheedle his way out.

'It wasn't me,' he said feebly.

Katherine said, 'Don't fucking lie, Mackie. I was there.'

Realising that tack wasn't going to work, he started apologising. I wasn't interested. 'Don't fucking bother apologising to me. Get your arse around there and fucking apologise to our Mam.' I let him go, and pushed him away. At that moment seven blokes rounded the corner. Mackie glanced at them, saw he knew them and got a bit brave. He puffed out his chest and said with a mocking laugh: 'Only kidding. I'm not fucking apologising to your fucking slut of a mother.'

He leaned forward and pushed me in the chest. Before he'd finished my hand flew up and whacked him in the face. Blood poured out of his bust lip. People were coming out of the pub to watch the action. Within a few seconds Mackie and I were scrapping, lunging at each other as the crowd egged us on. Suddenly my kidneys exploded – someone had booted me from behind. As I shot bolt upright in pain a couple of Mackie's mates grasped my arms and pulled them tightly behind me. I was struggling to get free, and Katherine was doing her nut. Brave Mackie then had a free shot. With his meaty fist he gave me a bust lip to match his, and a second swipe in the eye, but as he was coming in for the third punch I managed to kick him in the balls and he collapsed to the floor.

Katherine, who'd never been in a fight in her life, had seen enough. She skip-jumped and booted the crouching figure in the head. She was magnificent. Mackie's mates left her alone, thank God. Instead they dragged me out into the street and flung me up against a café with a grille pulled down over its windows. Just as well, or I'd have smashed through it. Then we heard the whine of a squad car, and the crowd swiftly broke up, just before I would have got my battering. Katherine and I marched off in the opposite direction. I was covered in blood and my eye was starting to throb. I knew I'd have a shiner. My kidneys were tender and blood was foaming in my mouth, but I was happy. I'd achieved my task. I knew Mackie wouldn't be back. As we turned the corner into Steel Road, our Mam was waiting on the front doorstep with her hands on her hips.

'Hiya, Mam, what you doing out here?' I asked casually.

Her eyes bulged as she saw me. 'I bloody knew it,' she said. 'I can read you like a book. Are you both all right?'

She pushed us inside and we gave her the lowdown on the fight. I spent the night in the front room with a baseball bat, just in case Mackie had the bad sense to come back. He didn't. The next morning, mission accomplished, I got the train back to Yeovil.

As the course date drew closer, I washed and ironed my kit over and over again. My fears were growing stronger. What if I failed? I'd never failed anything in my life, and the shame would have been difficult to bear. I carried on training, pushing myself up hills and round circuits. If I was hurting, that just served as an incentive to go faster. When the pain got so bad that to quit was almost the only option, I thought of our Mam and the shitty life she'd had, and all the abuse she'd suffered at the hands of Eric. I had only one mission: I had to do it for her.

The night before I left for the course I phoned our Mam. I hadn't told her what I was up to, but now I was off for three weeks I had to say something. I said I was going training in Wales with the squadron, and left it at that. She told me Dean had seen Eric in the King's where we used to play as kids. He'd followed him into the toilets and beaten the shit out of him. Eric had staggered out and tried to escape, but Dean had gone after him and finished off the job. Our Mam said that when she'd run to see what was going on Dean was bashing Eric with a heavy shovel. There was blood everywhere. Our Mam had wiped it off Dean and the shovel, and got someone to take him home before the police arrived. Eric was now in intensive care.

Dean and I hadn't seen eye to eye for years, but when I heard this story I felt almost close to him. I would have done exactly the same thing to Eric if I'd had the chance. After I put the phone down I felt very downcast. I could have done with happy family thoughts while the tension of the course was looming.

I knew that my future was down to my mental attitude. I'd trained as much as I could; now my nerve had to take over. I felt utterly alone with my thoughts as I swayed along in the train heading north. I was on edge, and suspected everyone I saw of being a staff member checking me out, watching me, listening to me.

I arrived at a branch station for the pick-up. Three four-tonne army trucks were parked next to a uniformed sergeant with a clipboard. A dozen of us got off the train, and we were detailed into the trucks. Ten subdued lads were already sitting on wooden benches in the back of mine, and in the far corner was a heavy-set woman with a blonde bob. The majority of the blokes were in their mid to late twenties, and were wearing smart civvies.

Everyone avoided eye contact, psyching themselves up for what would come next. The grapevine had told me that Camp One was tough, unremitting and filled with abuse. After a five-minute journey the truck passed through some electronic steel security gates and the brakes squealed as we pulled up in the camp parade-ground where about sixty people, including a few women, were doing press-ups on the tarmac. The chains raced through their bearings and the back flap slammed down with a crash. Four PTIs were waiting to pounce. Then it began. Abuse, and a lot of it. A bloke in a bright green beret yelled, 'Come on, you horrible lot, I'm not waiting all day for you. Fucking move it!' The other PTIs added to the chaos, screaming conflicting orders. 'Stand to attention! Sit down! Stand up! Do thirty press-ups!' There was no time to think or to adjust. You were in their power, compelled to obey their orders. Make the mistake of eye contact and you'd be singled out for special attention. It was a massive shock, but I knuckled down to it. No one had promised a picnic.

Gradually a sense of order prevailed. We were told to form a squad and stand to attention. All our bergens were in a heap along with our grips – one numpty had brought a suitcase covered in stickers from worldwide holiday destinations.

'I want you all to know you are the scruffiest, shabbiest, most pathetic intake I've ever seen,' snarled the Warrant Officer. 'Look at the state of you. Staff Sergeant, take over. I can't even be bothered to look at this bloody mob.' The WO was a squat, muscled man in his early forties. I later discovered his name was Smithy and he'd done many campaigns for the SAS, including the Iranian Embassy siege in 1980. He was a very good organiser and a superb team leader. Although he worked hard and played hard, he had a wicked dry sense of humour, but back then he was the epitome of the bust-a-blood-vessel drill instructor, yelling at us and giving us a hard time. Six years later I would work with him on a bodyguarding job in civvy street.

I was disorientated by all the commotion, but I kept my head. This was obviously part of the inevitable process of wearing us down. And we'd only been there for ten minutes. Another PTI, who I later knew as Chris Muscles, took over. A fine figure of a man, he had blonde hair and a triangular torso. The perfect bundle. He was wearing a sharply pressed, brilliant white vest, and looked like an advert for Persil. I was totally focused, senses alert, geared up to obey every instruction this hard-core Adonis might bark at me.

'Get down and give me twenty press-ups. Move it!'

I was down and pumping before he'd finished speaking. Persil stalked around, like a lion eyeing its prey. Whenever he came to a woman – I counted eight of us in all – he told her to put her knees on the tarmac and carry out simplified press-ups. At Yeovil the girls with poor upper-body strength did those, but I would always do proper press-ups, with my whole body suspended in the horizontal. I'd trained with the field gunners, and didn't want to look pathetic. Now I was a bit pissed off by this special treatment, but there was no option but to comply. (I later discovered that Persil had a theory that if women did full press-ups they could develop a pot belly.) But as long as you're huffing and puffing, it doesn't matter what position you're in. I soon realised that the whole philosophy of Camp One was pushing yourself 110 per cent. You could be the slowest man in the battalion, but if you gave it your all you'd have a better chance of passing than the fittest man who just coasted along.

We did grid sprints, burpees and running on the spot. All the while the instructors in PT kit were stalking around the parade ground harassing anyone who caught their eye. Just as we finished one set of press-ups, someone else would take over, booming, 'Too slow! Give me another twenty!' Then we'd all be on our backs doing sit-ups. Then squat thrusts. Abuse showered down on us continually. 'What's wrong with you useless bastards? Do you really think you're going to pass? You're all pathetic.' I filtered out the words. It was all part of the game, a charade designed to intimidate and wear us down. If I could continue to view things impassively, I knew I'd make it. There was only one solution, and that was to tune out the abuse.

After forty minutes it finally stopped. Like prisoners of war, we were marched into a grey breeze-block admin building for processing. Our mug-shots were taken, and we were issued with a personal number. I was 105, like the Peugeot, but I felt more like a Land-Rover – all torque without fancy bodywork. Eager to do the right thing, I addressed the guy who was processing me as 'sir'. Too late, I realised my mistake. If you're a Warrant Officer you're a sir; if you're a staff sergeant or below, you're a staff. Army ranking was unfamiliar, and I could not get it into my brain. Every time I made a mistake over the next few hours I had to do twenty press-ups as a penalty. Usually I was already being yelled at to do something else, so the tasks quickly accumulated, and soon I owed a debt of eighty press-ups.

We were ordered back to the parade ground to collect our stuff and told to go to the barracks to change into BFT kit – T-shirt, denims and trainers. I'd carefully wrapped white plastic tape round one of my bergen straps the night before so I could identify it quickly. Watching other people scrabbling to find their bags, I felt rather pleased with myself as I ran over to my bergen and swung it up and over my shoulder. I nearly broke my back. Someone had loosened one tension strap and undone the other completely. The same thing was happening to people all around me. One of the DS

(Directing Staff) must have tampered with all the packs and bags while we were in the admin building. The bergen hit the floor. It weighed about seventy pounds, and was very solidly packed. I had a lot of kit: two pairs of boots, two pairs of denims, two pairs of combat trousers, three green army shirts, three T-shirts, two pairs of jogging pants, two woolly jumpers, two combat DPM jackets, a combat peaked cap, a webbing belt with ammo and water pouches, two waterbottles, half a dozen pairs of M&S knickers, three pairs of thick Arctic socks, three pairs of thin cotton socks, three sport bras, a towel, paper and envelopes, a compass, a ruler, a summer sleeping bag, a packet of fags and a cuddly toy. (Actually, I'd sensibly left Troglodyte, my pink panther, at home.) Although there was no edict forbidding us from bringing jewellery or make-up, I'd left all that at home too. I did have a toiletry bag containing Wash & Go shampoo – my hair doesn't need much attention; Ponds facial wash, which doesn't dry out my skin; Ponds body moisturiser – I have very dry skin, and if I don't moisturise after a shower it resembles flaky pastry. And I never went anywhere without Oil of Ulay facial moisturiser – our Mam always used it, and because she had great skin I copied her. With the addition of Sensodyne toothpaste for my sensitive teeth, the bergen was bloody heavy. But at least I could lift it. One of the other girls told me later that her boyfriend, a Marine, had packed hers for her the night before. When he'd first put it on her she couldn't stand up. She hadn't trained with it, and didn't know how to handle it.

There was one amusing moment in the scrum when a young Rupert scooped up his bergen then leant over to pick up his suitcase. As he clutched the handle it fell open, and all his neatly-pressed striped Savile Row shirts tumbled out onto the tarmac. People were hobbling to the barracks clutching armfuls of laundry and staggering under the off-centre weight of their bergens; if you stood still to sort out the straps you were bollocked.

The women's accommodation block consisted of eight sets of metal-frame bunk-beds with green plastic mattresses on a bare concrete floor, flimsy orange and green cotton-print curtains and a bank of steel lockers. In the washroom outside were three showers without curtains, eight sinks and some old-fashioned toilets. A sink and a bunk-bed each. Luxury. But there was no time to enjoy the facilities. We were expected back on the parade square within five minutes, so we had a mad rush to unpack everything into the lockers.

The BFT was what I feared most. If we had to do a short explosive dash I had the muscle to power away from other women, and could keep pace with the fastest men. But when it came to longer distances I was knackered almost as soon as I'd begun.

Still, I was completely focused on my mission; there was no room for anything else. As we ran the first mile and a half in a squad along a tarmac road and through a wooded area, I was breathing so noisily I thought my lungs would explode. The PTI drew level with me and shouted, 'Are you all right, 105?' I nodded, and concentrated on planting one lead weight heftily in front of the other. The first mile and a half is supposed to be a combination of jogging and speed-marching, a gentle warm-up for the second half, but we'd started off at a sprint. I couldn't believe it. I tried to suppress my gasping, but because no oxygen was reaching my legs I had no option but to open my gullet and pant aloud to keep up. The PTI dropped back and hissed in my ear, '105, I dream of women like you.' The pace eventually eased off, but it had taken me every ounce of determination to make it back in time. This was just a BFT to everyone else, but to me it was the world. There was such a fine line between failure and the chance to carry on and prove myself in other forms of endurance and strength of body and character.

As I reached the finish an instructor shouted out my time, eleven minutes seventeen seconds. I was devastated: I was seventeen seconds over the maximum allowed time. As we all lined up in order of finishing the course, I felt my body flood with depression as I waited for the inevitable RTU (returned to unit). But when I looked at the sweaty, heaving bodies in front of me I realised I was the first woman home. Surely they couldn't bin all eight of us? It was a glimmer of hope. About seven guys were binned without compassion, but only after Persil had abusively quizzed them on why they'd bothered to turn up in the first place, and labelled them wankers. Their drooping shoulders spelt humiliation and defeat. But I had made it. With my stumbling block behind me, I felt fired up to achieve anything. Why the hell had the other girls been so slow? I didn't know and I didn't care, I was just relieved they'd dragged behind.

Gratefully I fell into bed at midnight, but we were in for more surprises. At about four o'clock the lights flashed on, and I awoke with a start as a swift kick made noisy contact with the foot of my bed. The room was filled with shouting female instructors ordering us out of bed and yelling at us to hit the deck and do press-ups. One moment I was in the protective cocoon of my gonk-bag, the next, before I'd even had a moment to wipe the sleep from my eyes, I was spreadeagled on the stone-cold concrete and pumping away. Our lockers were being raided. One by one we were ordered over to them as our possessions were examined. We had been told to bring nothing with our name or unit on, or any kit that would connect us to a certain unit. A spew of clothing was flying in all directions. All the other women had come from the Army, so their stuff was a bit worn. Mine was fresh from stores and still had its rigid creases, so it stood out among the general chaos. Our personal possessions were scrutinised: writing paper, pens, stamps and Tampax were all acceptable. But as soon as the instructor picked up an innocuous plastic bottle from my wash kit my heart sank. Brufen tablets are a military cure-all issued by sick bays, with the power to sort out anything from a headache to appendicitis. They are also good for hangovers. Neatly stuck to the bottle was a label saying 'Wren Ford, HMS *Heron*'.

She held the offensive object up. 'What's this, then?'

'Brufen tablets, staff.'

'Why have you brought them? Are you ill?'

'No, staff.'

'Why are your name and unit on them?'

'Don't know, staff.'

'You fucking don't know? Are you stupid or something?'

I didn't answer. She twisted the cap off the bottle and poured the tablets onto my bundle of kit on the floor, then chucked the empty bottle into her bin liner. I could have kicked myself, bloody idiot that I was. But there were worse roastings going on. Several girls had brought teddy bears with them. Another had photos of her boyfriend inside her wash kit. There were even diaries and name-tabs in uniforms. But I couldn't slag them off, I'd been just as stupid.

When there was nothing left in any of the lockers the instructors yelled, 'Sort out this bloody mess, get into your PT kit and get down to the parade ground.' The floor looked like a jumble sale as we briskly sifted out our knickers from our ammo pouches. Then we ran down to one of the training areas on the beach for three hours of beastings (hard physical training) near the sand-dunes.

It was still dark, and the air was heavy with drizzle. Only three days before I'd felt as fit as an athlete, training with the best the Navy has to offer and fitter than I'd ever been, but now I was back in bag-of-shit league, gasping with the rest of them. I always gave PT my all, but sand just saps your strength. We did sit-ups in the freezing cold Irish sea, our exertions illuminated by the half-moon, then press-ups in the soft wet sand just beyond the breakers, before running and fireman's lifts, which were really hard going. I'd done circuit training with the field gun crew who run the cannons up and down at the Royal Tournament, but that was like nursery playtime compared to this. I told myself to stop thinking and get on with it. The constant abuse washed over me. I knew I wasn't a 'fat bastard' or a 'waste of space', however often I was told the contrary.

At 7 a.m. we were told we had thirty minutes before we had to be back on the parade ground. I had a quick shower and guzzled two pints of rancid powdered lemon juice and a humungous fried breakfast, which all tasted wonderful. We were split into groups of about thirty-five, and for the next three weeks we studied first aid, map reading, weapon recognition, vehicle recognition, driver training and firearms training. At least twice a day we also got severely beasted with exhausting PT sessions including assault courses, orienteering and stretcher runs along the sand-dunes.

On the second Tuesday of the course, beneath a blistering sun, I pounded up and down the shoreline as part of a six-man squad running two abreast for an hour and a half. Every few minutes the men at the back would run to the front and grasp the sticky wooden handles of a stretcher loaded with jerry cans sloshing full of sea water. I was already knackered when we'd hit the sand, which was soft and deadening. My legs felt disembodied and refused to react to the messages my brain was sending them. I was wearing DPM trousers, a T-shirt and high-leg combat boots. My webbing contained water bottles which were bashing against my arse, and my green T-shirt was soon black with sweat. It starts down the spine, moves to the top of the chest and spreads down under the arms. Everyone else was also drenched, and a cloud of evaporating sweat followed our progress up and down the beach. We all stank. I hadn't brought any deodorant with me, as it would have taken up valuable space in my bergen. It didn't bother me: I wasn't there to smell sweet, only to pass the course.

I had a standard-issue SLR (self-loading rifle) – ten pounds of unwanted baggage – slung over my back, and I was trying to grip the stretcher with my slippery left hand when I saw a blond bloke in the squad up ahead collapse onto his knees in the sand. He'd obviously thought, 'Bollocks to this.' As we heaved past I saw that his face, like mine, was a concrete grimace. The instructors recognised the signs. They didn't bollock him because they could see he was genuinely on his chinstrap. If you bin yourself there's no slagging. Instead you get an 'OK, mate, get back to camp and sort out your kit.' We never saw Blondie again.

No two days were the same, except in three consistent respects: relentless mental torture, physical exhaustion and verbal abuse. One instructor called Bob – or 'Cyborg', as I soon dubbed him – always seemed to be having a go at someone, but I was most often singled out for his insulting treatment. He was a mega-fit, tall, blond northerner who would sidle up to me and whisper, 'You'll be back in the Navy soon, back in the slow lane.' I tried my best to ignore him.

There was little room for friendship with my fellow internees.

Conversations were limited to, 'All right, mate, how are you getting on?' Nor did you trade names. I was always 105, never Sarah. There was no time for niceties or personal details. Even at meal-times we were surrounded by DS breathing over us. The regime was as severe as a military detention centre. Even though we were training for special duties we all had to be smart; the staff had hair so short you could see their scalps. The boys had to close shave, and the girls had to tie back long hair if they had it – I had an easy life with my skinhead and James Dean quiff.

Frequently on parade, groups of numbers would be called out. Sometimes the numbers corresponded to those of us who would be staying. At other times, hearing your number meant you were binned. But you didn't know which group you were in until after you'd been segregated. Deep down I knew I was doing well. I just hoped they saw that I had the right attitude.

We were undergoing regular beastings over twelve miles, often strapped to a log with five other men. We ran everywhere; the only time we were allowed to walk was from the cookhouse to the barracks. After a few days we caught on to the fact that sleep deprivation was a core component of the course. We got just four hours of gonk at night. If we went to bed at midnight, we'd be up at four; bed at two meant up at six. The intention was to wear us down physically and mentally. Nevertheless, I was totally focused and just pressed on. I was never tempted to bin myself. I was able to somehow detach myself from all this deprivation, which, after all, was a means to an end. 'Don't let the bastards get you down' was a mantra that could have been created specifically for me.

One area where morale was always high was the cookhouse. They didn't cut you short on food. It was brilliant, and you could scoff as much as you could shove in – unbelievable-sized plates were demolished. I ate more than I had ever done in my life. It was pure stodge city: fried eggs, bacon, huge plates of sponge pudding with custard. It didn't matter what it was, I stuffed myself with it. I needed it. On one orienteering exercise over eighteen miles I'd taken a wrong turning and ended up doing about twenty-four. On another one we had to rattle off complex number and word memory-retention phrases while navigating to grid refs. We'd be told something like: Tom Flaherty has got seventeen geese, he lives at number 83 Monaghan Road, where his four brothers and seven uncles visit every second Thursday. We had to take all this in while concentrating on remembering the six-digit grid ref. The faster you got there, the less time you had to forget the phrase. Then it was on to the next checkpoint, and at each one we had to spew out all the phrases so far. The final grid ref was back at the camp cookhouse, where the instructors were waiting to hear the lot. I was sweating so much that I dripped all over the DS's notes. Her tight little face burst into life as she hissed, 'Don't you fucking sweat all over my paper.' It wasn't loud, but it was hard enough to intimidate, and more effective than any of the male insults. But Liz, as she was called, ended up becoming a good friend. She was very helpful and very professional, having been in Special Forces for many years. As hard as nails, she'd operated in the toughest detachment of 14 Company and was also a former weightlifting champion in civvy street.

One day I was drying off after a shower when I noticed some dark patches on my hip. I rubbed them with the towel, thinking it was dirt or a bruise, before I realised it was a shadow where my hips were sticking out. My body had undergone a metamorphosis. I hadn't thought I'd had any fat to burn off, but I must have had.

One night at 2 a.m. we were told to get down to the classroom to watch a video, which would be followed by a questions session. The crackly black-and-white film, scored by age lines, flickered into life. A BBC presenter dressed in fifties gear was standing in a Himalayan bamboo plantation and talking in the most boring monotone I'd ever had the misfortune to hear, about the use of the plant by the locals. I looked around the nice, warm, soporific classroom, and saw that everyone was desperately attempting to stay awake. The threat of being binned was always looming. My eyes started closing, and I did the noddy dog as I jerked awake. All around me, heads were dipping and popping back up again. Stare at anything too long when you're knackered and it starts to shimmy. I felt as if I'd been on an all-day drinking session. But drink, like sleep, was a distant memory. For forty agonising minutes of sheer boredom I focused just to the side of the screen. Afterwards I somehow filled in my answer sheet. We later found out from one of the DS that the answers were always binned without being read. This was no lesson about memory retention; it was intended purely to disorientate and wear you down. As I left the classroom Cyborg came over. 'If you can't hack it, just tell me,' he hissed. 'You can catch the first train home tomorrow, I'll personally buy you a ticket.' Maybe it was because I was a northerner, or perhaps it was just my gender which troubled him. In any case, I reckoned it made him feel good to humiliate people. It was how he got his kicks.

I did well in weapons recognition classes. We had a slide-show at which we had to identify the weapons and provide details. Anyone can recognise an Uzi or an AK47, but once an obscure one flicked up, a sub-machine gun with a distinctive square butt. I knew it instantly; this was one I recognised from my handy W.H. Smith guide. It was a Carl Gustav 9mm, a Swedish weapon. I felt well pleased with myself as I prattled off the answer. I also enjoyed the R-to-I (resistance to interrogation) classes, which gave us pointers on how to cope if we were ever captured by terrorists.

As Camp One progressed the no-hopers were gradually pruned out. The abuse began to ease off, as a recognition that those of us who remained showed potential. We were having more instruction, and less beasting.

Luke, our firearms instructor, was from G Squadron of the SAS, and he was gorgeous. His eyes were blue, but his left one had a fleck of brown in it. He had a brilliant attitude and a passion for firearms which readily communicated itself in his enthusiastic teaching. 'You're here to learn,' he said as he introduced us to the 9mm Browning. 'I'm not here to give you grief.' On my first firing attempt on the outdoor ranges I got a four-inch grouping over thirty-five metres shooting from the prone position. When he checked the targets, Luke was gobsmacked. I couldn't understand the fuss. I'd just done what he'd instructed me to do.

But where Luke was a delight, Cyborg, who was also in the SAS, remained my nemesis. One afternoon after pistol-grouping practice he singled me out as we were all getting into the wagon.

'Where do you think you're going?' he snarled.

'Back to camp, staff.'

'Not in that, you're not. Go on, start running. You need the exercise.' I had no choice but to bite my lip and start off on the one-mile run. I started wondering if my achievement on the ranges was adding to his irritation with me. By now I suspected that he was lacking in testosterone, and had a problem with strong women. I presented some form of threat to his masculinity. He was the sort of man who would control a weaker woman and try to dominate the tough ones from his position of power. He probably had a small dick, and was no doubt shite in bed as well.

One day Cyborg got under my skin deeper than anything else at Camp One. We'd been shooting, and as usual I'd done quite well, but he started to abuse me. 'You might think you're a fucking good shot, but you're on your way out, you're failing. You're crap and I can see through you.' He said it calmly and with such menace that it was as if he really meant it. He hit a nerve. Was I really about to be binned? I turned my back as the tears threatened. I tried to hold my breath, but the pressure mounted and my emotions welled up. I started walking back to the firing point. I wouldn't let the bastard see me cry. I had to get away before he got to me. Ron, one of the other instructors, asked if I was OK. As I took a breath to get the words 'Yes, sir,' out, the tears came. I quickly organised myself and rubbed them away. From then on I would imagine Cyborg in the sack, trying really hard but getting nowhere.

After two and a half weeks two of the girls had been binned, so there were six of us left. We learned to cross barbed-wire fences while wearing a bergen and holding a rifle, without leaving any sign or pinging the wire. It was difficult to balance, so we helped each other. Camaraderie and teamwork were coming into play. You had to be capable of coping alone, but also of mixing into a group.

One night we were told to pack our bergens because we'd be up at 4 a.m. for an exercise. Just after four we met in the gym and did an hour's PT before breakfast, then we were each handed a cardboard lunchbox which we stashed in our bergens. At 5.30 we clambered into the four-tonners for a two-hour drive to an army camp. I didn't pay much attention to where we were going; it could have been High Wycombe or the Himalayas. All that mattered to me was getting through. On arrival at our destination we filled our water bottles, put them in our webbing belts and took our packed lunches to the training area, where we were divided into groups of three. We were told to conceal ourselves and observe the area, which was vast, gently undulating and full of long coarse grass and bracken. We found a good dip and squatted down. We took it in turns to keep watch. We spoke only to tell each other it was time to change stag. We didn't risk any chit-chat – for all we knew there was a DS crouched in the long grass keeping tabs. Beyond us was a ridge on which some farming activity was going on, and a man and a dog walked past on the top of the hill. Whatever we saw, we faithfully wrote it down. About four hours later we decided to have lunch. I opened my box. There was an apple and a single thin slice of white bread wrapped in cling-film, cunningly disguised as a sandwich.

'God, I need to pee,' said Gail, one of the two girls with me. 'What should we do?' We decided she should stay low, move a couple of metres out and do it there. That became our ablutions area. The cling-film on the fake sandwich was obviously for wrapping up any shite, but luckily my bowels remained inactive. The sun began to beat down, and we were roasting. We had no idea when we were going to be lifted out. At tea-time we heard a shout: 'Come out and fill up your water bottles.' Looking around, I could see little heads bobbing up in the bracken all around. We quickly gulped down what water we had remaining – we'd been conserving it, not guzzling it – and filled up. Two hours later a DS strode into view two hundred metres away and started talking at a patch of bracken. We couldn't hear what he had to say, but we realised it was a binning session as the other three girls sheepishly emerged. Clearly there had been some organisation involved in choosing which girls were in which trio. As the hours ticked past, another few batches were binned. It was so systematic that I got the feeling they were already on the list before the exercise began.

At nightfall we were still there, trying not to move about or make a noise as we observed the area. We'd got brave enough to have a laugh about the joke lunch we'd been given, but a very quiet snigger it was. Dawn, the other girl with us, had an orange, and was constantly nibbling microscopic bits of skin off it, just relishing the colour and the thought of the taste. By now it was fucking freezing lying on the ground without protection – we'd been told to wear only a shirt, jumper and combat jacket. By midnight my bones were cold to the marrow, and I was rubbing parts of my body by rote to warm myself up. We were taking turns to do two-hour stags, and by about 4 a.m. were all snuggled up together like little rabbits in a burrow to conserve heat and taking turns to be in the middle. It was too cold to sleep, but at least when I wasn't on stag I could rest. It was a stressful night. If we'd failed to spot some activity we could have been issuing our own one-way travel warrants.

At 7 a.m. the DS suddenly shouted, 'Right, come on, you lot. Over here.' Numbed after so many hours of immobility, we creaked and groaned to our feet. My left ankle, which I'd broken six years ago in training, was aching badly having been so chilled.

By now our numbers were down from the original 120 to seventy or so, but despite our knackered state, once we were back at camp we were shown no remorse, but were immediately ordered down to the assault course by Persil. Apart from the phony sandwich and the apple, I hadn't eaten for twenty-seven hours, but I began dragging myself over the high wall and through the tunnels. My body was weak and I was light-headed. Because my bones were stiff there was a possibility of injury, so I concentrated hard. Gulping for air, I pulled my weary body up the scramble net which stretched twenty forbidding feet into the sky. A six-footer in his mid-thirties, with salt-and-pepper hair and a moustache, who I was to know later as Sparky, was also dragging himself skywards. I'd already spotted him as a good bloke, who liked to present himself as a bit of a bumbling idiot. He was like the proverbial naughty schoolboy, a real Just William, always getting into minor bother. I was fit for a girl, and he wasn't so hot for a guy, so we were quite well-matched, and had ended up together on runs a few times. As we neared the top of the net, the rope burning my hands and making them redden and itch, his leg shot through a hole and he teetered over backwards. I grabbed hold of him. 'Come on, mate, hurry up, keep moving,' I urged him before a DS caught sight of us. 'Thanks,' he gasped back.

Soon he dropped well behind me. I was blindly going for it as hard as I could. Physical exhaustion had moved me onto a different plane. I was going over the net again, on my third circuit, when I heard the DS shouting, 'Are you deaf or something?' As my concentration cracked I realised everyone else had stopped and was running back to camp. In my exertions I'd filtered out the rest of the world.

Our numbers whittled down to sixty, we were driven back to Camp One for the progressive driving segment. We were taught emergency procedures such as controlled handbrake turns and J-turns, where you evacuate a situation by reversing aggressively and slewing round before screaming off. Learning how to get from A to B the safest, quickest and smoothest way – in that order – was also crucial. Despite the intensive driving instruction, more operators are killed in traffic accidents across the water than by terrorists.

We were in groups of four: instructor, driving student and two more students in the back. I'd done four test drives, and was starting my fifth, revving round the red and yellow roads which snaked through the gently undulating landscape. I was reading the road and telling Phil, the instructor, what I could see. 'Ninety-degree right-hand bend,' I said as I flicked my eyes to the speedo. Seventy-five miles per hour. Approaching the bend I braked hard. Fifty metres before I entered it I dropped a gear to third, and felt the car surge. I took it smoothly into second. The revs ran high and the engine was whining, but there was plenty of traction should I need it, and I was well in control. Wind whistled through a small gap in the offside window. Touch the brakes now and I faced a flip into the ditch faster than a chef could toss a pancake. But I wanted to maintain speed, otherwise you're not really pushing yourself. I fixed my eyes on the bend, my body bowing with the car like a reed in the wind. Tension prevailed. This was no boy-racer's day out. You had to read every nuance of the road and react fast. There was no margin for error; half a tonne of metal is a very unforgiving weapon. I saw the road open up, but I was still nervous as hell. I wouldn't have dreamed of doing these speeds on winding country roads before the course. I could only hope I'd been trained well enough to know how to react should I meet oncoming traffic. My mood wasn't helped by the scorching sun and the other nervously sweating bodies in the car.

I moved up to third gear. 'School-crossing sign. Right-hand turn. Sharp left-hand bend eighty metres.' I'd seen an emphatic set of black-and-white chevrons urgently pointing that way. After taking the bend I changed up to fourth to rest the engine and slowed to forty as I neatly pulled around an old man walking his dog. 'Minor crossroads. Humped-back bridge.' I climbed to sixty-five and took the bridge with a stomach lurch. 'Clear road.' I was back up to seventy. Trees and hedges were skimming past in a blur of green. 'Sweeping left-hand bend.' I dropped to third and nudged out over the white line to start taking it. My eyes were glued to the hedge at the apex of the curve in front of me. 'More speed,' said Phil calmly. I was doing seventy-five miles an hour, but going even faster was necessary to provide that extra few precious seconds to get back in my lane should I meet any oncoming traffic. Going slower might feel safer, but once you're over the line it's far more hazardous. I pushed my foot down hard, and I was fully over the white line, with the speedo up to eighty and my heart pounding.

I gunned around the bend and took in the concealed entrance on the right, fifty metres away. A lump caught in my throat and my heart skidded as I saw the red cab of a tractor inching its way out. Phil shouted, 'Pull in!' What the fuck did he think I was trying to do? I yanked my left hand down as hard as I could. The car was flying, and it rocked violently as I shot back into my lane. The net effect was that the bend was now tighter, and our weight was well over on the outside wheels. I kept the speed steady. I was already in danger of spinning or leaving the road, but braking at this stage could be fatal. The car urgently wanted to travel sideways, and by touching the brakes I'd be granting its wish.

As we powered back onto the straight and I let go of my breath Phil said a quiet, 'Well done.' I didn't need to hear it. Praise embarrasses me; I'd rather have the sweet sensation of inward satisfaction than someone telling me their opinion. I continued reading the road as the guys in the back let out sighs of relief and briskly wound down their windows. After a few minutes the sweat had stopped trickling down my chest and my heart-rate had slowly returned to normal.

FOUR

MAXIMUM DISRUPTION

AT FIVE IN THE MORNING, after an hour of beasting, we were loaded into four-tonners for an unknown location. We were pushed out at 9 a.m. with maps, grid refs and fully laden bergens, and told to get ourselves to an FRV (final rendezvous). After only three hours' fearsome tabbing over the tough scrub and rocks of a rugged mountain range, I'd developed a fearsome blood blister the size of my heel. Every footfall made me wince with pain, and my shoulders were soon adding to the intense discomfort. A woman's collarbone is more pronounced than a man's, and that and my bra straps were combining under the pressure of the fifty-pound bergen to create deep welts on my shoulders.

Eight hours later I arrived at the FRV. I was hungry, my legs were tired, my shoulders sore and my blood blister more than a bit uncomfortable. But there was no time for rest. We were immediately loaded back onto the four-tonners and driven to a woodland area about an hour away. Here we slumped gratefully to the ground and waited it out. Rumours were flying from people who'd been on the course before, or who claimed to know someone who had, that we were now up for the first of the interrogations. I tried not to listen; it was all hearsay and second-hand gossip. I'd brought six of the potent, bright pink Brufen tablets on the tab with me. I'd already taken four, but now I swallowed the remaining couple, just in case.

I was sitting next to Dave, a northerner, ignoring an officer who was also in our huddle. Dave and I got on really well. He was a bit of a joker, and was always making light of the situation. But the hushed whispers of the other groups reflected the nervousness in the air. It was the not knowing. There was no way of predicting what would happen next. But that was all part of the training; the psychological component – which the DS referred to as 'dislocation of expectation' – was crucial.

An instructor appeared and started detailing people off. I watched them disappear through the forest in the direction he had indicated. Too soon it was my turn. 'You're next. Off you go. Through there and into that building.'

I got to my feet, slid my right arm through the tighter of the two bergen straps, slung it onto my back and tightened the left-hand strap. I had to walk on my toes, because I couldn't put pressure on my blistered heel.

I was physically drained, but my mind was alert as I set off down the path leading out of the clearing. It was a grim, grey day and the trees towered over me. Down towards the end of the path on the right-hand side I could see the edge of a red-brick building. Through the trees to my left was the whitewashed stone of an outbuilding. Beyond and between them was the three-storey white-painted building the instructor had indicated. The path widened out into a small gravelled courtyard. I was feeling very apprehensive about the inevitable interrogation. It was like walking into an abyss.

As I passed the corner of the outbuilding on my left I saw the blur of black balaclavas and combat kit. Suddenly a group of four or five men roared onto the path and jumped on me. My stomach churned in terror, and I felt the fight-or-flight chemicals coursing around my system as they threw me hard onto the ground. There was commotion and shouting, but despite my attackers' agility and the speed of their assault everything was happening in slow time. My brain was working faster than my body could react. For that split-second as they rushed me I thought, 'What am I going to do? Should I do a runner? Do I struggle? How many are there? How big are they? Have they got any weapons? If I did a runner, where would I go? Are there more of them?' The mental processing took half a second, not nearly enough time for my body to put any of it into motion.

Then I was hitting the ground and they were on top of me, bundling me into the gravel. I was pushed backwards as they stripped me of my bergen. My arms were wrenched out of the straps and I landed with a thud on my back. One of them produced a rough hessian sack, dragged it over my head and tied it securely around my neck. I felt the raspy texture and inhaled the mildewy smell. Glints of light twinkled through the weave. Having my sight removed was the worst part, I felt vulnerable and helpless. I couldn't breathe freely because of the choking thickness of the hessian. I tried to kick my legs and flail my arms, but they were all effectively pinned down.

I felt tugging at my feet and heard the sound of my shoelaces being pulled out of their metal eyelets. Then I was roughly dragged to my feet and thrown forward. Someone grabbed me under the armpits and yanked me along and up some steps, my feet trailing behind me. My captors spoke not one word, which heightened the terror I was feeling. Even though I knew that this was just an exercise, the sense of unpredictability was very real. I had no handle on these people. They seemed so detached and professional because of their calculating coldness.

I sensed I was being dragged down a long corridor. I could feel the space and hear the echo of my scuffles bouncing off the shiny walls. If you can't see, your other senses take over and supply you with additional information. After about twenty metres one of the men barked at me to stand up. Before I had a chance to do so I was roughly pulled upright by a violent tug under the armpits. My arms were yanked behind my back and held tightly in two less than delicate armlocks.

'Close your eyes! Look at the ground!' barked one of my captors. The hessian sack was pulled off and replaced with a canvas blindfold. I was pushed, with my arms still locked behind me, through a doorway and into what felt like a large room. There was a horrendous, disorientating crackling noise seeping from every direction, as if every inch of the walls was conducting the sound of a badly tuned radio. Its pitch, frequency and volume were unwavering. There was nothing in the white noise to focus on, but it was just loud enough to drown out normal conversation and disrupt your thinking.

I was pushed to the floor and my legs were crossed for me. My hands were placed on the back of my head. Someone yanked my shoulders to ensure my back was straight and growled, 'Stay there. Don't move.' For the first few seconds obeying this instruction wasn't a problem. But because my fingers weren't linked my shoulders were soon tensed up under the strain of supporting my arms, and developed an agonising dull ache. I knew that if I could just let my elbows slouch down it would relieve the pressure from my shoulderblades. After what must have been about twenty minutes I dared to relax a bit. No sooner had my elbows dropped an inch or two than they were yanked back up. I realised my captors were hovering over me. I would have to be very devious if I was going to move again.

The more I was subjected to the white noise, the more it drove me nuts. It was difficult to focus on anything else. From the moment I'd arrived I had tried to focus on clues. Was there a window? Where was the door? Could I feel a breeze, or sense any interesting smells? Anything to provide me with a fragment of information to help me orientate myself.

The pain in my shoulders was desperate. After another ten minutes I decided that the inevitable slap back into position would be worth it for that precious second of respite. I gently leaned forward to take the pressure off my lower back, and was immediately pulled back into position, which didn't seem so bad. From then on I allowed myself a moment's relaxation every now and then. But after what must have been an hour and a half of this torture I relaxed my elbows again, and was rewarded with a swift and accurate kick to the kidneys. The pain was like a bullet next to my spine. I was more cautious with my rest breaks from then on.

Some while later two of my captors picked me up and bundled me over to the wall. Were they punishing me for moving? My legs were kicked apart and my hands were splayed so that my body was making a star shape. I was pushed against the cool, smooth wall, and for a moment I allowed myself the luxury of thinking, I can handle this. But soon it all started again, and a new set of muscle groups started to complain. It was not so much a pain as an excruciating ache, like painting a ceiling for hours on end with your arm constantly above your head. Coupled with all this, my blood blister was still killing me. I was not having a good day out.

They changed my position every so often, with what seemed like an uncanny ability to recognise when I was just about to collapse under the strain. I continued to force myself to think about other things. The blood blister was a good focus.

It was difficult to gauge time. After about three hours, when I was again sitting on my arse with my hands on the back of my skull, my captors half-lifted, half-dragged me to my feet. We were off again, my feet trailing behind me. We went up a couple of steps, around a corner, down a corridor. Every time my left foot bumped the ground my blister started complaining again. I tried to hold that leg off the floor as I was dragged silently through the maze, but then my thigh muscle started up as well, which went some way to blocking out the gyp my foot was giving me.

Then we stopped. A door in front of me opened and I was dragged into a warmer room. As the door closed I could sense floorboards giving slightly underfoot, which was an improvement on the cold concrete of the holding area. The biggest joy was the silence: there was no white noise. I could hear several people milling about. The boards creaked, and I picked up the almost imperceptible sound of rustling clothing. Although I still couldn't see anything, I sensed less menace. I was marched to the centre of the room and pushed down onto a wooden chair – not normally very comfortable, but right now – luxury.

'Close your eyes while we take off your mask,' said a quiet voice from about five feet in front of me. Aha, so this is the nice-man routine, I thought. The blindfold, which was held on by Velcro, was whipped off. I opened my eyes and blinked to adjust to the light. It seemed bright, although it probably wasn't. I quickly scanned around. On the polished mahogany desk in front of me was a clutter of papers illuminated by a desk lamp. Behind the desk sat a young man with a grey rollneck wool sweater, a black jacket and a thick black beard. He didn't look particularly menacing, but then, nor was he smiling in welcome. The blokes who had dragged me in were standing behind me. I could hear their breathing as they recovered from pulling my ten-stone bulk into the room.

The man behind the desk spoke quietly. 'I hope my friends are treating you all right?'

Don't get dragged into anything, I thought. Remember, you're only allowed to say the big four: name, rank, number and date of birth.

The light flickered, and I heard someone moving behind me. Was it my captors? Or was someone else hiding just outside my peripheral vision? All my senses were on overdrive. As my eyes adjusted to the light I was trying to take in as much of the room as possible.

'What's your name?'

'Ford.'

'What's your rank?'

'Wren.'

'Wren. Is that spelt with a "w" or an "r"?'

'I cannot answer that question.'

His voice was encouraging. 'Oh, come on, surely you can tell me how to spell it?'

I stayed silent.

'What's your official number?'

I paused. I didn't want to answer straight away. I wanted to give myself some time, wanted to drag the inevitable process out. I only had four simple things to remember, but the longer I gave myself to think about them, the less chance I had of messing up.

A few seconds passed. 'W135578T,' I said slowly.

'Was that an "Echo" or a "Tango"?'

Another trap. 'I cannot answer that question.'

'So, what's your name then?'

His voice was changing now, getting harder, faster. I told myself to ignore the pressure and to proceed at my own pace.

'Ford.'

'Date of birth?'

'13.11.65.'

'Did you say thirteen or thirty?'

I stuck to the stock blocking phrase. I was beginning to worry about every damned question. Could fucking up and saying 'yes' or 'no' get me binned? I wasn't going to take the chance.

'I cannot answer that question.'

'13 November 1965, eh? How old does that make you then?'

'I cannot answer that question.'

'Don't be silly – if you can tell me what your birthdate is, surely it's no different to telling me how old you are?'

I ignored him.

'Oh well, suit yourself.'

I could hear a chair being scraped across the floor behind me. Then the door creaked open and a woman in her mid-forties came in with a plastic cup of coffee. I saw the steam snaking out of it. Bet that's not for me, I thought.

'Thank you,' said the interrogator, taking the cup. After a greedy sip, he turned to me once more. 'How did you come to be in the area?'

'I cannot answer that question.'

It might have been a bit monotonous, but at least in this new environment I was warm, I was comfortable, I wasn't being kicked. Things could have been a lot worse. I stuck resolutely to the big four for thirty or forty minutes. All the while, he was nonchalantly sipping his coffee, smoking his cigarettes and not offering me a thing, the bastard.

Then suddenly it was over. He gave a dismissive nod of his head, which clearly meant 'Take her away.' My captors replaced the blindfold and started manhandling me out. I let my body go floppy. I wanted to rest my arms and legs for a few more precious minutes. Why not let them do the work of carrying my weight? As I was thrust into the corridor I allowed myself a fleeting mental slap on the back. I'd done all right. Just keep your head down and crack on, I told myself. Then I was back into the holding area and reintroduced to the joys of white noise. I was certain it was louder than before. I was launched into the stress position routine, and during the next few hours I got several more good kickings as I fine-tuned my stance.

Soon the urge for a wee was really building up. I tortured myself for about an hour. Holding onto the contents of my bladder was a distraction, something to focus on, but now it was at bursting point. I didn't know what the score was. No one had briefed us on toilet procedure. So I just took action; I put up my hand and waited for one of my captors to respond in whatever way he saw fit.

I heard footsteps. 'I need to go to the toilet,' I said quietly. It must have been the right thing to do. Two of them grabbed me as usual, one on each arm, and dragged me out of the building and across a courtyard. I could feel it was night-time; there was that fresh-air feeling. I could feel its chill on my exposed skin. I was dragged into a smelly toilet block, and my blindfold came off as I was shoved into a cubicle. I kept my eyes shut tightly though, and dropped my head down. I was fearful of being binned if I saw anything.

I was busting, but as soon as I was on the cracked plastic seat I just got it done. It was bliss to sit down, but I didn't fanny about. Maybe I should have used the time to relax, but I didn't want to do anything to jeopardise my chances and find myself being given a one-way train ticket back to Yeovil.

About an hour after my toilet excursion I was dragged out again. I knew the ropes by now, and sensed another interrogation. We followed the same path to the same room, but this time when my blindfold came off I was positioned with the polished desk behind me. In front of me was a concertina cotton screen supported by a chrome rail near the ceiling. After I'd had a few moments to register this, my chair was spun round, and I faced the bearded man again. It was a very effective way of doing things. I'd been shown my fate: clearly there was something nasty behind the screen. While I came to terms with that, we went through the big four again. Then there was a new question.

'Where were you going when you were captured?'

'I cannot answer that question.' What was behind that curtain? Was it the torture chamber?

'In your bergen we found spare clothing and a wash kit. Where were you planning to sleep?'

'I cannot answer that question.' Don't be soft. That would be against the Geneva Convention, I reassured myself.

Then he changed tack. 'Go behind the screen and strip off.' The command was muttered like an afterthought. The thought of getting naked made me feel less than comfortable. We'd been told during our training that if we were asked to do anything we considered inappropriate, we could refuse. Obviously, I'd much rather not have stripped off, but if going behind that screen and taking off my kit was what was required to pass this course, then there was no way I was going to kick up a fuss. (I later found out that one of the female Ruperts had refused, but an official had been called in to explain that the command was kosher, and she had relented.)

I looked around at my captors before I rose to my feet, trying to suss out their locations. There was the emotionless officer behind the desk and the two oafs who'd brought me in. But what the hell. I already felt vulnerable. Having no clothes on couldn't make me feel worse. After all, they were in control, not me. I got up and slowly walked behind the screen. There was nothing there but a wooden chair. I started taking off my clothes as quietly as possible, so as not to give the men in the room the thrill of rustling fabric.

When my trousers were off and my shirt half unbuttoned, I heard the door opening and footsteps approaching the screen. My pulse quickened. Around the screen strode a stout nurse with a severe haircut, comfortable shoes and a lived-in face. In her hand was a blue zippered bag. She nodded for me to keep undressing. As I did so she held out her hand for my garments, and methodically searched each seam and pocket before draping them over the back of the chair. When I'd handed her my knickers and had the embarrassment of her giving those the once-over, I was left standing there, fully naked. I could think of hundreds of other predicaments I'd rather have found myself in, but I didn't give a shit what she thought of my body. It was in pretty good nick anyway. She gripped the crown of my head and started rifling her fingers through my spiky crewcut, peering at my scalp. Then she pushed my head back and told me to open my mouth. I gave her a quick blast of unbrushed teeth. She peered up my nose, then spun my head and checked my ear canals. I felt very vulnerable standing there, being treated like a dirty object. She moved on to my body. I knew I was reeking of BO, and was covered in sweat and dirt from the furious tab, but that was her problem. I half expected her to reach into her bag and spray me with disinfectant. She splayed my hands out, scrutinising the webbing between my fingers, lifted my arms and looked at my torso.

She seemed satisfied, but I was well aware there was one bit she'd left out in her meticulous search. Sure enough, she opened her bag and drew out the pair of latex surgical gloves I had expected. She snapped them efficiently onto her hands.

'Bend over the chair,' she barked. I leant over and involuntarily tensed up. She shoved her finger up my arse without ceremony. This wasn't very nice for me, but I doubted it was too nice for her either, which made me feel slightly better.

'Get dressed,' she said as she took off the gloves.

I dressed as quickly as possible. During the search, I had been focusing only on her actions, but now I realised that all this activity must have created a horny thrill for the boys on the other side of the screen. When I emerged I was put straight back into the blindfold, so there was no eyeballing, which helped to hide my embarrassment.

Then it was back to the by now horribly familiar stress positions and white noise. I tried to think nice things, pleasant thoughts about being alone on an empty northern beach with a dramatic coastline and wheeling seabirds. I thought about our Mam. This was nothing compared to what she had been through. After a few seconds, though, the screeching would slam me back into focus. White noise doesn't set your teeth on edge, like fingernails scraping a blackboard. It just slowly drives you insane. It gets inside your brain, and there's no escape.

The stress positions were really doing me in. After another

couple of hours I was beginning to fall apart. The main pain was in my back and shoulders, but my arse was also numb and cold from the chill concrete floor. And, of course, there was the fucking blister, throbbing for Queen and country. How much longer did I have to go? I reckoned I'd already been here for about ten hours. 'Don't fuck up now,' I told myself.

Another interrogation swiftly followed. Then, a couple of hours after that, my captors roughly manhandled me for the fourth time. The stress was really building, even though I knew the form by now. It was the same routine, but this time I was dragged to a different location slightly further away. There were even more steps to bash my blister into.

At the new location I was pushed down onto a seat with a cushioned pad. Hell, it was almost comfy! All I had to do was keep my head and not fuck up. I reckoned I'd done all right so far. I'd been up forever, and was seriously tired. I prepared to really focus on what was going on. When the blindfold came off it revealed an unshaven, aggressive-looking face just six inches away. Cold blue eyes were leering into mine. Then the face began to spit and yell abuse. 'You fucking bitch! Don't fucking think you're going to waste my time any more! I've had enough of shitty little bitches like you! If you don't answer my questions properly, or give me any crap whatsoever, you're gonna get it!'

The shock factor was intense. By comparison my previous three interrogators had been child's play. He had sticky-out ears, so I dubbed him Wingnut. He was glaring contemptuously at me. A fluorescent strip in the ceiling cast a cold blue light over the room. I shifted uneasily, and scanned my environment for clues. A Venetian blind was pulled down over the window, so it must still have been night-time. This room was less cosy than the first interrogation chamber. Where it had been all brick, floorboards and polished wood, this was whitewashed breeze-blocks and grey formica.

Wingnut was blasting out insults. 'You pathetic, ugly cunt, I bet you haven't even got a boyfriend. No bloke would come within ten feet of an ugly, smelly cow like you.' For a minute or two he screamed abuse as he paced around me. He used every swearword and derogatory name under the sun, but unfocused abuse like that is easy to shake off. I just sat there passively as he banged his fist so hard on the desk his coffee cup rattled. This seemed to make things worse. His eyes were wild and he was red in the face with all that bellowing. He was a young, tough-looking bloke, but the veins in his neck were popping out like worms. Then he stopped the torrent of abuse, drew his leg back and smashed his foot into my chair leg. The chair spun back, throwing me around. He was trying to get under my skin, trying to piss me off. I made my face register nothing. I didn't want to give him a single foothold into my psyche. He shut up and walked behind me, resting his meaty forearms on the back of the chair. Then he started screaming in my ear. All the time he was asking questions and I was giving him the old 'I can't answer that question' routine. This incensed him.

'Your friends have told us what we need to know, and they're out of here. They're warm, they've got food and drink, they're safe. Now you, you stupid ignorant little fucker, why don't you just tell us what we want to know, then you can go and join your pathetic mates.' He was really frothing at the mouth now. There was a rotten stench on his breath. For a moment I thought he might be telling the truth, but then I remembered the days when my brother Dean was told the same type of thing by the police during questioning. It had always got him into worse trouble.

'So, one more time. What are you doing here – and if you say to me one more time, "I cannot answer that question"' – he parodied me – 'You won't know what the fuck's hit you.'

Every time I said it, it really fired him up. He'd got wilder and wilder. I was beginning to quake, wondering whether this really was a trial interrogation or some grisly mistake, and I really was a prisoner. The man was menacing, out of control. He'd been going strong now for what must have been twenty minutes, and I was getting nervous. I was tired physically and mentally. I was hungry. I needed a drink. And he was beginning to get to me. I was like a sponge, just passively soaking up all his aggression. Don't fuck up, Sarah, I thought.

I took a deep breath. Well, here goes, I thought, and gave him what he wanted to hear. 'I cannot answer that question,' I said quietly.

He exploded. He frothed at the mouth and pounded his fists on the table, screaming at two stooges by the door, 'Get this fucking scum out of my sight!'

I allowed myself an exhausted little thrill of achievement. I'd won. I'd beaten him. His anger was a perverse form of compliment. I'd denied him the pleasure of breaking me down.

I was blindfolded again and dragged back to the cold concrete floor and the white noise. As I sat there, I ran through the events of the evening and wondered how I'd scored. I did a mental check on my body to see how it was faring, and tried to shrug off the exhaustion running through my brain. Then, much sooner than the last few times, I was picked up again. This time the approach was different. I was still blindfolded, but I was walked out of the building quite politely, not dragged backwards. It was morning; I could see flecks of light through the tightly woven blindfold. I was marched back across the courtyard into another building. My heart fell. Another move to a second holding area or another interrogation cell. I was led to a chair and the blindfold was pulled off. A man was crouching over me.

'Do you know who I am?' he asked.

'I cannot answer that question,' I said. He repeated the question. Then I saw a familiar face and a white armband on his DPM shirt. We had been told during an R-to-I lecture at Camp One that this designated a non-participant – an umpire, in fact. I couldn't believe it was all over so suddenly. Where was the wind-down? I nodded. Yes, I did recognise him.

'Well, who am I? What's my position?'

'You're the security officer,' I said cautiously.

He nodded. 'Right, good. The exercise is over. Grab yourself a cup of tea. This gentleman is going to debrief you.' He indicated a middle-aged guy in nondescript civvies.

I sat with the debriefer for ten minutes, talking through what had happened over the past ten hours. The aim of the interrogators wasn't to break us down, but to introduce us to different techniques that we might need if we were captured for real. Well, that was the theory. The Provos weren't well known for sticking to the Geneva Convention when they caught undercover operators. You only had to think of Robert Nairac, who'd been lifted from a pub carpark in 1977. He'd been viciously beaten before they got bored and murdered him. Nairac was widely thought to have been the Liaison Officer for the SAS squadron in South Armagh, having previously been one of the first members of 14 Company.

The debriefer told me that I'd done fine on Exercise Red Boar. Another hurdle passed. The relief was enormous, and the tea was nectar. As I slurped greedily from my cup I looked around at the other survivors. No one said a word. We looked in shit state, really knackered and drained. I breathed in the fresh air, heard a bird singing outside, and felt relieved to have got this far. Including the fearsome tab which had preceded the interrogation, I'd been at it for twenty-nine hours, and my body was pungent evidence of that fact.

In the female accommodation block I plunged into the shower. My hair was a doormat of knots and grime; every crevice of my skin was ingrained with dirt. After thirty minutes of feverish scrubbing I thought I'd shifted most of it, but when I dried my hair the towel still came up dirty.

We hurried over to the cookhouse and I shovelled a huge fry-up onto my plate: sausages, eggs, bacon, tomato and fried bread, washed down with a pint of milk and a mug of tea. Although I was routinely consuming a bodybuilder's diet, the weight was still dropping off me. I dunked my sausage in the egg and put it to my lips, but anticipation turned to nausea. I couldn't face it. Instead I necked the tea and milk, and followed it up with fruit juice. Downing liquid after endurance is critical; food could come later.

By now we'd found out where we were: a training area in the Welsh borders used exclusively by Special Forces – us and the SAS. It was a scene of rural bliss: gently undulating, sparsely populated countryside. There was no indication that the innocuous country lane, identified only by a milk-chocolate National Trust sign, led anywhere other than to a picnic site. After a couple of miles the hedgerows on either side thickened into well tended twelve-foot walls of dense green foliage, backed by high fences topped with razor wire. The only giveaway was the huge red mast with a red winking light.

Stirling Lines in South Hereford, home to 22 SAS, was equally well hidden, set down a small suburban side street between 1930s bay-fronted semis. Again, the only clue was a radio mast and a red-and-white striped entrance barrier.

At the countryside training area there were outdoor and indoor shooting ranges; an assault course; several training buildings, including a four-storey block known as 'the Embassy', where the SAS and SP (Special Projects) teams practise assaults on buildings, like that used to end the Iranian Embassy siege in May 1980; a grounded Trident for aircraft assault practice; a climbing tower, abseil wall and forty-metre 'death slide' – a high wire you're shackled to for a steep descent using your own bodyweight. The whole area was dominated by a forested hill overlooking the driving area and a network of gunge-filled sewer pipes for crawling through.

We made our way to the lecture room in the classroom block. After the exertions of the previous three weeks our original 120 comrades had shrunk to a shattered fifty-one, including three women: Dawn, Gail and me. We took our seats. The CI (Chief Instructor) was looking uncharacteristically benevolent.

'Congratulations for getting this far,' he said. 'You've made it to Camp Two.' There was a collective sigh of relief before he outlined the next six weeks of fun and games. He finished with a warning. 'The beastings are over, but you've got a lot to learn, so knuckle down and concentrate. It's about to get very intense. After the weekend you'll be heading over the water for NIRTT [Northern Ireland Reinforcement Training Team]. The good news is, you can have the weekend off.'

I was chuffed to bits; I hadn't expected any time off. Before we could go, the CI indicated that now was the time to come out of the closet and get our own names back, in place of the impersonal numbers we'd used so far. He worked his way through the throng in the lecture theatre. Any people with duplicate names had to offer alternatives on the spot. My mate Paul was the second Paul in the room.

'Think of something else,' said the CI.

There was a pause before Paul renamed himself: 'Sparky.'

'Sparky it is then,' said the CI. 'Are you sure?'

'Yes, sir,' he replied. It must have been strange for Sparky to be calling the CI 'sir'; after all, they were both warrant officers, albeit from different units. Following the exertions of the past three weeks Sparky was looking pretty rough; it must have broken his regimented heart to look that way, without a tin of boot polish in sight.

The other two girls who were still on the course had surprisingly un-Ruperty names, despite their la-di-da accents. They were just plain Gail and Dawn. No Hooray Henriettas here! 'Sarah' earned a snigger: rough-and-ready types like me are supposed to be called Tracey or Sharon, it seemed. Dawn was a petite blonde with straight collar-length hair. She'd been having big problems carrying her bergen over the mountains. Her shoulders were virtually non-existent, and even though she'd padded the straps out she still had massive grooves permanently carved into her collarbones. She was the one who'd refused to get her kit off during the interrogation. She was very helpful and always had one of those toothy upper-middle-class can-I-do-anything-for-you smiles. Gail was substantially more fleshy than Dawn, with collar-length dark brown hair and strong features. She looked quite rugged, but although she was an outdoor horsey type, she could be rather clumsy.

Now all I had to worry about was my painful blood blister, which had grown to the size of a golf ball. I went over to get it sorted by a medic. Of all the people with a needle, it had to be Cyborg. I could have cried. He looked at the big red blister, and curled his lip with relish. 'Do you like pain?' he asked. Not really, I thought, but I'm going to get it anyway. He quickly popped and drained my heel, which made me squirm, then filled his syringe with Tinc Benz. There were no niceties in the sanatorium. As he plunged the needle into my flesh I was hanging off the ceiling. Tears exploded in my eyes. It was like having a cattle-brand searing your skin. Yup, I was certainly still alive.

I hobbled back to the mess to pack my kit, and got a lift down to the local station with the Military Transport lads. I was excited to have passed, but was doing the noddy dog all the way to Yeovil. Every time I dropped off I was back in the stress positions.

Chris was at the station to meet me. We melted into each other's arms, but our tender embrace didn't last long.

'Bloody hell, what have they done to you?' he said, holding me at arm's length. My physique had completely changed. All my excess fat had turned to muscle. I was lean and tanned, and I'd got a better six-pack on my abdoms than Chris. After a brief visit to the house we went out to the Bull Inn in Ilchester and propped it up. It was after the third vodka that the world went wobbly and blurred at the edges. I still hadn't had a proper meal, my senses were dulled; I was wiped out, sick with tiredness. I drawled, 'I've got to get some sleep.' The second my head hit the pillow I was out.

I was crouched down behind a three-foot wall with an M1 rifle, firing repeated rounds into the mist at a vague moving target. I was sweating with stress and breathing heavily. Chris was next to me and I was trying to hand the gun over to him, but he wouldn't take it. Then he was waking me up and holding me tight. 'It's OK, you're with me. You're having a nightmare, darling.' I was tense and confused. I'd never dreamed about weapons before.

The weekend passed all too quickly. Sunday afternoon saw us setting off for Swindon station in plenty of time. But then we hit traffic. Chris drove like a maniac. If I missed the transport, I risked getting binned. I couldn't believe I had jeopardised everything. Then, just as we were on the home straight, the blue flashing lights joined us behind. Chris accelerated into the station. I leaped out like a woman pursued by Serb militia and hurtled into the ticket area, panicking like ten men. I was five minutes late, and there wasn't a soul to be seen.

'Have there been loads of people in big army trucks?' I asked a cleaner.

'Yes, they left five minutes ago.'

'Bollocks!'

Like a blue-arsed fly I shot back out to Chris, who was by now heavily embroiled with the cops.

'They've gone. You've got to drive me to Lyneham,' I yelled to Chris. 'Officer, I've got to go. Book us later.'

It turned out that Chris had already been working the Northern Ireland angle. Obviously it worked, because the copper said, 'No problem, follow us.' They were loving it. They put on the flashing lights and gave us an escort over the forty miles. When we arrived at the camp, sirens blaring, the police pulled up and gave us a wave.

I ran into the waiting room, where all the students were milling about. I dashed up to Smithy, the Chief Instructor. 'Sir, sir, I'm really sorry I'm late.' Then the big question. 'Am I binned?'

He gave me a broad smile. 'No, but your kit's gone back to Hereford.'

Chris was loitering in the shadows. I gave him a huge hug good-bye and whispered something really dirty in his ear, then went over to the lads to scrounge some kit. I begged and borrowed: DPM kit, denims and boots. None of it fitted, but I didn't care. After a scare like that, I was just glad to be there. As long as the fashion police didn't spot me I'd be OK.

We landed at Aldergrove, the military and civilian airport in County Antrim, near Lough Neagh, then drove to Ballykinler down winding country roads. It looked a bit like Cornwall, green and gently undulating. After ninety minutes we reached the spectacular Mountains of Mourne. My bed that night was in a corrugated-iron shed.

It was a busy time. The NIRTT course is a compulsory training package for all army bods heading across the water, from padres to paratroopers. There were lectures on patrolling, PVCPs (permanent vehicle checkpoints), explosives and terrorist weaponry, and a grounding in regular forces agencies. One area of the camp was called tin city, and it was here that we learned patrolling, four to a brick. We learnt techniques for entering and leaving a secure compound, and studied how to use lamp-posts, doorways and even six-inch kerbs as cover – lie prostrate in the gutter and there's less of a target for the snipers.

At this stage the mechanics of the 'Det' – as the DS referred to the unit we were joining – were still shrouded in mystery. I wasn't exactly sure what I was letting myself in for. But we plugged on. I was sent along with four other lads to Londonderry for four days to help man a PVCP (permanent vehicle checkpoint). My uniform didn't fit, I didn't look right, and I hadn't yet mastered the army jargon. Everyone was curious to know what I was doing there. I couldn't start gobbing off, it might have been a test, so I just pretended to be extremely introverted and quiet.

But at least I missed my mate Jill's wedding. Her bloke was a pathetic little shit. Two years and a child later they went their separate ways after he'd dipped his dick in a fishwife from Grimsby.

Back on the mainland at Camp Two, we passed through the training area's electronic security gates and into the large, well guarded site. We were split into two classes for photography and driving. Four unfamiliar faces had joined us: Del, Bobby and Mark were SAS, Dippy was SBS. Soldiers who've already qualified for service with 22 SAS or the SBS can volunteer for Op Spice (a tour with the Det), and undergo the same training as us, bar Camp One. Tough, experienced blokes, they'd already proved their physical prowess. The Det provided them with an extension to their soldiering. It gave them skills which would add to the capability of the operational SAS squadrons, complementing their training in advanced surveillance techniques and enhancing their all-round expertise. But just because a man is SAS doesn't mean he'll automatically make it through. A non-infantry bloke could come out much better than a Regiment guy. There are certain necessary qualities, which boil down to the ability to be a sneaky bastard, necky enough to fit in anywhere. You could be the world's toughest soldier and fail the Det on aptitude. Blending in as inconspicuously as possible is crucial; potential recruits have been turned down on the strength of a mole or birthmark.

A Det operator has to be able to spot a player and not flinch. A Regiment bloke might have an ingrained tendency to glare and eyeball. You can't predict how anyone will react. The SAS aren't used to being in the public eye. They operate in covert environments behind closed doors, where they might never mix with local communities.

Del and Dippy were in their early thirties, Bobby and Mark in their late twenties. At the start my perceptions were the same as Joe Public's: I thought the Regiment guys were going to be superhuman gorillas climbing walls. But from day one they treated us as equals and showed no cockiness or bravado, although they didn't suffer fools gladly. None of them were big-headed. If they were, they wouldn't have been right for the job. You work hard and play hard, but there's no room for self-congratulation. It's vital to get on with the next task at hand.

Cyborg took us for what he told us would be just a gentle introductory jog around the area, rolling hills covered in dense woodland. Ten swift miles later I realised that although we weren't up for any more beastings, the onus was on us to maintain our level of fitness. I once again promised myself I'd quit smoking.

Then it was down to more technical work. We had a lot to learn. By the end of the course, six months later, we were expected to be able to drive, navigate, use comms, be prepared to go foxtrot and eat a takeaway curry all at the same time. But for now we just concentrated on getting ourselves from A to B using the three rules of Progressive Driving: safety, speed and smoothness.

In photography we studied low light and infra red. Photographic evidence is a crucial component of surveillance, but there was time to mess about and indulge in some trick photography. Stephen, later to become a Det boss, did a double exposure and printed up a grainy self-portrait of himself giving himself a shag.

On the first day of Camp Two we were issued with 9mm Browning Hi-Powers complete with three magazines, IWB (inside the waistband) holsters, magazine pouch and three blank rounds of ammo. This was a significant moment. From now on the Browning, cocked and locked (the safety catch on, with a blank round up the spout), would be with me all my waking hours. It was the first thing I reached for in the morning. At first I was tense in public, worried about the ballistic equivalent of VPL (visible panty line). I was always checking to see if my weapon was concealed effectively and not peeping out from beneath my jacket. Although carrying the gun was a pain in the arse, sometimes literally, it was crucial to our training to be relaxed, comfortable and confident when tooled up.

We raced through the segments: dry and live firing, rifle firing, assembly and disassembly of weapons, weapon recognition, ballistics instruction. I crammed in all this information, hoping my brain would sponge it up. When your life, and those of your mates, can rely on your speed of reaction with a weapon, using it has to be second nature. You have to be able to respond immediately. You cannot afford mistakes.

One afternoon I was in my room practising dry firing by aiming for a spot on the wardrobe when all of a sudden the air exploded with a heart-stopping crack. There was a cloud of tell-tale smoke drifting around my head, and a dull sensation reverberating in my ears. I was shitting myself. An ND (negligent discharge) is a major cock-up. If it had been a live round there could have been serious consequences. I had the old sledgehammer lurch to the heart, and my pulse soared sky high. 'The gun just went off, m'lud': that's how people justify an ND. It's as feeble as saying the kettle made a cup of tea, or the computer wrote a letter by itself. I'd taken the gun from its holster while it was still loaded with a blank and pulled the trigger. Now I was panicking big time, trying to plan how to work my way out of this. I dashed to the window, unlocked it and fanned it back and forth to try and dispel the smoke. At any moment I expected a bang on my door and a 'What the hell's going on here?' Seconds turned into minutes, and the rebuke still hadn't come. Of course, blanks don't make half the racket of live rounds, but I assumed that the noise would have drawn immediate attention.

I stuck the gun back in the holster and ran over to see Del, one of the Op Spice guys. He was an Australian, and a very strange man indeed. A bit of a nutter, he would always dry fire in his mirror, and whenever he had a bad draw he'd shout at himself and dish out twenty press-ups. He had a very regimented mind, very tick-tock, highly tuned, but he was surprisingly encouraging to me. He failed the course, but later wrote me a letter from a regimental tour somewhere in the Middle East: 'I'm not there but I'm keeping up with you.' I knew I could count on him to sort me out.

'Del, I've just had an ND,' I whispered, as if I was admitting that I'd picked up VD. The blank round had to be replaced somehow, as its absence was sure to be noticed during the next routine inspection. Del was nonchalant, but still managed to rattle off a response which sounded straight from the pages of an SAS textbook. He was quite incapable of sounding like anything else. 'Tonight. 2100 hours. We'll run over the training area and sort it out. RV with me at the entrance to the blokes' block. Don't worry, NDs happen.' Our op was tasked.

That night we pounded along on our evening jog. My biggest concern was keeping up; Del was intensely fit, and my running was still shite. Fortunately, after only two and a half miles we turned into the SAS training area on some scrubland. We stopped outside a single-storey red-brick building which was used for house assaults and blank firing. It was still light and warm as we stood in its shadow and waited. When we were certain no one else was around, Del found some bits of wood, propped them against the wall, then hoisted himself up ten feet and scrabbled through a broken window. He dropped down inside, and I could hear him moving around. When he re-emerged and jumped back to the ground, blood was dripping from his arm. I asked to see it, but he shook his head. 'It's just a scratch,' he said. It was no scratch, blood was pissing out, but I knew better than to mention it again. He opened his palm: six blank rounds which he'd collected from the floor. My panic drifted away from me. From then on this was my little secret with Del. At least I'd saved myself a VC (a voluntary contribution of a tenner to the beer kitty), but more importantly I wouldn't have to explain what a prat I was.

I was quite good with a gun. Whether it was a static target at two hundred feet or a moving figure at five paces, my rounds made neat groups. Sparky and I competed with each other, but I always came out top. To aim at a moving target you had to calculate the distance, the speed of the target and of the bullet. I was amazed by my abilities, and indulged in a bit of fake showing-off. When I kept on getting the best scores, people began to take notice, especially when they discovered that I'd never shot before. For these boys with their toys, this was an irresistible challenge. Everyone wanted to take me on. They were significantly more competitive than if I'd been just another bloke. Combat shooting might have a lot to do with 'visio-spatial' awareness – the ability to make snap judgements in three dimensions – but although I must have had this latent ability, nothing could substitute for the hours of dry practice I'd been putting in.

Shooting said a lot about a person. Gail was a bit erratic, but whatever went wrong she could always find someone or something to blame it on. This appeared to piss the instructor off more than her lack of marksmanship. Harry, another guy on the course, was a good shot, but a bit of a loose cannon on the ranges. He was a quiet bloke, and I'd always suspected he had a mysterious centre, and once I saw him shooting I never trusted him again. He was trigger-happy, and without an ounce of humour. His eyes were too cold for comfort. Phil was binned for being a crap shot, which was a shame because he loved to sing golden oldies on the range. But maybe it was for the best – he always stank of sweat; torrents of it used to pour off his shiny forehead like a waterfall. The players would have sniffed him out at a hundred paces!

I was really going for it now, totally focused and involved in my training. One afternoon we were practising punch and shoot techniques with Mad Max, our unarmed combat instructor, in the killing shed. We had to punch the bag and simultaneously draw our pistols. The bags were suspended on hooks in a row, like carcasses in an abattoir. Max's sidekick, Kev, was teaching us uppercuts, roundhouses, hooks, elbow strikes and knee strikes. I'd taped up my hands to stop the friction of the gloves tearing my skin, and sweat was streaming into my eyes as I pummelled the bag, giving it rock-all and picturing Cyborg's smug face. Kev sidled over to watch me.

'Don't go at it so hard,' he said gently. 'You'll be knackered. Pace yourself.' It was weird to have an instructor tell me to slow down after all the rigours of Camp One, but I didn't risk letting out the slack.

A few days later I was partnered with Del for a strangling exercise. The little Wren and the big soldier. You sat back-to-back waiting for the command, at which you had to flick round and grapple each other. No doubt Del found this pairing quite comical; he'd been in the SAS for five years, and ambush was his game. On 'go', I spun round, clamped my palm on his bollocks and slapped my other hand over his mouth. I was squeezing his knackers so tightly that he wasn't going anywhere, and he was in too much pain to organise any retaliation. The instructors were impressed. Only a girl could have got away with such upfront action. Afterwards, Del was great about it.

'Well done, mate, you had me there,' he said with a toothpaste-ad smile. I'd nearly ripped his knackers off, and here he was giving me a herogram. No attitude problem there.

We were gelling together into our own little clique of Sparky, Joe, Bobby and me. They were good-looking lads, always cracking jokes, and Sparky in particular was brills. We were all giving this course every last ounce of our determination and helping to motivate each other.

After the basic package there was a binning session and a weekend off. Eighty-two had been binned so far, and there were thirty-eight of us left in groups of twelve or thirteen for the intermediate stage. Binning had become more polite; there was no public slagging, just a quiet dressing-down.

Up until now, the Det had been an enigma. It had been up to each of us to put together our own jigsaw about what it might involve. Then one afternoon we were handed a fairly strong operational clue. The instructors had always acted as targets, and we were used to being tasked to hare after them down country lanes. This had always seemed a strange discipline, but now we were instructed: 'Follow, but don't be seen. Then report on what you saw.' I liked the sound of that.

I also enjoyed heli photography, where we had to take aerial shots from varying altitudes and develop our own prints. On one otherwise perfect image I was dismayed to see some tiny white dots disrupting part of the image, until someone pointed out that I'd got a flock of sheep in focus.

Intermediate CQB (close-quarter battle) training took place at Sennybridge, a massive MoD training area in the middle of the Black Mountains, where you can fire and manoeuvre with live ammunition. After a hard day on the ranges with the G3s and HK 53s – the standard Special Forces support weapons in Northern Ireland – we were in need of some excitement. A big oildrum was burning to keep us warm, and Joe wondered what would happen if we chucked in a round. Then, inevitably, came the aerosols and the bangers and flashbangs (stun grenades), until we had a jumping barbecue going, with explosions popping up into the night sky. The toilet was forty metres away, a wooden box with a long drop. You'd just get yourself nicely settled when a flashbang would land outside and give you all the encouragement you needed.

One great outing was a trip to a nearby army range. Once we'd done our tests for the day, which involved firing a rifle at targets from fifty to two hundred metres away, we had some fun. We'd loaded up masses of firearms from the armoury back at camp. It was a magnificent haul, of which any terrorist would have been proud. There were sub-machine guns, carbines, assault rifles and sniper rifles, with plenty of ammo to burn up. I had some particularly exciting moments with an old Thompson sub-machine gun, otherwise known as a Tommy gun. I also experimented with a Scorpion VZ61, a sleek Czech machine pistol, just seven inches long and the smallest SMG I'd seen. I liked it because it was so cute, and it didn't have the oomphy recoil of the meaty G's. The G3 is an awesome rifle with plenty of muzzle flash and powerful recoil. Green army units often whinge about Special Forces having all the good kit, but the fact of the matter is that you need the right gear. After all, you can't block the heat with a chocolate fireguard.

FIVE

COVERT ATTRACTION

THINGS WITH CHRIS had begun to come apart at the seams. He'd slipped to the bottom of my things-to-do list. With Camp Two well under way, and me in with a chance of passing, we were facing up to the possibility of me being away in Northern Ireland for a long stint. The reality was that we'd been leading separate lives for some time. I didn't think about him much, and anyway, I was dismayed to realise that I was falling for one of my CQB instructors.

Every time I saw Luke, my firearms instructor, I started to feel fired up, and even when my eyes weren't clapped on him I couldn't shift him out of my head. He was a six-foot Irishman who'd been in the Regiment for fifteen years, with an accent to die for, bundles of enthusiasm, a sleek, fit body and jet-black hair. His blue eyes were framed by gorgeous long eyelashes, and his permanently suntanned complexion glowed. He never treated his students badly, and he could relate well to anyone, creating immediate respect for his ability to take command of a situation. But he didn't view respect as his God-given right.

I'd discovered that he was an Aries (I'm Scorpio). Did that mean we were compatible? But Luke was an instructor, so I didn't dream of doing anything about my feelings for him. There was an unwritten rule that instructors and students didn't fraternise, and I had no desire to jeopardise my future. He didn't pay me any particular attention, although I could sense that he liked me.

One Friday we were cleaning weapons and preparing to go on leave when Luke asked us what we were all doing for the weekend. Joe sparked up with his plans of going down town to pick up birds and get drunk. Matt piped up, 'My fiancée is a good Catholic girl, so I won't be doing anything until we get married. Can I join you, Joe?'

'That's the right attitude,' said Luke with a laugh. 'Practise on a Prot, marry a Catholic.' At that moment our eyes met, and Luke self-consciously wiped the smile off his face. Later he told me that he'd wanted the ground to swallow him up. I'm a Protestant.

Things with Chris weren't helped when he picked me up at Yeovil station the following day. He gave me a quick hug and, looking a bit shifty, said, 'We're going to stay in a hotel.'

'That's a nice thought, but all I really want to do is go home, have a bath, eat and mellow out.'

There was a pause, then he came out with it. 'Well, we haven't got a home any more. We've been evicted. I've bagged up all your stuff.'

I exploded. 'Fucking hell, Chris. I'm here on a weekend to recharge my batteries and we've got no fucking house? What happened?'

Sheepishly he explained that he'd let the rent drift. He tried to calm me down by telling me how lovely the hotel was, but I was seriously unimpressed. Because I hadn't been around to keep everything organised this wanker hadn't had enough sense to keep things running smoothly. I'd had enough. I didn't want a man who needed leading. Inevitably, the weekend was a disaster. The tension between us ruled out any chance of relaxing.

When I found myself feeling relieved to be back on the course on Monday morning, and hoping to catch a glimpse of Luke, I realised it was time to call it a day with Chris. As he was now of no fixed abode, it took me a couple of days to track him down and tell him the news over the phone. He wanted to meet up and talk it through, but I briskly said, 'No, I've made a decision. That's it. I'll pick up my kit some time.'

Three days later we were all in the camp's bar, which was under the girls' accommodation block. Luke was on duty, and I couldn't take my eyes off him. I hung around at the end of the bar, sipping my glass of red wine. He was closing the bar down and I was one of the last to leave. I crept back down the stairs just as he was coming out. My palms were sweaty and my throat was dry.

'I thought you'd gone to bed,' he said softly. My heart was thumping. I grabbed hold of his hand. 'I wanted to say goodnight properly.' My voice was trembling as I reached up to give him a chaste kiss on the cheek. This man had the power to bin me. What was I doing? Was he really worth the risk?

He grabbed hold of me and pushed me up against the wall, out of the way of the glass doors. Instead of irritation, his face was a picture of aroused disbelief. 'My God, I've fancied you since Camp One,' he breathed. 'My feelings were so intense I wondered if you'd realise.'

'Mine too,' I whispered. 'I had to say something.' We clutched each other and snuck out into the chill night and over to his car. We drove out of camp and up to the woods, to a secluded spot under the bright, starlit sky. We were dying to get at one another, but as well as ripping each other's kit off we talked a lot. We were up there a couple of hours, and knew only too well we were jeopardising both our careers. He was a passionate man, keen and able to pour out his feelings in a great burble of emotion. I already knew he was single, from the general chit-chat on the range and in the bar. He'd been married once before, to an Irish girl, and he had a seventeen-year-old son.

The cork was out of the bottle. We both knew how we felt, but we were also aware that we had to be intensely careful until the course was over. Next morning we were back to normal, pretending there was nothing there. We started seeing each other as much as possible, unable to deny the strength of our feelings. It was such an intensive course, with so much to learn, that we were mainly confined to meeting late at night. I'd borrow Dawn's car and we'd arrange to meet in guest-houses in the area. Then I'd drive back to camp before first light and sneak back to my room. I was permanently knackered, but Luke was worth every moment.

We were now down to three classes of nine, and were beginning to put together everything we'd learned so far. Advanced surveillance consisted of going foxtrot and mobile, working on your own in a car as part of a team doing stake-outs. Four cars would follow an instructor acting as the target. We had to relay his movements over the net to the guy manning the ops room at camp. All the time, instructors were driving around watching us to see how we were doing. The key was not to be obvious to a third party. Basically that meant no reversing out of dead ends, executing three-point turns in cul de sacs, or flashing torches around. We had to look like normal traffic on the road.

Heading south towards Abergavenny one night, I picked up the target in a layby and we boxed him in, so that between our four-car team we were ready to follow him in any direction. At 11 p.m. the target went mobile. We picked him up and tailed him at sixty miles an hour down an A-road. Things were going fine until he turned right, and headed towards the mountain range over which I'd tabbed before the R-to-I. I was responsible for the target, and this would be a real test of my map-reading ability. I was one up (solo in the car), and whipping around winding country roads while trying to navigate.

Map reading at night while driving presents its own set of problems. You can either put on the interior light, which would be a dead giveaway to other vehicles, or hold a torch in your mouth. As I drove along giving my torch a blow-job, I was clipping the target on the bends, judging it so that I didn't emerge onto the straights until he was out of sight. If you're map reading properly you know he can't turn off, so being unsighted shouldn't present a problem. The other cars in the team were following me.

I rounded a tight bend and saw telltale red tail-lights. He'd pulled over to the left, just in front of an unlit junction. I had to keep moving, and gave 'Stop, stop, stop,' over the net to let Andrew, the backing call-sign, know that he now had the target in sight. Andrew turned right down the crossroads to a position from which he could see the target. I was covering west, and pulled up once I was unsighted. The other two cars, including Sparky and Gail in car three, needed to turn back and cover the way we'd just come.

I came up on the net with, 'Zero Delta, I'm covering towards yellow four-one.'

Car four came in: 'Zero Tango, I'm covering back towards the main.'

Sparky was ominously silent. The desk operator spoke up. 'Romeo Zero, which option are you covering?'

There was a few seconds' tension before Sparky came up, very flustered, with, 'Wait one [back in a minute].'

The commentary continued. Andrew told us the target had got out of his car, opened the boot, and was leaning against the rear passenger door. Inside the boot he'd spotted what looked like a small cement mixer. Terrorists will use anything, including coffee grinders, to make up bombs. Two minutes later the ops room came back on. 'Romeo Zero. Your location?'

'Zero Romeo, we're geographically confused. Wait one . . . You stupid old bag, you should have known it was a dirt track.'

'I bloody well told you where to go, but oh no, you wouldn't listen. Why did you have to do an eighteen-point turn anyway?'

'Make yourself useful. Get out and push.'

The ops room tried to cut in to get Sparky and Gail's bickering off the net, but Sparky was blissfully unaware that his pressle was stuck down in the transmitting position. Then it released itself, and Andrew gave an urgent: 'Standby, standby. The target has done a 180.' I spun round and headed back.

Andrew, call-sign Oscar, followed the target past Sparky's location and came up with, 'Zero Oscar, that's Romeo in a ditch. The target's just passed him.' There was a note of humour in his voice.

Sparky had once told me, 'I'm always in the shit, it's just the depth that varies.' On this occasion he'd lived up to his assessment. Back at camp, after he and Gail had been pulled out of the ditch by recovery, he had a lot of beers to buy. That was the rule of training. If you had a cock-up you either made a voluntary contribution or got a crate of beer in. Sparky explained that they had taken their first option, a left-hand turning, and Gail had planned to take them around three sides of a square to face the right direction. But Sparky had ignored her and done a 180, misjudged it and crashed into the ditch, revving like mad to get back out. He got a bit of slagging from the DS for not admitting the problem. The moral of the exercise was 'honesty is the best policy'. The only safe way to deal with fuck-ups over the water is to be frank. There's no glory in being afraid to lose face.

Advanced CQB took place over eleven days, and Luke made sure we packed a lot in. On the walls of the classroom he'd hung cross-sections of various weapons. Around the edges were work benches with cleaning kit and a compressor to blow a jet of air into the awkward parts of the guns. The room had the warm, sweet smell of gun oil. Sometimes Luke would jot slogans on the white-board: 'Aim at nothing and you'll hit it'; 'Shoot fast, don't miss.'

One day, down on the range, Luke was filling his magazine, swigging a brew from the urn and immersed in friendly banter with the trainees. They were teasing him for being an old bloke – he was forty-one – when he turned on them and said, 'I can outrun you, outshoot you and out-fucking-shag you.' Fortunately he didn't turn to me for confirmation!

One morning we set up chipboard doorways, walls, kerbs and windows to simulate a street. The range was all live firing and the bullets would embed themselves in sandbanks to the front and sides of us. As I was milling around having a general chat with Gail, Joe, Dippy and Harry, an explosion cracked out from the front of the range, six metres away. A 7.62 round impacting into a bank makes an awesome boom. Live ammunition continued to hurtle over our heads and slap into the bunkers.

Harry screamed, 'Contact front!' We'd been paralysed for a frac-tion of a second by the disorientating noise, which brought the automatic adrenaline rush of fear. But instantly we were up to speed and detailing ourselves off into pairs. Moving to cover, I took the nearest chipboard doorway to my right, breathing in the smell of stale wood as Gail joined me. Harry and Dippy took the left-hand side. The shots had come from the instructors on a rise at the back of the range. Now we were into our well-rehearsed groove, laying down rounds to the front of the range. I was firing at one of the cardboard targets with my Browning, blasting out full-metal-jacket roundnose bullets. The object of the exercise was to move as quickly

ABOVE My brother Dean and me, aged three and two.

LEFT Dean and me plotting to catch birds in the back yard of Ashton Street.

BELOW Us four girls with our prized possessions.

First school photograph. I'm ten, and deeply protective of the little 'uns (left to right: Jane, Katherine and Melissa).

With five kids, every day was wash day for our Mam.

So proud! Immaculate in
my Wrens uniform.

Training at HMS *Daedalus* (front row, centre) to become an AEM (Aircraft Engineering Mechanic), November 1983.

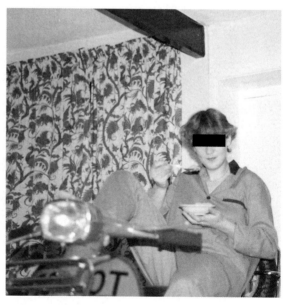

ABOVE Protecting my scooter from the winter frost while sharing a hovel with Dean and Tel at HMS *Heron*, Yeovil.

LEFT Aged twenty. A skinhead was to replace my quiff within a few weeks.

Receiving my N.I. Medal from the boss of 45 Commando RM, whilst practising my cheesy Rupert grin.

'Don't worry, lads. I'll get supper ready.' Me on one of the many pre-Det training sessions.

Across the water in summer 1990. South Det geeks posing in front of our Gazelle.

LEFT 'Right lads, listen up!' Teaching the admin staff basic firearms technique.

BELOW LEFT Luke and me at a regimental dinner in 1990 before things started to fall apart.

BELOW RIGHT After signing out my sexy legs I was propping up South Det bar waiting for a lift to Belfast.

Congratulating Taff on numerous hours of flying time. I was with him for most of them!

The South Det lads and me down at Ballykinler range keeping our skills up to scratch. I'm clutching my HK53 with extended stock and twenty-five-round mag.

The horror of our lucky escape. More operators are killed across the water in road traffic accidents than by enemy action.

My watercolour
painting of weary troops
returning from war.

Posing up the Mourne Mountains on
a much-needed day away from
the compound.

Jock after running
me ragged across
the mountains.

Me and Joe during the ill-fated skiing trip to Bavaria.

My partner Jed enjoying a day off at one of Ulster's beautiful tourist spots, Strangford Lough.

Tooled up with my 9mm Browning, HK53, Op Gracie and a bag of maps after a routine aerial surveillance.

"Go out into the highways and hedges" and compel them to come in ..."

Official Det memorabilia, quoting St Luke.

as possible to the back of the range, away from danger, while giving each other cover. Gail was in front of me, and screamed, 'Coming through!' The boys were laying down lots of fire from the other side of the 'street' ten metres to our left. There was shouting and chaos as Gail came out of the door, crouched down and ran past me. For a split second while she crossed my arc I stopped firing, as we'd rehearsed. We'd been trained by the best men in the world, but I could easily harm her if I made the slightest error of judgement. This was the real thing. You don't get this in the green army. If we didn't act as a team, and she ran into my line of fire, it could be goodnight Vienna.

As a round enters a body it dumps a massive amount of kinetic energy, creating a pressure wave of body fluid and destroying tissue. It's that hydrostatic shock which kills. A straight kill can be achieved by targeting the neurological areas. If the round hits the ears, eye sockets, under the nose, or the base of the skull, the brain usually stops immediately and your target won't know a thing about it. The secondary area is the cardiovascular centre mass, which we had been trained to view as the target zone. The neurological area is difficult to hit with precision in a combat situation, but a direct hit to the heart, lungs, chest or throat will normally cause almost immediate death. Hollywood always shows people who've been hit clutching their chests and bleeding profusely, but that doesn't often happen with modern weapons. Your nervous system would be involuntarily wriggling you about like an epileptic having a seizure, and you'd have no time to splutter out that final clue to your comrades or sentiment to your lover. Hits to the arms and legs can also kill, but it will be a much slower death. There's a widespread misconception that if you are hit anywhere with a bullet you will die. This is simply not true. In many cases a high velocity round will pass straight through the body, causing very little trauma or injury.

The British Army and Special Forces use a fairly small range of ammo, but each is of full-metal-jacket construction, in accordance with the Geneva Convention. A copper jacket covers the lead core of the bullet, enabling greater velocity to be achieved. Special Forces do not use any form of hollow-point or 'dum-dum' bullet, as popularly portrayed. Rounds have the ability to swiftly despatch an enemy target if accurately placed, and this is where the many hours of highly specialised marksmanship practice pay off. There is no magic calibre or bullet that can circumvent dedicated training.

As I continued firing, Gail made it to the next available cover behind me. I heard her laying down fire and prepared to run, her bullets passing three feet to the left of my head. I squatted down, lower than a snake's belly. Gail wasn't the world's best shot, and I wasn't going to take any chances.

'Coming through!' I yelled as I prepared to run through her arc of fire. I pointed my pistol to the heavens. The second rule of firearms is: never allow your muzzle to cover anything you're unwilling to destroy. (The first is: treat all firearms as being loaded.) I spun round, keeping as close to the wall as I could, and ran in the crouch position to the next cover. Live ammo whistled over my head. As I tore past Gail I could see the rally point, a brick wall at the back of the range. Good. Hard cover for me to hide behind.

The boys were doing the same routine on the other side of the chipboard street. I could hear the firing as I charged behind the brick wall. I laid down more rounds, taking one and a half seconds from shot to shot on my magazine change. Dippy came screaming up to join me from the other end of the wall, pumping sweat and looking like a man who'd run a half-marathon. Pressure makes you breathless as your body floods with adrenaline. I saw Gail flick her head round to check the rally point.

Gail yelled, 'Coming through!' and started to run, but I looked on with numb horror as she ran out in front of the rally point, instead of up the side. She screamed 'Stoppage!' and I saw her fumbling on her mag change, unaware that she was about to enter our arcs of fire. Her pistol was pointing at Harry, who was working his way back to cover down the left.

My finger was still on the trigger, and all of a sudden Gail was moving right to left in slow motion, waddling like a duck across my arc of fire. When something like this happens your brain speeds up, giving the impression that time has slowed down, and your reactions and senses are heightened. As she entered the arc my finger had taken up the first pressure on the trigger. I was lined up on the target, but this woman was filling my sights. I felt my finger moving in the wrong direction, and realised that my brain was forcing it back. I was aware that I had somehow managed not to squeeze out the shot. Suddenly hands crashed onto my back. I heard the tail end of 'Stop!' in my peripheral hearing. Then the slow time was over. I snapped back into real time. There was shouting and commotion. Gail arrived panting at the rally point. The instructors were leaning on me. I looked at my finger, which was off the trigger and lying along the pistol frame. This was evidence that my brain had created an automatic reflex for every eventuality. My subconscious had taken up the tools of the training and pushed them one step further. I flicked up the safety catch and holstered the Browning.

I was very wound up, but Gail just stood there, getting it from all sides. Had I been alone with her I would have lamped her. I was drained, wound up. I needed a moment to reflect and think what might have been. Gail appeared blind to what she had just done, or rather not done. She wasn't apologising or cursing, instead she was feebly attempting to justify herself.

'What the fuck do you think you were doing? I could have slotted you!' I yelled. But Gail couldn't admit blame. Instead she burbled on about her mag change, when the real issue was running past two arcs of fire and pointing a loaded weapon at a team-mate. Luke and Ron were shouting at her too, irate that she was blaming other people rather than being clued up about her failings in the contact. She didn't get a formal bollocking, but from then on the instructors kept a close eye on her. I certainly wasn't volunteering to be partnered with her again.

This was nothing compared to the course which followed us, when someone shot an instructor twice – in the thigh and shoulder. Everyone yelled for the medic, but the medic was lying on the range writhing in agony. SF training is a big boys' game, and there will always be casualties. Since the end of the Falklands War in 1982, nine SAS soldiers have been killed in training accidents, compared to five by enemy action, four in the Gulf and one by the IRA. If you sign up for the training, you can't ignore the risks involved.

We packed up for lunch and headed for the cookhouse, where some SAS lads were wearily queueing up, having just completed a strenuous training exercise. After scoff we sat in the television room for fifteen minutes with our brews watching *Inspector Gadget*, a children's cartoon about a character tooled up like a cross between James Bond and the Six Million Dollar Man. It was a favourite among us would-be Walter Mittys. Then the reverie was over, and it was back to the explosive world of turning bullets into brass (empty cases).

Four days later we were on a debussing exercise (getting out of a vehicle in a pressure situation). We were required to drive onto the range, head for the nearest cover and lay down fire while retreating from the contact. As we came to a halt, gunfire exploded over the roof. I jumped out of the back seat and headed for cover five metres away on the left-hand side of the range. Harry and Bobby, who was driving, leaped out of the front of the car and ran to the other side. Once I was behind the chipboard shack I spun round and started giving covering fire with my Browning. Dippy was still inside, and having difficulty exiting; his foot appeared to be caught between the seats. Just as he freed it, he staggered and fell onto the tarmac clutching his stomach. In disbelief I saw blood spurting all over the ground. I tore across to Dippy, who was writhing in pain. As I ran I heard the instructor scream, 'Stop the exercise!' My brain was working overtime. I was certain I hadn't hit Dippy, but where could the shot have come from? With a chill I realised that I was the only person who *could* have shot him. My two team-mates were on the right-hand side, and he was well out of their line of fire. Yet I was certain of my sights. He must have shot himself as he stumbled out of the car.

I was the first to get to him. His white T-shirt was soaked with blood, his face chalk-white. 'Get the medic!' I screamed.

'He's not here!' shouted Cyborg. This was desperate. I looked at Dippy, whose blood was seeping onto the ground.

'Get the medical pack!' shouted Sparky. All hands were now on Dippy, laying him down, trying to find out where the wound was. His body had gone into shock, shaking and shivering as he mumbled, 'I'm shot, I'm shot, someone give me a drink.'

There was blood everywhere. I fumbled around the small of his back for the exit wound, but couldn't find it. I had to stop because he was in urgent need of a compress. All I had on was my jeans and T-shirt, so I started pulling my top off. At that moment Luke came pounding across the gravel with the medical pack. Everyone was shouting. I heard: 'Who shot him?' and yelled back, 'It wasn't me, I could see where my sights were. He must have shot himself.' All the while I was fumbling with Dippy, who was well into shock and moaning dismally. The range car screamed up and skidded on the gravel. Ron, the instructor, leaped out, examined Dippy briskly and decided to immediately pick him up rather than wait for an ambulance. I looked at the blank faces around me. We were all drained, but each of us was still justifying why we weren't responsible.

Ron had heard enough. 'Cut it out. There's a bloke who's been shot, and it's one of you bastards. One of his own team-mates. Unload your weapons and hand them over to Bob.'

The firearms post-mortem would work out how many rounds we'd each fired and where the bullets had embedded. A single shot would remain unaccounted for, the one which had hit our mate. We drove back to the classroom in stunned silence, nervous about the impending grilling, and hoping desperately that poor Dippy would pull through. Soon the lawyers would arrive. I was certain I wasn't responsible, but in everyone else's eyes I'd already been tried and found guilty. There was just no way that the round could have come from the others, and we all knew it. But I was equally certain that it hadn't come from me. My range skills were just too sharp by now. I knew where my rounds were heading. We trudged forlornly into the classroom area, where one of the surveillance instructors was hanging around. 'How's it going? Everyone happy?' He hadn't heard. I spoke up in a hyper-frenzy. 'No, Tim. Dippy's just been shot. They've taken him to hospital, we're having a debrief.' His face fell and he followed in behind us.

The atmosphere in the classroom was dire. There was a good chance that Dippy wouldn't make it through. We were told he'd lost over three pints of blood. We sat down, eyes front, and ran through the events for half an hour. Who did what, who moved where. It was the worst day of our training. After we could add nothing more, Luke said, 'We've got someone else who might want to say something on the subject.' I turned around, expecting to see the lawyers filing in. Instead there was a rattling sound from the metal cupboard at the back of the classroom. Out walked Dippy with a big grin on his face.

'Fucking hell! You bastard!' I cried. I could have throttled Dippy. He'd been set up beforehand with a blood bag and instructions to burst it as he debussed.

Then came the congratulations. We'd laid down our weapons correctly, sorted out the casualty, and I'd been about to rip off my T-shirt to staunch the blood and reveal my bra straps to the world. I wanted to know if I'd specifically been set up. Later, Luke reassured me that it was just by chance that I'd been on the left-hand flank, and that the exercise would have taken place irrespective of who'd been covering that option. 'You're my wonderful young woman and you're doing very well. I'm very proud of you.' Nevertheless, I still slapped him about a bit.

Luke and I only had very short periods of time together and that heightened the intensity of our relationship, as did its clandestine nature. We would have known if anyone had guessed about us, and certainly the other two girls hadn't.

Luke lived in a large eighteenth-century house he'd bought in a village not far from Hereford. He sneaked me there one Saturday afternoon. It was very much the spartan, uncluttered house of a man, although he'd decked it out in some wood panelling that he'd liberated from an old church, and there were some fine pieces of heavy, dark antique furniture. He had a vast open fireplace, six feet long by five feet high. I'd perch on the side of the grate and he'd show me photos taken throughout his SAS service. In his twenties and thirties he'd been a good-looking man, and his features had weathered deliciously with age.

During our CTR package we were given a target described only as 'a large house with outbuildings on the outskirts of Hereford'. When the lads drew up their report they said the building looked disused and uninhabited. I decided to keep my mouth shut, rather than risk disagreeing with their assessment; Luke wasn't too chuffed about the clinical description of his treasured home.

During CQB we were taught how to do house assaults – forcibly entering a building, shooting the bad guys and rescuing a hostage. The theory was that, in the event of an operator being snatched and held by the boyos across the water, we could go in and get him out. In reality such assault work would most likely be up to the Troop: the élite SAS team permanently based in the Province, with whom I was in training. But we covered all options, just in case.

On one occasion I was in a team of four. Our brief was to rescue a fellow operator. Tom was first man in, I was second, and Greg – known as 'Sexpest' – was third. Rob acted as doorman – it was his job to kick, axe or shoot the door in and give back-up cover. Ron had set up the bulletproof room, one of nine in the three-storey building, with various targets and items of furniture. We were tooled up with 9mm Brownings and MP5Ks – a compact 9mm SMG – and raring to go. Tom gave 'Three–two–one–GO.' Rob shot up the door lock. Tom bundled in to the right and I followed swiftly, covering the left flank. We both took out the targets in our arcs of fire. Greg hovered at the door, awaiting our order to search the room and ready to step in if either of us had a stoppage. Keeping my Browning holstered as back-up, I put two rounds from my MP5K into each of the three targets in my field in the upper chest area. Then I saw him. Sitting on the window ledge was Tim. I couldn't believe what I was seeing. Fortunately the targets had been placed in such a way that we wouldn't have naturally shot in Tim's area. I was relieved to see that he was wearing full body-armour, but I was still gulping in shock. On the command, Greg came in and did a methodical sweep.

Even when you think you've got all the targets, there's always the possibility of a loose cannon concealed behind a couch or in a wardrobe.

'All clear!' Greg shouted. I moved forward, grabbed hold of Tim and pulled him outside to safety. He was indeed a brave man. I wouldn't have wanted to sit there like the circus knife-thrower's stooge with all that hardware raining down around me. The whole operation had taken no more than eight seconds from entry to extraction. The aim of a successful room assault is the element of surprise coupled with speed and accuracy. Tim's presence had certainly been a surprise.

Later that day Luke introduced us to the delights of flashbangs – 'stun grenades', which disorientate the occupants of a room into which they're lobbed. They'd been used to great effect in the Iranian embassy siege. As he chucked one in amongst us I thought the heavy artillery had arrived. The thing was so loud it sent shock-waves slamming through my body, shaking my bones far worse than being next to the loudspeakers at a heavy-metal gig. It flashed so brightly and irregularly that it felt as if it was soldering my retinas. It would stun an unsuspecting terrorist big style. Across the water we would also have a similar stun device attached to our vehicles, activated by a button inside the car as you debussed. Flashing and banging, it would buy you valuable seconds in which to flee or assume a firing position.

The advanced CTR segment essentially required us to sneak up on buildings and have a cheeky look at what was going on inside them. One of our missions was to enter a printers in Hereford, gather some photographic information, and extract covertly. Our TOG (time on the ground) was set for 3 a.m., well after the pubs and nightclubs had emptied, so there was little danger of interference. Everyone in Hereford helps Special Forces. Local farmers let us use their land, and businesses give us permission to go in and do OPs (observation posts) and CTRs (close target reconnaissance) in the interests of national security. It's all good PR for them.

The printing company was a three-storey brick building dating from the turn of the century. Joe was in charge of the operation, and would go in and do the CTR with Sparky. Paul and I were doing the OP by acting as a couple. This is one of the ways women can be useful to Special Forces. Politically incorrect as it might sound, a man and a woman can snog in a doorway and not draw attention. It would be much harder for two men, or a single male, to find an excuse to linger. No one told me that fake clinches were a good gambit: it was obvious.

Frustratingly, I'd learned that across the water I wouldn't be allowed to do CTRs. The hierarchy had banned women operators from doing certain things, and for some reason having boobies and no Adam's apple meant CTRs and rural OPs were out of bounds. There was no logic behind this; it was just the way it was. You don't get het up about something you can't change. Not bucking authority was part of having the right personality for the Det. Had the government allowed women into the main core of the SAS I'd have been the first recruit, but I couldn't get worked up about the fact that my gender barred me. It's the same as when people ask me what it's like not having a dad. It's an irrelevant question. What's it like having a dad?

So there I was, on the other side of the street, stuck in a shop doorway with Paul, pretending to snog him every time we heard someone walking past, while both keeping a lookout. I might have been tempted to give Bobby a real kiss – he was a big, strong, good-looking fella – but Paul, short with a big nose, wasn't my type. On the dot, Sparky and Joe were dropped off after we'd given the all-clear. They walked briskly down the street in normal clothing – dark jeans and bomber jackets – brushed past us and made their way into the building. The DS had given them the key and the alarm code. They locked the door behind them, letting us know their precise location over the net as they worked through the pitch-black building. They made it to the office and informed us they were in, when the ear-splitting scream of an alarm sounded off. Paul and I looked disbelievingly at each other. Surely it couldn't be from our building? We heard nothing from Joe, so we informed the ops room that an alarm was going off and asked Joe to acknowledge. 'Roger that, we're coming back out.' It should have taken

Joe and Sparky about eight seconds to exit. After two minutes I got on the net and nudged them: 'Lima Delta. Exit clear.'

Sparky came up on the net. 'Roger that. We're having a few problems getting out. We're locked into the office.' I couldn't believe it. Sparky was slap bang in the middle of yet another Just William escapade. Outside we were dead calm, but they were obviously running about like headless chickens, trying to pick the locks and checking for roof hatches. Eventually Angus, the DS, went in and let them out, and then we all extracted.

It was always Sparky, and the general consensus was that that was the last time he went up front. But this time he'd gone by the book, doing what he'd been briefed to do. It wasn't his fault that since the owners had handed over the key for the exercise they'd put in further security. Either that or the CTR staff knew full well, and had left out details of the self-locking door as just another part of the test.

There was another binning session, and the intake was down by ten, to a total of twenty-seven bods out of the initial 120. Consistently poor map-reading under pressure, an inability to reach the minimum score on the ranges, and leaving obvious signs on CTRs were typical reasons for being binned at this stage. But a couple of people we'd thought were doing well were also booted out. We could only assume that there were significant flaws in their general aptitude, although we were never told. The tension of uncertainty remained for those of us who were left. Significantly, no one ever praised us. We had to be totally self-reliant.

We were well aware that we still faced the second R-to-I exercise, known as Red Dragon. It's a vastly more unpleasant 'simulated terrorist interrogation' during which we would have to maintain a cover story in the face of mental and physical abuse. Where members of the SAS were trained to be physically strong, Det training concentrates on psychological strength. We would face a greater risk of being kidnapped due to the clandestine nature of our work. We often did surveillance in close proximity to the terrorists' homes, with no escape if things got tough. Recruits to the army's covert agent-handling unit in Northern Ireland, which also operates close up to the terrorists, go through much the same R-to-I process.

Rumours had been flying around about Red Dragon, but I'd tried to switch them off. It'd happen soon enough – no need worrying about it just yet. Then one crisp November night we were on an exercise driving around the area, one up. The general feeling was that this was it, but I'd tried not to get too worked up in case it wasn't. I received an abrupt command over the net: 'Zero Delta, make your way to the three-storey building on the Garraback range. Enter and go through the second door on the left.'

Fucking hell, this was it. I did a 180 spin and went back the way I had come. I glanced at my watch: 6.53 p.m. As I drove, I counselled myself. I'd been in shit state on the last R-to-I. My mental state was much better this time round. I wasn't knackered and I had no blood blister. I'd got this far, and I could push through another obstacle. I wasn't cocky, I just felt fresh and confident. I gave myself a quick mental injection of strength-of-character juice.

The range was silent, and there were no other vehicles around. I cut the engine, took a deep breath and thought, 'Don't let the bastards get you down.' I was grateful that I was well fed and watered, but regretted the fact that I was smartly kitted out in skirt, tights and court shoes. I was up for a long night.

I walked towards the heavy wooden door, which was already open. The lights were on in the hall. At the end of the bulletproof corridor was a lift shaft. A door led off the right of the corridor, and there were two more to the left. As I padded apprehensively down the smooth concrete corridor, every nerve in my body was straining for clues. I opened the second door on the left and went inside. The room was dimly lit; I could just make out the shadows of furniture, but nothing more. I'd taken only four paces inside when the lights flicked on, blinding me. Six beefy men wearing balaclavas and boilersuits ran into view and straight for me. I was sighted only for a split-second and felt the overwhelming presence from all directions. They knew what was coming next. I didn't have a clue. Then a hessian sack went over my head, and rough hands seized me. A rope was looped around my neck and yanked tight. People tugged and pulled at me, ripping off my gun and mags. My clothes began to tear. I was disorientated. Everything was chafing hessian. The fabric of my blouse ripped, my arms were yanked back and it was pulled over my shoulders and shredded. I felt fingers clutching at the elasticated bottom of my sports bra, but they let go. I later found out that Liz had signalled that it wasn't a halter-necked top, although it looked like one. Other hands were ripping off my shoes. My American tan tights were like rice paper as huge hands grabbed and shredded them. There was nothing a spot of nail varnish could do to repair those holes. The top button of my knee-length grey skirt popped, the zipper was ripped and the skirt yanked down my legs. My arms burned because of the friction caused by the guys restraining me from behind. I tried not to struggle. There was no way I could escape. I just let them do it to me. My heart was beating, my mouth was dry.

I was now naked except for my sports bra and knickers. It was bitterly cold and I could feel the goosepimples forming, but before I had time to start shivering my limbs were briskly stuffed into overalls. Then my hands were pulled behind my back and plasti-cuffed. I was dumped on the floor and my feet were also trussed up with plasticuffs. I felt vulnerable and helpless. In such situations the natural instinct is to protect your face and torso, but with my arms tied behind me there wasn't too much I could do, although I'd have gone foetal if I could. It was all over in less than fifteen seconds. I could feel my moist breath collecting damply on the hessian in front of my lips.

I was picked up under my armpits and dragged outside. The next thing I heard was the doors of a van opening, and I was launched into the interior, crunching onto the soft warmth of a pile of motionless bodies. I felt like a faceless carcass. The only sound was the diesel engine ticking over and my raspy breathing. Then the doors closed with a slam. 'Can everyone breathe all right?' a gruff voice enquired. Gail spoke up with a muffled 'Yes.' The owner of the gruff voice lurched across me, his elbow jabbing me in the ribs, and there was a dull thud as he winded Gail. 'Who told you that you could say "Yes"?' barked the voice. As the fist made contact with her solar plexus she let out an involuntary 'Ugh.' So he whacked her again. 'And who said you could say "Ugh"?'

As the van sped off there was lots of fear sloshing around inside. We had no idea where we were going, what we were up for, when the next physical abuse would arrive and in what form, but it was a fair guess who was doing it. A highlight of the season for the SAS squadron in training at Hereford was when they were offered the chance to beat up the 'Walts'. I was swallowing every few seconds and controlling my breathing. I tried not to think about the Camp Two folklore of broken bones and bust noses from the R-to-I.

After lots of disorientating high-speed left and right turns the van suddenly stopped. I heard the crunch of feet on gravel and the back doors were opened. I was dragged out and thrown onto hard, stony ground as if I was a sack of rubbish. I landed awkwardly on my elbow and saw a minor constellation of stars as my neck tensed to protect my head from slapping like a melon onto the ground. Other bodies were dropping all around with sickening thuds. I concentrated hard in an attempt to reorientate myself. I'd been dumped on damp and smelly concrete. I got a whiff of animals and cow dung: a farm. It's vital to find clues to help orientate yourself, indeed it's the only way to feel less vulnerable. I lay absolutely still as I heard the van pull away. There was complete silence, just the quiet of the November night. As the cold worked its way over my skin I began to shiver. Without shoes or socks my feet were numb with cold, and the overalls were stinking and soaked with cow slurry. There wasn't much point in trying to move, I was trussed up like a Christmas turkey.

Footsteps crunched towards me from different directions. My stomach tightened. Was one of those boots about to be planted in the back of my neck or my kidneys? I reckoned I was overdue for a good kicking. My whole body spasmed in anticipation as the feet stopped just inches from my nose. I was dragged up and pushed into a huddle of shivering, swaying bodies. I heard the rush of water. Then it hit me, pummelling me from all angles. It was completely depersonalising. I was no one, just a shrouded object being hosed down with icy water in a farmyard. Freezing, barefoot and drenched. The hessian sack stank of mildew. Water dripped off my sodden hair and face, running down my neck. Where the hessian rubbed my skin it was coming up sore and itchy. After a minute the water torture stopped. I was dragged across the gravel, pushed upright and leaned against a post. Then a hand slapped the back of my head and my face obediently smashed into the post. I tasted the salty blood filling my mouth. The plasticuffs were slashed so that my arms could be yanked around to embrace the post, which was the diameter of a lamppost, and I was re-plasticuffed.

Nervously, I felt my split upper lip with the tip of my tongue. My front teeth had made a neat half-inch cut in the flesh. It didn't hurt too much, and there was no point feeling angry about it; there wasn't much I could do.

I stayed there for what must have been an hour, with my bare feet on the cold slimy ground. I could sense a breeze at waist-height which was a few degrees warmer than the near-zero temperature elsewhere. I surreptitiously shifted my hands a few inches up the pole to warm them. The breeze had a farmyard smell and I realised it was coming from where the pigs were. It was a soothing image, and I held onto it as my whole body froze and shook, like a prisoner in some Siberian gulag.

After a while I became severely worried about my toes. I'd managed to acquire frost-nip in Norway in 1987 – the first stages of frostbite, when your toes go white and lose all feeling. It had been minus 40 degrees and Keith, a bloke I was going out with, had been drinking 90 per cent proof illegal home brew when he decided to sit in the snow and not move for love of me. I'd been wearing jeans, trainers and a padded jacket. It had taken me forty minutes to drag him out of a gully and up a hill to the Wrens' quarters. The alcohol in his body had been cooling off his core temperature and he'd been going down with exposure and frostbite. When we'd got inside I'd shouted for some of the lads who were illegally visiting to help me. They'd seized hold of Keith, whose lips were blue by then, and started warming him up with their body heat by rubbing and holding him. As soon as I could I'd yanked off my shoes and had seen three bright white gleaming toes. I'd said to one of our mates, 'Quick, give me your armpits.' We'd sat there for twenty minutes with my toes jammed underneath as I felt the burning sensation of my blood returning.

Keith was a headcase, and was really clingy. One day I got so fed up with him that I'd said, 'Oh, for fuck's sake, do something manly,' so he'd stepped out of the first-floor window of his barracks and broken his leg. Another time he'd drunk eight pints of bitter in two hours and threatened to drive into a brick wall if I didn't stay with him. I was so pissed off that I'd told him to get on with it.

Now Keith was proving useful for the first time, as a distraction of sorts. After about half an hour trussed up against the pole my spine felt as if it had turned to an iron rod. I could hear someone nearby groaning, and the whimpering moans of one of the girls. But I wasn't doing too badly. After all, I was just standing there with a hessian sack over my head. This was nothing compared to the stress positions from the previous R-to-I, although I was still numbed and cold.

After what must have been an hour, someone cut the plasticuffs on my feet and wrists, and shoved me into an armlock. I hoped we'd be going somewhere warmer. The guards dragged me about twenty paces before turning left into a building where, joy of joys, the Philharmonic White Noise Overture awaited me. Although I couldn't see it, the building felt more agricultural than army. After another eighty paces or so we turned right down a corridor and into a small room. I was pushed down to a seated position on a wooden pallet and my arms and feet were strapped onto it. I could neither sit up straight nor lie down because of the bindings. It was an enforced stress position.

I was left there for what seemed like three hours, hearing, inhaling and tasting the white noise. It swirled around inside my head and dominated every thought. Denied any visual input, the only sense I was aware of was my hearing, which was magnified, making the noise twice as bad.

I used the time constructively, distracting myself by creating a cover story which I could bring out, fact by fact, when necessary. My overalls were still damp and slimy, my body was coated with goosebumps and my tongue felt like a soggy piece of cotton wool. Every now and again I heard the rustle of clothing as my captors wandered in silently to observe me. I couldn't shift position because of the bindings and my mind was in a frenzy, not knowing when the yelling would start. My thoughts drifted to John McCarthy and Terry Waite and what it must be like for real hostages.

Someone came into the room, untied me and frogmarched me to another room. The sack was pulled off. The room was brightly lit, and two men in balaclavas and leather jackets were scrutinising me. One of them carried a crappy AR180 – the classic IRA assault rifle. I flicked my eyes back and forth, without moving my head, to see if there was anyone else lurking.

After the initial questioning – the old name, rank and number routine – my inquisitor's manner hardened and the questions became completely focused on what I was doing, where I was going, why I had special gear in my car. This was a test of my ability to maintain a cover story.

'I know you're a member of a team,' he said sharply. 'What are their names, what are their vehicles, what are their VRNs?'

'Sorry, I don't know them that well,' I lied.

'Why are you operating in this area? What unit are you in?'

'Signals. We're all signallers.'

As the questioning intensified I tried the rag doll approach. 'I don't want to be here. I want to go home,' I whined.

He kept up the pressure. He'd lifted all my kit from the car: maps, weapons, comms, the lot. I wasted a lot of time struggling to remember the VRNs, which of course I knew straight off. As they had captured our vehicles, I wasn't giving away any secrets there. The interrogation lasted about twenty minutes. I stayed completely still, answering in a limp monotone. The worst was yet to come. Hooded again, I was led stumbling back to the pallet. We went through this little routine three or four more times until my inquisitor decided he wasn't having any more of it. He wanted more information. I stalled. 'Please give me a drink. My mouth's dry. I can't speak any more and I need to go to the toilet.'

'You're not going to the fucking toilet until you speak to me.'

I started to cry. I was putting it on, but it didn't take too much effort. I thought he might feel sorry for me or dismiss me as a pathetic little nobody. All the time I was planning what to say next.

'Look, I'm pregnant, that's why I need to go to the toilet. I need something to drink. My mother's ill, I haven't got a husband.' I tried to look as hopeless and insignificant as possible. But soon my bladder was genuinely bursting. It was about eight hours since I'd last had a leak. I started crying and pleading for the toilet.

'You're not going to the toilet and you're not getting a drink,' he barked.

There was no other option. I pissed myself. It was five seconds of delicious warmth as it seeped through my overalls, ran onto the chair and dripped down to the concrete floor. He hesitated for a second; I'd genuinely surprised him. I started to cry and moan.

'Do you think I fucking care if you piss yourself, you disgusting little tart? It's you who'll have to sit on it all night.' He was back up to speed.

I couldn't have cared less about my pissy overalls. At least my bladder was no longer aching, I'd got warm and I'd made a mess. I wasn't at all embarrassed.

'Get out of my fucking sight,' he said.

The time dragged by as I enjoyed the comfort of my pallet. We must have been about ten hours down when one of the blokes marched in, untied my hands, grabbed my chest and shoved me over backwards. I was freaking out. Was I up for a kicking?

Then he barked, 'Sleep!' My eyes must have closed as he said it. MoD rules for R-to-I exercises stipulate that students should get one hour's sleep every twelve. I awoke feeling refreshed, despite the fact that I was straddling the pallet with my head on the concrete, inhaling the vapours of the stinking sack. All too soon rough hands yanked me and bound my wrists again. This time my captor was over-zealous with the plasticuffs and I could feel my right hand swelling up. The more I squirmed, the tighter it got. I was praying someone would come in and notice before it seriously restricted my blood supply.

This time I faced a different balaclava-ed inquisitor in the interrogation chamber, a well-spoken bastard who immediately started yelling at me. 'We want some fucking information out of you – do y'hear me?'

I was dragged through a door and into a small room. A man was standing by the window with a cordless high-powered drill in his hands. He shoved it towards me. 'You've fucking had it coming to you, Brit bitch. It's about time you met my friends Mr Black and Mr Decker.' I felt nauseated. I'd have thrown up over his feet if I'd had anything in my stomach. I was certain he wouldn't drill me – would he? The line between reality and fiction was getting a bit blurred, not least because he had a strong Belfast accent and was clutching a drill with intent. He flicked the switch and pushed the whining tool towards my face. Unseen hands grabbed me tightly from behind. I could feel terror soaking my body. 'You fucking bitch, you're going to get it now.' I was very scared by this time. What the hell could I do? After thirty sickening seconds while he bobbed and weaved the screaming drill at me he suddenly got pissed off with his game of cat and mouse. The blokes behind dragged me back to my pallet. Half an hour later the hessian sack was yanked off me and one of my captors was thrusting bread and water into my face. I took greedy bites and generous slurps.

The slats of the pallet were carving deep hollows onto my back-side. I remembered watching Tel and Dean chopping up pallets for firewood in the house at South Petherton, near Yeovil, never dreaming that I'd end up strapped to one. After a couple of hours I felt someone checking the tension on my plasticuffed wrists and ankles. A hand touched my shoulder and I tensed up. Then I heard a whisper: 'Keep it up, darling girl, only about three hours to go now.' It was Luke's gorgeous, reassuring Irish accent. He'd given me that single, crucial fact – a time scale. I must have been there for about twenty-one hours, and at last the end was in sight. Still, I was overcome with embarrassment. I was wearing pissy overalls, my head was in a hessian sack, I was tied to a pallet. I certainly wasn't looking the best for my man. Was Luke hiding a secret bondage fetish?

Several hours later I was armlocked and walked out to the holding area. Gentler hands removed my mask. In front of me were Liz and Luke. I could see real concern in their eyes. To have got this far in the training meant that I was suddenly being viewed as a prize commodity. They were trying to ascertain whether I'd cracked or not. Throughout the interrogation, two doctors and two psychiatrists had been on hand. Although the intention of the R-to-I was to put us under severe pressure, the medical professionals watched out for danger signs. While we were tied to our pallets we were constantly monitored by closed-circuit TV and a permanently live telephone line.

Liz spoke slowly. 'Do you know my name? Are you all right? How do you feel?'

I looked at her. 'Yes, I'm fine, Liz. Anyone got a fag?' Luke lit a Marlboro for me.

'Not half as bad as the first one, was it?' I said. Liz looked incredulous. Presumably everyone else was coming out flaky. I was no superhero. I didn't know why I wasn't in a worse state, but this one just hadn't got to me as much as the first R-to-I, which seemed to bemuse the instructors.

Because of all the physical evidence our captors had found – weapons, comms and so on – we'd had to think about our cover stories and be creative. Apparently me pissing my pants had really impressed the DS, who reckoned it showed I wasn't prepared to compromise or give anything away to my interrogators, even at the cost of a certain amount of humiliation. Having said that, I'd had much worse mental beatings in the past, and also the luxury of Luke's reassuring presence towards the end. But the training was clearly doing its job, and I was a lot tougher than I had been before. I felt a rush of confidence: I was going to be able to do this job.

After twenty-four hours of lying on that pallet I felt I deserved my huge scoff, shower and sleep. Next morning was Remembrance Sunday. I dressed in my nice tan tights, court shoes, white blouse and brown skirt, teaming it all with big, painful red welts on my ankles, wrists and neck. As I stood in the local village church, watching Luke who was looking delicious in his regimental number two dress uniform of khaki jacket and trousers and sand-coloured beret, I was annoyed by the warbling bugler. He was playing the Last Post so badly that I felt more angry than I'd been at any time during the R-to-I.

My relationship with Luke was growing in passion. We had a favourite Victorian B&B in Leominster, ten miles north of Hereford, which was run by an old lady who always put us in the blue room. There was a huge brass bed, an old-fashioned water jug and china bowl, and fresh flowers on the chest of drawers. There wasn't a view, and even if there had been we wouldn't have had time to look at it. It was great to have some time alone together. Unfortunately our nights were always broken at 5.30 a.m. when I'd get up to sneak back to the mess. By the time the girls were waking up I'd be snoring. I was struggling by on two hours' sleep a night, but it was worth it because I was besotted. Luke was completely different from all the other blokes I'd been out with. He was liked and respected by everyone, and he was close to my ideal. On the outside he was a rough, tough guy, but inside he was extremely sensitive.

Luke was never afraid to tell me how he felt. 'I appreciate you being frank and open with me,' he whispered one night as we were drifting off to sleep. 'That's how it should be. We have a beautiful relationship, and there should never be anything we can't talk about. We should always discuss our fears, problems and doubts before they create barriers between us.'

My theory is that SAS men create a vision of the perfect relationship, as a contrast to their lives of controlled aggression. But their ideal is fundamentally flawed. They think they need a base, a solid foundation, and in pursuit of this dream they are drawn to the sort of woman who is happy to stay at home and provide them with security and a conventional home life. So they get hitched young to a local girl, buy a small house with a strip of lawn, and have a couple of rug rats. But their wives can't hold their interest, for reasons they don't fully understand. The couples are separated more often than they're together, so they break up, and the pattern repeats itself again and again. SAS men have a passion which can't come out at work, and if it doesn't have an outlet in their relationship, it festers. What they really need is a woman with her own life. When they find her, and their passion gets a focus, it's fireworks.

Luke and I certainly recognised a special something in each other. He was sixteen when he left his small village in Ireland and came to London to join the army. It was there that he'd seen his first inside toilet and an escalator. Like me, he was driven to better himself.

We had one day of situational awareness, where we had to drive around a target area confronting all sorts of problems, including roadblocks and potential ambushes. The purpose was to test our decision-making under exacting conditions. It was very tense. Afterwards we watched a video of the exercise in the classroom. Seeing how my team-mates coped provided interesting insights into their characters. When Dippy walked into a potential ambush he managed to talk himself out of it. The pattern had been set – Dippy liked the sound of his own voice.

Then it was three weeks of really working our arses off for the exercise phase, the final part of Camp Two. We were on the ground operating like a Det, with OPs, two ops rooms, surveillance teams, CTR and heli work. Again I got very little sleep, no more than six hours' gonk in every twenty-four. And we often worked through the night, simulating the conditions that we would face over the water as closely as possible. There was now no room for a personal life. You had no choice but to sharply focus on the job in hand. If you don't concentrate you fuck up.

We also worked closely with the SAS, as we would for real in Northern Ireland. We were tasked to do surveillance jobs and CTRs, and if we found evidence of 'terrorist activity' the SAS would be called in. It was a very intensive period – we were always on the ground following someone or watching something.

My twenty-fourth birthday, in November 1989, was marked by two events: the Berlin Wall had fallen, and I was up for the final exercise, or Camp Three. It lasted ten days, and took place around the Birmingham area. There were now only sixteen students left, and we had control of the dummy players for twenty-four hours a day. This training segment was taken very seriously, and all the head sheds (Special Forces bosses) were present at the briefing, including the Commanding Officer of 22 SAS and the SAS lieutenant colonel with overall responsibility for our training. Vince Phillips, an SAS sergeant, conducted part of the brief in his distinctive Swindon drawl. Within fifteen months he would die of exposure as he, Chris Ryan and Mal M attempted to evade Iraqi forces after getting separated from the infamous 'Bravo Two Zero' patrol in the Gulf War.

We were tasked to do surveillance and gather information on 'known players' for a week. We discovered that they were planning to do a hit, so we called in the SAS to carry out the reaction. It went like clockwork; we all worked together in unison and everyone was operating at their best. The Troop, as the SAS are always called over the water, had confidence in us, and we in them. The many aspects of our training had dovetailed to create a responsive, professional unit.

I'd spent almost six months of my life preparing for this, and I was on the verge of getting across the water. I was about to enter a world where I would have to put my life on the line on a daily basis. Any ounce of extra concentration I could invest now could make the difference between survival and fucking up, or fucking up for someone else. The real terrorists wouldn't make any concessions for us. If we messed up, they wouldn't apologise before gunning us down.

Putting together the arsenal of skills we'd learned was satisfying, but right up to the end people were still being binned. As usual, it was impossible to predict who'd make it. Dawn didn't. She was pretty good at most aspects of the job, but just couldn't get to grips with CQB, however hard she tried. But instead of being binned, she was a 'retread', and went back on the next course. She wasn't too aggrieved. She knew better than to argue the toss, and I had a sneaking suspicion that she was slightly relieved at the chance of some more training.

Cyborg had taken to giving Dawn a hard time about her lack of firearms skills, but that didn't stop him getting in his digs at me. During a first-aid lesson, when we were all sinking IV lines into each other's veins, he couldn't resist telling Tom to be careful not to get any of my blood on him. 'You don't know where she's been,' he said spitefully. A few weeks after that Cyborg suddenly left the camp, after giving Dawn one too many hard times. We speculated that he'd been disciplined for his bad attitude. Although I didn't gloat, I had a secret smile at his disappearance.

After the final exercise we packed up and drove back to the camp in convoy. We sorted out our kit for the imminent journey to our respective Dets in Northern Ireland, while the SAS guys went drinking. Jock earned a black eye just for chatting to the new wife of one of his old regimental mates.

The next morning we had a brief from an operator called Ted at the technical branch, who filled us in about all the devices used across the water. We assumed that we were all in, but even at this late stage Abel, a Rupert with ginger hair, was binned. It didn't make sense; he seemed the same as any other Rupert. But the good news was that I had made it. The original intake of 120, including eight women, had been whittled down to twelve blokes and two women, one of whom had achieved the highest CQB score. Some people said I was a natural, which I resented. I'd spent hours practising and fine-tuning my technique until it was automatic. My student report graded me with 100 per cent for my pistol final assessment.

Luke wrote: 'This outstanding student has continued to progress to a level of marksmanship which puts her in overall first position on assessment shoots. Sarah has a strong professional commitment which is reflected in the quality of her performance. In stress situations her physical determination and natural ability are evident in her actions which are calm and positive. She has the respect of her fellow students where her talents are consistent and appreciated. This cell has little hesitation in grading her "A" in view of her commitment and progress.'

Even more terrific was the big piss-up we were all planning, and the fact that Luke and I were planning to go overt. That night saw us at the Pal-u-drin Club, a bar inside Stirling Lines, the home of 22 SAS, all togged up in our posh clothes. I was wearing a black skirt, a very expensive little number, teamed with a black and red bolero jacket. My ears glittered with diamante, I was in three-inch heels, and my battered, bruised legs were neatly camouflaged in sheer barely-black stockings. I'd painted my face, and was so incognito that no one recognised me. I'd even done my hair. Miss Glamour-Puss! Sparky and Joe couldn't believe it, and were both pestering me for a snog and a feel. It wasn't a case of fancying them, but I had a quick dance with any of my team-mates who were sweet enough to ask. I felt more relaxed than I'd been for six months, and was surrounded by like-minded people in a social setting.

After a great evening of chatting, drinking and dancing came the slow dances, the old ten to two club. But this time I didn't have to search for a man with a pair of willing lips. He was there. We caught each other's eyes for the umpteenth time. He was looking gorgeous in his black dinner-jacket, red cummerbund and silk bow tie. 'Will You' by Hazel O'Connor sang out, and Luke strode over, took my hand and led me to the dance floor. As we entwined, and started kissing, all eyes were on us. I felt so wonderful and so proud. There was nothing anyone could do to change that.

Mind you, afterwards Sparky pretended he'd known all along. 'No you fucking didn't, Poirot,' I laughed as I slapped him.

SIX

ACROSS THE WATER

AS THE COURSE NEARED its end, the instructors gave us more information about the four detachments which operated over the water as part of 14 Intelligence Company. The info drifted in bit by bit, inevitably coloured by which Det each instructor had come from, and was the subject of much friendly banter. South Det covered a large rural area including Tyrone and Armagh, and therefore got the most action. North Det, covering the north of the Province, was the equivalent of the outback, with little activity and zilch on the excitement scale. East Det, whose area included Belfast, was somewhere between the two – and was perhaps more notable for its endless piss-ups. Another group had been set up in South Det in 1988 to work against paramilitary racketeers, but had evolved into concentrating on the terrorists in South's area. They were located in an A-frame adjacent to South Det, in the same compound. Because of their original role they had dubbed themselves 'the Untouchables', and the name had stuck.

One of the big misconceptions about the IRA is that most of its funding comes from America. In fact the larger part of its money is raised by various forms of criminal activity in Ulster and Eire. Apart from the traditional sources of funding – bank robberies, post office raids and payroll snatches – the terrorists, be they Republican or Loyalist, also run 'legitimate' businesses including bars and clubs, shebeens (illegal drinking clubs), unlicensed bookies and loan shark set-ups. They also make big money from tax and VAT frauds, scams with EC grants and loans, and from a multiplicity of thriving extortion and protection rackets. They've always steered clear of direct involvement in running drugs and prostitution rings, but neither side is above taking a rake-off from people who are.

Not surprisingly, this level of criminal activity absorbs a good deal of time and effort on the part of the paramilitaries. Most of the mainstream terrorists are too busy plotting their murderous campaigns to get involved with gangsterism, so the terrorists had specialists to run their racketeering operations, and the Dets were occasionally tasked to keep an eye on them.

I secretly hoped I'd be sent to East Det. It was all city work, and I reckoned I'd feel more comfortable in an urban environment, as my navigation skills out in the cuds (the countryside) weren't the best in the world. South seemed to be the Det to avoid. Although they got the most media coverage, because more incidents took place there, they were known to be women-haters who thought the Det was no place for the female of the species. Even the colonel in charge of our training admitted to me that South had a reputation for being misogynists, and one DS told me, 'South don't need, want or have women.' And for three years they hadn't had any. Their mentality was perhaps due to their being the only Det to share their accommodation with the Troop. Although I've always felt more comfortable with men than women, and have spent all my adult life in a male environment, I had no desire to spend my time among women-haters. What would be the point of all my training if I wasn't going to be used? Yet I was intrigued by the fact that the DS from South were particularly animated, outspoken and professional characters.

East and North's work consisted of almost 100 per cent surveillance. South handled most of the rural work, incorporating CTRs and OPs, which in the operators' opinion made it much more macho. A South Det DS told me that a North or East success would just mean lots of arrests, whereas a South success would, almost by definition, be more terminal.

One by one we were called in to see the training major to be detailed off to our Dets. Gail was going to North. The bad news was that I was to head to South. My heart sank. What had I done to deserve this? I'd just passed one of the most formidable Special Forces courses in the world, and all my finely honed expertise was going to be wasted on a place where I'd be stuck with chauvinistic Neanderthals.

Outside I found Liz, with whom I'd built up a good rapport. I was trying not to look too disappointed at my destination, but she could see how I was feeling. 'I'm going to South,' I said glumly. Liz had been the last woman to do a stint there, three years earlier.

'Don't tell me – the map reading! Don't worry, I was the same as you. You'll be getting lots of practice in it.' I told her it was the sexism that bothered me more than the navigation, and she gave me one of her really dirty laughs. She was a tough little fucker. Short, stout, Cockney, muscled, she swore like a docker. 'They'll fucking put you through it! But don't worry about it, mate. They're just a bunch of chauvinist pigs. You'll be all right, but you'd better get your drinking up to scratch, 'cos you'll be in the bar a lot. If they start anything, just drop 'em. Show 'em who's boss.'

I tried not to let my posting get to me. Maybe they didn't want me, but the fact was that I'd passed the course. Now it was up to me to prove myself. My philosophy has always been to judge each individual on their own merits, and that was what the lads in South would have to do with me. I had no choice but to go and do my best. I reckoned that if I was good enough to pass the course, I'd be good enough for them. Anyway, the boss wouldn't have sent me if he didn't reckon I was up to it.

The chief instructor, Smithy, asked us each to write out a will. I left everything to our Mam – not that I had much to leave, only a few favourite bits of jewellery and my book of poems. I put down our Melissa and Grandma as executors. If I was killed the MoD would cough up a few thousand pounds to cover funeral expenses. There would also be some money in the kitty if I'd had children, and we were encouraged to take out life insurance from one of the limited number of companies with the financial balls to take the risk. We were press-ganged into joining SASA, the Special Air Service Association. Everyone who goes through the system gets to pay up their £20 fee. SASA looks after ex-members and the families of those killed in action, much like the British Legion or the RAF Association.

The fourteen of us left the camp on a bleak, grey December morning. There was a skeletal outline of trees against the stark sky, and the wind was scurrying in frosty eddies across the parade ground. The seasons had changed twice since we'd started the course, and I had also metamorphosed. So much had happened. Summer and the beastings of Camp One were a distant memory.

Luke was heartbroken that I was leaving, and I missed him already as he stood in the shadows watching me heave my bergen and suitcases into the coach. He was wearing a fleecy American flying jacket, and he looked gorgeous and sad, with his hands deep in his pockets to ward off the cold. It was very hard for me to leave him. I felt like a teenager being whisked away from a holiday romance. We'd been together through the toughest six months of my life, and rather more intimately for the past seven weeks. He'd seen me at my weakest, lowest, most physically drained and unattractive, but he still loved me completely. I felt that he could gaze into my soul and touch me. I was utterly miserable, even though I knew I'd only be gone for ten days before my Christmas leave, and then he'd be waiting for me at Leeds airport.

Luke waved forlornly as the coach pulled out of the gates and drove towards RAF Lyneham in Wiltshire. I was deep in thought about the challenges that lay ahead, and barely with it as we made the short hop across to Aldergrove. As we landed, rain was spitting onto the fields in that gentle Irish way. We were loaded into a van for the journey to South Det. I felt lost and lonely. I couldn't even see the countryside because the windows of the van immediately misted up.

The compound looked like something out of *Star Wars*. As we drove towards the enormous metal A-frame building all the fluorescent lights were blazing, and there was a sense of scurrying activity and quiet efficiency. The vast studded-metal twin doors were open, and the cold wind was rushing in. Multi-storey Portakabins and brick buildings were dotted about under the A-frame roof, which was supported by giant iron girders.

Men were wandering around with mugs of tea in their hands. Others, carrying bundles of papers and dressed in scruffy civvies, were walking briskly out of bashas and running up stairs, their boots clanking on the metal steps. Vehicles were constantly on the move. I felt very insignificant in this alien, artificial environment as I pulled out my bergen, which contained my kit, and a suitcase holding my ghetto-blaster and some Gerald Seymour and Jeffrey Archer books, as well as photos of our Mam, my sisters and Luke. All the rest of my stuff, including bedding, was still bagged up at Chris's mess following the eviction.

Operators were detailing off my team-mates for their journeys to the other Dets. I didn't know when I'd be seeing them again. But staying with me in South were Greg, Dippy and Stephen. Sparky was only going next door to join the Untouchables, so it would be easy to keep in contact.

Greg, Dippy, Stephen and I followed an operator upstairs to the ops room for the start of a whistlestop tour of the compound. The ops room, nerve-centre of all South Det operations, was a twelve-foot by ten-foot office lit by two fluorescent tubes. The team were out on the ground when we entered, and I could hear activity on the net. We'd been practising the net code for months, but the real thing sounded like Swahili, it was so slick, fast and efficient. Nothing made sense. I felt completely swamped; how would I ever catch up? Paul, the ops officer, a slim, dark-haired fella in his mid-thirties, was nevertheless noting everything down from his position behind a vast L-shaped desk covered in two-by three-foot maps of the area under a glass sheet. Paul, wearing earphones and gabbling into a desk-mounted mike like the despatcher in a minicab office, was 100 per cent focused on what he was doing. On the wall were 1:50,000 maps and enlarged aerial photographs of the area, pictures of known players and lists of vehicle details. In the secondary ops room next-door was the same set-up, and one of the bleeps was also monitoring the net, to back up Paul. We crept out quietly and into the spooks' (intelligence) room where we met Aidan, a big friendly northern fella who was head spook.

The amenities in the A-frame were geared to a highly physical lifestyle: gym, shooting range, squash court, and the all-important bar. The cookhouse looked and smelt like grease city, with a menu consisting of chips and beans – the only alternative was to go hungry.

Next I was introduced to the functional delights of my basha, a grey Portakabin against the external wall, forty metres from the ops room. The place was heaving. It contained a threadbare lime-green carpet, a horrible teak-effect wardrobe, a metal bed with a green-plastic covered mattress, and a buzz-box (intercom) connecting me to the ops room and the rest of the A-frame. There was no other furniture – when old ops move out everyone rushes in and lifts anything that moves. The bath, stuck behind a partition, had a grimy ring and a mat of hair wedged in the plughole. The toilet was a no-go area.

As I had no gonk kit – my precious duck-feather duvet was among those possessions bagged up in the Marines block at Yeovil – I had to get a couple of grey army blankets, the sort that look as if they've been made out of recycled newspapers and itch as much as loft insulation, out of stores. I had a quick clean-up, stashed what stuff I had and slung a couple of the ratty blankets over the windows. Then I went straight across to the bar, where the lads were coming back off the ground.

They arrived in dribs and drabs and got themselves bottles of beer. I stood nursing a can of Tennants, feeling like a total novice. They seemed so slick, impressive and polished. Among the operators were a couple of pilots, a few Troop blokes and some admin staff. I watched and listened. You don't want to come across as gobby when you arrive at a new place. After a few minutes one of the operators turned and looked sourly at me. Jimmy was a short Scot with straggly long hair and a droopy moustache who was greedily throwing back his bottle of Becks. He looked at Dippy, Greg, Stephen and me in turn.

'I see we've dipped out here, then,' he said eventually. 'We've got a fucking Rupert and a tart. So out of four ops, we've only got two.' I kept quiet. Arsehole. It wasn't as if Stephen had the word

'Rupert' tattooed across his forehead; it was just that the operators in the Det take a keen interest in the progress of the people in training, hoping they won't end up with any of them. Jimmy was one of the Op Spice guys, and had been in the SAS eight years. He turned out to be a fair bloke, but his opening conversational gambit didn't encourage me to go out on the beer with him.

'How many have they got in East and North?' This was Kevin, a Canadian who looked as if he'd stepped straight out of *Harry's Game* in his scruffy gear. He looked like a tramp, the sort you'd expect to see in a café making one cuppa last all day. He was unshaven, dressed in rags, and should have been arrested by the fashion police. In the A-frame there's an ops bin – before going out on an op you can delve in and drag out some clothing to wear on the street. Kevin had spotted this bin as a nifty convenience, and modelled its contents all the time.

Clearly he had been hoping for more manpower as well. In one sense he and Jimmy were right. Stephen wasn't going to end up on the ground, he was destined to be a head shed.

'Fucking women,' said Kevin, looking through me. 'Can't do CTRs, can't go one up. Well, at least we've got someone to make the tea and do the washing up.' Despite the nature of his comments, I could sense humour there. Not being able to do CTRs or go one up was a bummer. But Kevin was wrong to assume I was excess baggage. It wasn't my fault that I wasn't allowed to do certain things, and it was very frustrating not to be able to put aspects of my training into practice. Some bureaucrat had made this decision, and there was nothing I could do about it. There was no physical or mental reason why I shouldn't be able to carry out the same tasks as the blokes. Women in North and East went one up; it was only in South that we didn't. Most of the blokes apparently thought that if women were in the Det they should be allowed to take a full role. It was only the young lads and the fossils who thought such rules had any point, although they were unable to provide convincing reasons why. I longed to say, 'Don't have a go at me, have a go at the guys at the top,' but I kept my trap shut. Let them work me out.

For the first four or five days Greg and I stuck together. We sorted out our 1:50,000 maps of the massive area, almost five thousand square miles and it all had to be spectrumed, spotted and waterproofed with clear Fablon. Spotting was a way of speeding up map reading and shortening radio messages. Key junctions were marked with coloured self-adhesive labels and given a number corresponding to the master maps in the ops room. This meant that instead of having to give a six-figure grid reference or a description of where you were, you could just give your location as 'red two-seven', for example, which simplified everything. It might sound very *Blue Peter*, but it actually required a lot of concentration. It was up to us how we divided up our maps. I decided to make one very large one – soon nicknamed the Monster Map – of East Tyrone, and a number of town plans.

We were issued with our personal weapons, radios and vehicles. Comms were installed in our cars by the bleeps, who did a great job. Everything was hidden, with pressle switches wherever you requested them. They also fixed up each car with an engine cut-out switch, as well as brake and reverse light cut-outs. In drop-off and pick-up situations you didn't necessarily want your car to give away the fact that you were slowing down, reversing or stopping. Some of the operators used to treat the bleeps like dirt, and give them a hard time if their comms weren't perfect. I didn't have any time for that attitude. The admin staff were as vital to the war against terrorism as we were. There isn't room across the water for self-importance.

I signed out a grey Renault 5 – a 'woman's car', and took it out for a play. I spun it around with some handbrake turns, and threw in a few wheel-spins for good measure. Later in my tour it was replaced with a Peugeot 405, which was so damn big and heavy I could barely do a handbrake turn. It was bright red, and was known as 'the fire engine' or 'the big red bus'.

My firearms were a 7.65mm Walther, a neat and easily concealable pistol; a Heckler & Koch (HK) MP5K, a compact 9mm double-grip machine pistol; an HK53, a 5.56mm assault rifle; an HK-G3, a 7.62mm assault rifle; and two 9mm Browning Hi-Power pistols. This might sound like a lot of hardware for one operator, but each weapon had a specific role to fulfil. The Browning was our primary weapon, which we carried at all times outside the compound. The second Browning, which would usually have an extended magazine attached, was kept in the car. When driving two up (two in a car) I would put the Browning in my hip holster and stash the HK53, with double mag, in the footwell. The 53 is halfway between a sub-machine gun and an assault rifle, and I used it as my main support weapon. With its butt extended it's accurate over a much longer range than the pistol, firing higher velocity ammunition in either single shot, three-round bursts or fully automatic fire.

The chauvinist attitude kept cropping up over the next ten days of my induction. Sometimes it was blatant, but there also seemed to be a couple of closet sexists. Paul, the ops officer, could never deal with me sincerely. He would speak to blokes normally, in his West Country accent, but would insist on patronising me, as if even talking to a woman was a waste of his time. I soon developed a theory that this was a kick-back from being dominated by the women in his life. But, as in any group, there were enough good blokes with the foresight and sense to see how a woman could be an advantage in certain situations.

During this time Luke was my release. I'd phone him up at least once a day. But there were three hundred miles and the Irish Sea between us. We counted the hours until we'd be reunited. Every other day cards would turn up from him in pastel-coloured envelopes. Luke wrote that he was feeling physical pain that I had gone, that he was only happy when I was with him, and that I was the only true love he had ever known. His tender words seemed at odds with his tough SAS exterior. But on the phone he remained helpfully pragmatic. When I told him about the stick I was getting, he said: 'Oh, fucking take no notice. You can shoot the arses off them any day. Give 'em time, they'll come round.'

The Troop guys I'd met at the training camp, Jock, Big Marty and Wee Phil, were very supportive. They'd worked around me for the past three months, and knew that I was strong, competent, professional and able to take care of myself. We were on the same wavelength: work hard, play hard. In general, the Troop didn't have any hang-ups, and were brutally honest in their assessment of people. If you were shite, they'd tell you. Big Marty was vast in all senses of the word – he had a huge personality and a physique to match. A Scotsman, he was a good Catholic boy and a dedicated family man with lots of children, as well as being a good soldier and an all-round nice bloke. Wee Phil was a short, quiet, family man with a wife and children in Hereford. In his spare time he would make beautiful pieces of furniture for his missus. When he wasn't toiling over a lathe he was driving us nuts with his guitar playing. He and Big Marty liked and respected me, and were always giving each other a friendly slagging. Marty would say, 'Phil reckons there's a terrorist behind every pint.'

The split lip that was my free gift on the R-to-I hadn't been the worst of it. Having my head smacked into the concrete post had dislodged a tooth, and now it was really playing up. During the first week across the water it developed into a throbbing abscess, the most excruciating pain I'd ever experienced. But despite the fact that it was making my whole head feel as if it would explode, I had no time to see a dentist. There was always something to do: sorting out maps, zeroing and cleaning our weapons, sorting out our holsters and cars, digesting info and getting orientated in the area.

The fact that, as new ops, we were up for Christmas and New Year's leave, meant that the other operators resented us. They would only get a couple of days off during the festive season. In their eyes we were just kicking our heels while getting up to speed in preparation for a month-long orientation in the new year. They'd obviously forgotten how intense the course was.

I flew back to England just before Christmas. Luke drove me to Yeovil to pick up my stuff from Chris, and I finally went to the dentist, who kindly pushed a four-inch serrated point into my mouth after drilling into the tooth. Then he lanced the abscess. The poison drained into my mouth and trickled down my throat. The release of pressure inside my skull was delicious. I felt comfortable for the first time in weeks. I spent a few days with Luke, then opened my pressies at home with our Mam, Grandma, Melissa, Katherine and Jane.

Luke gave me two tickets to Cyprus, and we flew out the day after Boxing Day for a week in the sun. One day my feet overheated in the busy market area of Limassol. I was always having trouble with them; skin was constantly flaking off and countless other nasties were always breaking out. Luke bought some ice cream from a vendor and soothed my hot, aching feet with it. It was then that I realised my heart was melting almost as fast as the vanilla ice cream between my toes. I'd fallen for him big time, and only now did I feel able to tell him that I returned his love. He was overjoyed, and we were like randy teenagers all week long.

When I returned to the compound in January, we really got stuck into it. We were now officially in, and making a contribution, so we didn't get so much verbal abuse from the other operators. We were facing a month-long orientation, during which we would learn the ground by heart, reading up on past ops, learning all about the players and their history, and getting an in-depth feel for the area. We'd go two up with experienced operators to help get all the crucial locations into our heads, and watch endless videos of the target areas – Dungannon, Moy, Armagh, Crossmaglen, Newry, Coalisland, Cookstown and Cappagh – so we could learn the spots and spectrums without being physically on the ground.

There were mind-boggling quantities of detail to assimilate, including an endless encyclopaedia of information on the players: their houses, vehicles, VRNs, relatives, backgrounds, political sympathies, past actions. The spooks supplied us with photos and potted biogs, and we'd watch videos of them taken at events like protest marches and funeral processions. Throughout this time we were also working hard at drinking lots of beer, always an important element of any training.

One day I was out on orientation with Archie, an older operator, when we realised we'd strayed across the border into Eire. This was a real no-no, the geographical equivalent of an ND. We were working for the British sovereign on British soil, and were tooled up in a surveillance car. As soon as we realised our error we accelerated back over the border – and kept it as our secret.

On yet another bleak, cold, depressing day – you quickly learn that the sun never shines across the water – I was out on orientation with Connor, who was showing me the bad areas around Cookstown, which has a reputation as a hotbed of violent Republicanism. As usual I was cramming info into my head when Paul sparked up on the net: 'All call-signs, this is Zero. For your information, news hot off the press: we've just had a success in West Belfast. Two operators from the Untouchables are fine and on their way back. See you in the bar later.'

To hear about a successful contact was exciting news. Real action, and we'd only been here three weeks. We wanted more detail.

Connor said, 'India, roger that, who was it?'

Paul came back. 'India Zero, it was Vic and one of the new guys, Sparky.' I was elated. Sparky was a hero, and he was OK. It couldn't have happened to a nicer bloke. Sharing successes over the net as they occurred was part of the Det culture. Boosting morale in such an environment is critical.

Connor and I went through the motions of our orientation for the next forty-five minutes, but we were keen to get back. Operators always want to be out on the ground working rather than stuck in the A-frame, but this time we were gagging to find out what had gone down. We screamed into the compound, did the customary handbrake turn, shoved our maps, HK53s, pistols and mags into lockers in the romper room, and grabbed a brew before heading for the Untouchables' bar, where we found the merry throng already doing some serious quaffing of ale. Joe and Bobby had come across from East. It was good to see them again.

There was no sign yet of Sparky and Vic, who were still with the flying lawyers. These army legal people, based in Lisburn HQ, need to get the whole story as soon as possible after a contact takes place which has the potential to go to court. That way they're prepared if a terrorist subsequently brings an action against the Crown for damage to himself or his property.

Finally Sparky and Vic turned up, and we got it straight from the horse's mouth. They'd been out on orientation around the Falls Road area of Belfast just before 11 a.m. when they saw two armed men wearing black balaclavas and black gloves – the uniform of the Provisional IRA – running into Sean Graham's bookies on the corner of Falls Road and Whiterock Road. Seconds later they re-emerged. Sparky and Vic had to make a quick decision. These were clearly dangerous men, up to no good. Sparky and Vic may have had some options, but these were severely reduced when one of the men looked in their direction and aimed his MP40 machine pistol (a Second World War German sub-machine gun) at them. In that split-second the decision was made for them. Within moments they were out of the car, on the ground and shooting, and the threat was eliminated. Another burst of gunfire took out the raiders' getaway driver at the wheel of his car, which had Irish plates. Sparky and Vic then melted away, unfortunately leaving behind a pensioner with a shoulder wound.

Sparky had been blooded, but he was pretty normal about it. There was no particular sense of elation that a clutch of players had been malleted, more a massive sense of relief that our guys were all right.

Within days we heard via Special Branch and forensics that the raiders hadn't been terrorists. Sinn Fein claimed that the three robbers were 'definitely not' Provisional IRA members, and local people said that two of them, Peter Thompson and Edward Hale, had previously been kneecapped by the IRA for 'anti-social behaviour'. According to the RUC, all three were habitual small-time criminals, with a total of thirty-six convictions between them. Their guns – a pistol and a sub-machine gun – were fakes, but were almost impossible to distinguish from real ones. The triggers worked, the cocking mechanism worked, and the sights were exact. Even the magazines were functional and could have been used in a real weapon. Only detailed forensic examination showed them to be incapable of firing live bullets. I defy anyone to identify a fake gun at that distance and in such circumstances. Police and judges in Northern Ireland have frequently made it clear that carrying a replica gun is treated as seriously as having a real one.

The headlines in the British newspapers were broadly condemnatory, running along the lines of 'SAS Kill Three Unarmed Men' – because of the clandestine nature of 14 Int, their work is always publicly perceived as being done by the SAS. Unwittingly, the robbers had handed the IRA a propaganda coup. Belfast councillor Dr Joe Hendron suggested that the robbers should have been taken prisoner instead of 'mown down'. Whining do-gooders, joined by Sinn Fein, demanded to know whether the British security forces were operating a 'shoot-to-kill' policy.

This was total nonsense. All our activity operated under the 'yellow card' rules, which govern soldiers' use of weapons and are regularly reviewed by the government. These rules apply to all units, and Det operators are in no doubt that any breach could result in a murder or manslaughter charge. Soldiers are permitted to open fire without warning only if they believe that by giving a warning they would be putting their own life or that of others in grave danger. Any soldier who disobeys this risks a military court-martial or even a civilian murder trial. Sparky and Vic had faced a split-second decision, and they had elected to open fire. It is not practicable for soldiers to shoot to wound. A wounded terrorist could return fire, and innocent bystanders could be put at risk. Had such a policy operated in Gibraltar in March 1988, that five-hundred-pound car bomb outside Government House might have been detonated by remote control. The Regiment got a lot of stick for the number of rounds they fired into the three IRA terrorists in Gibraltar – one of them was hit sixteen times – but once the decision has been taken to open fire, your aim is to kill, so as to prevent repercussions.

The month of orientation/incarceration finally came to an end – along with Nelson Mandela's twenty-seven-year imprisonment. The sad news was that Paul and Gail from North had been RTU-ed, having been found unsuitable for the job. We weren't told why – we could only speculate that once across the water they couldn't blend in, despite their training. I couldn't believe that even at this stage it was still possible to get binned.

I was up for two days' leave, and was desperate to see Luke. We hadn't been together since Christmas, and missed each other badly. The phone-calls and the letters went some way towards making us feel better, but they weren't enough; I longed to be in his strong, comforting arms. I was filled with excitement on the plane, and Luke met me at the terminal, looking gorgeous. There was nowhere else in the world I wanted to be. When we got back to his place he presented me with a huge bouquet of flowers and a couple of bottles of good red wine. Then he made me dinner. We spent most of the weekend in bed, either making love or saying how much we loved and missed one another. It was like a dream which I never wanted to end. Luke drove me back to Heathrow on a rainy Sunday night. It was heart-wrenching. We faced another four-week separation.

If you're in the Det or the Troop, the Hereford–Heathrow trip is something you get used to. The difference is that the SAS are usually off somewhere glamorous: Hong Kong, South America, Australia maybe. But we're always going to the same place: Terminal One, then fifty-five minutes of British Midland's Diamond Service back across the water. Back to the compound, back to the A-frame, back to the job.

Although Dippy and Greg had by now been fully accepted, Stephen and I were still the outsiders, still made to feel like spare parts. But the banter about me being useless and Stephen being a waste of a man was gradually becoming more good-natured. When they saw me in action on range days, some of the lads saw my firearms skill as an insult to their masculinity. The three operators who gave me the hardest time were the same ones who were always getting at the hard-working bleeps: Dippy, who up to now I'd always thought of as a mate, was constantly whingeing at them; Jack, an immature chauvinist from Lincolnshire with a good build and black hair; and Kurt, an ex-Royal Marine with streaked blond hair who fancied himself – I reckoned that, like many of the other ops, he had a hang-up that he wasn't in the

Troop. Proximity to the Regiment threatened him almost as much as I did.

One night in the bar, after everyone had enjoyed several beers, one of the guys started gobbing off again about my shortcomings. I'd heard enough. 'Look, you stupid git,' I said quietly but firmly, 'you should speak to the hierarchy who run this joint and make the rules. Don't have a go at me, it's not my bloody fault.'

He was slightly taken aback at my sudden outspokenness, and put up his hands in the surrender position. 'All right, don't shoot,' he said defensively, trying to deflect his embarrassment back at me.

A lot of info had been stored on the hard-disc drive of my memory. I'd studied the procedure for conducting covert surveillance from a heli with a vast array of James Bond-style kit. The pilots were a really good bunch of highly professional blokes. Now all that remained was to see which operator I would be partnered with. As I was banned from going one up, my partner would be crucial to the success of my tour. Eventually, the boss couldn't delay the decision any longer. One morning in the romper room he asked the operators, 'Does anyone mind partnering Sarah?'

Jed immediately spoke up. 'I'll take her.'

I was chuffed to bits. During orientation I'd been partnered with all the operators in turn, and Jed had stuck out for his stupid sense of humour and his amazing knowledge of the area. He was also one of the few who hadn't belittled me, except in good humour. Not like Jack, who'd given me a sermon within minutes of my getting into the car: 'I want to get one thing straight. I will never be partnered with a tart. South Det doesn't need women. It's nothing against you personally, but I won't consider doing it.'

The worst Jed had done was wind me up when we got back to the compound after orientation. 'Well, I've done my bit, now hurry up and get me a cup of tea.' I reckoned I could cope with that. He was a well-respected bloke, so he didn't get slagged off for volunteering to put up with me for the next seventeen months. If anything, the rest of the guys were grateful to him. At least he'd volunteered, which meant that no one else would be lumbered with me.

Jed's maroon Peugeot 505 fitted in very well for long journeys over farmland in an area where most locals had saloons or estate cars. We got hold of a child's seat and fixed it up in the back, along with a stacking bricks set and a teddy bear from the local market. I asked the bleeps for a switch on the passenger-side footwell so I could speak over the net while keeping my hands free. The car was duly wired up, but before long I realised it wasn't practical, after Jed and I had been slagging off the head sheds without realising my foot had slipped over the pressle and was transmitting every one of our anti-establishment sentiments. But although my own car had been nicely commed up, it was destined to sit in the compound gathering dust while I spent my time out on the ground two up with Jed.

My job had begun in earnest. I was a Det operator, and everything I'd done in training was now for real. My call-sign, which had been Delta in training, was now Sierra, and I was learning to react to it as automatically as I did to my own name. Our usual brief was to keep various players under surveillance, and I spent much of my working week going foxtrot in the bad-arse estates – discovering players building barbecues, for example. My gender was a huge advantage in these situations. In all walks of life women are perceived as less of a threat, and I could operate virtually anywhere that was required. But I was never tempted to let myself get even remotely complacent; I had no desire to get slotted for careless arrogance.

Day in, day out I was doing surveillance, driving the video vehicles into the estates to record the players' movements. You'd obviously be compromised if you sat gawping at someone's door for hours on end, so we were equipped with a hidden camcorder, with wide-angle and telephoto lenses. It would peep out of a tiny aperture in the vehicle, no bigger than a ball-bearing. Sometimes I'd drive a van cammed up to look like a works vehicle with tools, overalls and boxes inside.

I never went out on a surveillance without my Browning, spare mags and the HK53. If I wanted, I could also take the MP5K, but I reckoned two weapons and seventy-seven rounds was enough. I always wore personal comms hidden inside my jacket or in my customised handbag. Every day I was building up a storehouse of knowledge. The job was everything I'd hoped, and the Wrens and aircraft maintenance seemed a million miles away. Within a few months I was fully up to speed, giving and comprehending info over the net.

Jed and I were becoming great mates. Initially I'd worried that I might lose out by having to go two up mobile and wouldn't progress so fast, but those feelings soon disappeared. Jed was a brilliant operator, and I couldn't have learned any more by being out on my own. Driving two up also meant that I was always going foxtrot, so in that respect I got to do a lot more than the lads did.

Each operation had a name, and we'd be given intelligence from the spooks and Special Branch. We had to follow a target and report back on their actions, gathering more info to swell the intelligence agencies' knowledge of the known players and to help build up a three-dimensional portrait of the grassroots activities of the IRA. When there was no work on we stayed in training by doing hare and hounds. One of the operators would act as a target, and drive around the area with the surveillance team keeping tabs. In South Det we used beefy saloon cars because of the distances we travelled in a rural environment. A lot of East's work was based in urban areas, so they would drive small hatchbacks. Inevitably, South used their big, powerful cars as further proof of their macho image. They weren't impressed by city runabouts.

Every month I got leave, alternately seven and two days, and Luke and I would make the most of our brief time together. It was difficult for him to visit me, as he was working as an instructor on the Special Projects Team at Stirling Lines. He was always happy to do whatever I wanted, and fully understood if I wanted a quiet weekend at his house after a busy op, which could last anything from a couple of days to several months. There were usually a number of ongoing ops, and you'd do a stint on one before moving on to another. Leave came round quickly if you were working hard on good jobs, but if you were stuck in the A-frame on standby – or worse, forward mounted in a temporary base closer to terrorist activity – time dragged past.

One Friday afternoon saw us eyes-down in the briefing room. The intelligence was that the Provisional IRA had stolen an XR3i Ford Escort to do a job, and had it hidden in some ruins near Cappagh. The Troop were to supply a mobile intercept car for South Det if and when the car moved from its position, and I was part of the surveillance team that would be forward mounted at Castle Hill police station in Dungannon, a few miles from the XR3i. This would put us close enough to the action to react swiftly. As I was barred from driving one up, I flew up in the heli while the blokes drove. This arrangement meant that I'd be available to partner Jed, but if I was needed in the heli there'd still be a four-car team.

Dungannon is built on a hill, and the police station is situated on the peak. Vast iron double gates provide an ominous entrance, but Matt the pilot and I simply flew over the high blast-proof walls and touched down on the helipad. We were stuck in a grotty, stinking Portakabin about forty feet long by twenty feet wide. So many jobs went down in Tyrone that South Det needed a number of FMBs (forward mounting bases), but I reckon we drew the short straw on budgets for this one. That's just the way it goes with the Det; we get the barest operational requirements. The place was heaving. There was a kitchenette with two gas rings and a stinking fridge, a sitting area with a sorry collection of threadbare sofas, and a sleeping area with hard mattresses covered in green plastic. The carpet was thick with dust and God knows what; when you walked on it, clouds of disease-ridden dust particles would attack you. The air was always swirling with cigarette smoke. Every time we were forward mounted in Dungannon, one by one all the team members would go down with some horrendous disease.

Once we were installed, we just stayed put. We couldn't afford to leave the Portakabin for a minute. At any moment the players might decide to go mobile in their XR3i, at which point the OP team of Jed and Adrian, who were in situ with the trigger on the target, would give us the standby and we'd have to deploy in a matter of seconds. So Jack, Stephen, Kurt, Stephen 2, Greg, Matt and I just sat there in limbo, staring at the comms equipment. Watching paint dry had nothing on this.

We took turns to cook, using big shiny aluminium pots, and the day's culinary delights depended on what regiment the chef was from. The Paras would make airborne stew, the pilots Kamikaze curry, the Navy lads pot mess. We aren't talking about prime cuts of meat here. Instead it was a question of chuck in whatever you could find. Tins of baked beans and mushy peas, a chopped cabbage, salt and pepper, chilli sauce, brown sauce and stir. Tasty. When it all got too much, we'd have hot cans. Stab them with a skewer to activate the chemicals, and the beans and sausages self-heat in moments. You'd glow in the dark if you ate too many of those.

You can't do anything productive in these situations. Life becomes mind-numbingly boring. You just sit around and vegetate, waiting and wishing that something would happen. You can't even read the papers – there's no opportunity to buy them. Kurt and Jack would play cards while I read a Jeffrey Archer or the romantic poetry of Ella Wheeler Wilcox, or wrote my own poetry, pouring out my feelings on paper to Luke. Stephen 2 was the laziest, most laid-back person I'd ever met. He was a twenty-a-day man, washed down with gallons of sugary tea. He'd pretend to be asleep when it was his turn to get the brew on. Lounging around in a grotty chair in equally foul clothes, he'd ask me to bring the ashtray closer so he didn't have to stretch. Kurt had the world's smallest television, which relieved the monotony a bit. We'd sit in a huddle, staring at the four-inch screen. But despite the enforced close proximity there was no bickering, just lots of friendly banter. That was all part of the selection process. Det operators need to be able to pull out the adrenaline with a flourish when it's required, and switch off and wait patiently when it isn't.

It was mid-afternoon on day three, and we'd just scoffed a Stephen and Stephen 2 special. Neither of them were culinary experts – it had taken them hours to create the plates of brown stuff which tasted of vinegar and aluminium, and we were all feeling a bit queasy. If you scraped too hard on the pans it flavoured the meal, so we were stuffing down lots of bread to try to eliminate the aluminium poisoning.

Suddenly we heard Jed's whispered 'Standby, standby. That's three Bravos foxtrot towards the target,' over the radio.

Everyone slammed down their Mother's Pride, grabbed their kit and dashed for their waiting vehicles just outside. It was like the blur of activity in a fire station when the bell rings. My loaded Browning was already on my right hip in the black leather IWB holster, and the two spare mags were in their pouches. I picked up my loaded HK53 from its position slung over a chair near the door – it already had a forty-round curved mag on it – and grabbed my DPM combat jacket and my helmet with inbuilt mike. The last thing I reached for was my Dotty P carrier bag filled with maps. Two seconds later Matt and I were down the steps and haring across the compound to the heli, thirty metres away. But in amongst the flurry of activity was one calm figure: Stephen 2 slowly finished his Benson & Hedges before scooping up his jacket and running in slow motion towards his car.

The heli's rotors were already turning as I fastened up my five-piece harness. The Gazelle is a beautiful aircraft, small, sleek and very manoeuvrable, and it was much more exciting to be preparing for lift-off than to be stuck underneath with an oily rag watching someone else have all the fun. Once I was strapped in tight I plugged my headphone cable into the comms panel, and heard the familiar crackle of the net. The procedures were as smooth as a reflex. I was now in touch with the guys on the ground and with the ops room. They'd have got the standby at the same time as us, and would be just as hyped up. The Troop were also deployed, and were on the ground within seconds.

Matt was on the radio to air-traffic control. A whispered commentary was coming over the net from the lads on the ground. The rotors were whipping around and my heart was racing. This was it. It was up to me to get eyes-on before the OP team lost sight of the target. I organised my kit, angle-poising the GOA (Ground Observation Apparatus), a roof-mounted one-eyed

binocular that enables you to pick out objects on the ground. I
didn't fit the round-catcher onto the ejection port, because there
was no certainty that I'd be firing. If we did get into a contact I'd
immediately clip it on, to stop the empty cases from shooting out
with potentially lethal consequences. It's a rule in special operations:
the more chances you take, even if they seem trivial, the more likely
you are to screw up. If I had to open fire inside the heli I'd be
giving it rock-all, and there'd be more empty cases flying around
than pint glasses in the compound bar. If these were sucked into
the mechanics, or smacked the pilot in the face, they'd really spoil
our day.

Within moments we were airborne.

'Zero Sierra check.'

'Zero, that's OK.'

'Sierra mobile.'

'Zero Oscar, that's three Bravos entering target.' Time was
pressing.

Matt and I hovered above the compound for a moment, then it
plunged away beneath us. The weather was rapidly deteriorating.
The cloud was thickening and it was beginning to drizzle. I could
see Dungannon market square, which was packed with shoppers
peering out from under awnings. Then I looked across to Coalisland
and its mazes of drab little council estates. Our nose dipped and
we headed north-west towards Cappagh.

The Troop were on their way in with G3s and pistols, driving
two mobile intercept vehicles. Although the most likely scenario
was a mobile intercept, they were also ready with the kit for a house
assault or setting up an OP. They didn't know if their role would
last thirty minutes or four weeks, so it was imperative they were
prepared.

My plan was to head eight kilometres south of the target, reaching an altitude of seven thousand feet, from where I could conduct
surveillance on the XR3i. But I needed to get onto it straight away,
without giving the game away by being seen or heard in the target
area.

'Zero Oscar, all three Bravos complete Charlie One.'

All the call signs acknowleged Jed's transmission. I flicked my eyes to the altimeter, we were already at five thousand feet. I would have eyes-on in less than thirty seconds.

We made it to seven thousand feet. Through the thickening cloud, I could just make out Cappagh High Street. It looked like Toytown. From there I traced the road seven kilometres north-west to the target.

'Zero Sierra has eyes-on target building.' The team needed to know I'd found what I was looking for.

'Zero, roger.'

'Oscar, roger. Engine started.' Jed had heard the car spark into life. A few seconds later I saw it emerge from the ruins, a tiny dot in the distance.

Simultaneously Jed gave the word. 'Zero Oscar, that's Charlie One mobile.'

I watched as the XR3i crawled down a dirt track towards a small B-road, and gave the news over the net. I was now in control. The lads in the car team were listening in to my commentary, hanging back and preparing to take over if necessary.

Everything was going to plan except the weather, which was rapidly getting worse. My view of the ground was increasingly blocked by gusting cloud, and rain was pelting onto the heli's perspex bubble. It was an effort to stay sighted.

Matt brought us down to six thousand feet, just beneath the cloud base, in an effort to keep eyes-on. If the weather became any worse, we would be forced to fly so low that we'd risk being spotted by the target. Somehow, I'd managed to keep eyes-on for the past ten minutes, but I could see I was going to have to give up the trigger. It was time to call it a day.

'Zero Sierra, I'm going to have to drop this. The weather's shite up here.'

'Zero, roger that.'

Jack would have to take over at the next crossroads. 'Golf, Sierra. Can you, at yellow three-two?'

'Golf, yes.'

Just as well. I felt like Cyclops-head, having peered through the

GOA without a break. Such bad weather is an easy route to severe eye-strain.

While Jack and the rest of the car team took over, Matt and I gained some height and disappeared up into the cloud, but stayed in the area.

By now the target was heading towards Dungannon, via a meandering network of minor roads. The driver was clearly switched on to the possibility that he might be under surveillance, and was trying to cover his tracks. Little did he know! Matt and I stayed put, listening intently to the commentary over the net. A few minutes later, we heard some bad news.

'Zero Golf, Charlie One unsighted towards yellow one-four.' Jack was no longer eyes-on. This wasn't a major disaster – yet – but it was vital that he regained sight of the target immediately. He didn't.

'Zero Golf, I'm at yellow one-four. Negative Charlie One.'

Shit. He'd lost the target at a five-way junction. The XR3i could have been anywhere.

Immediately the car team split up to check all routes. If only we'd been able to bug the car, this wouldn't have happened. The beacon-receiving kit, known as Op Gracie, would have given us a clear signal indicating its location. Now we had nothing.

After a few minutes it was depressingly clear that the target had evaded the surveillance team. The boys were criss-crossing the countryside in the hope of picking it up, but after half an hour had passed, they still hadn't found it. It was very frustrating.

TCG, the police Tasking and Coordination Group in Portadown, spoke to the ops room, and Paul came over the net and told us to stay in the area. Then we heard him giving the order for the Troop to pull off and go back to the compound.

We waited for our order to turn back, but it didn't come. Clearly, nothing was going to happen if the Troop was pulling out, but our team was told to maintain our positions. Why the hell were we being left in situ? It didn't make sense. Either it was going down or it wasn't.

By now Matt was really getting concerned about the weather,

which was becoming ever more crap. He was wrestling with the controls to keep us in position at five thousand feet. Rain was hammering down on the bubble, and we were being battered about by the wind in the increasingly thick cloud.

'It's not looking good,' Matt muttered. 'If it gets worse we're going to have to fly on nav aids.'

I took the decision. There was no action on the ground, and even if there had been, the cloud was so thick that we wouldn't have been able to see anything. The Troop had pulled out, and it was time to follow them. I spoke briskly into my comms. 'Zero Sierra, we're heading back to the FMB. It's no good up here for the heli.'

The job was folding. Matt and I headed back to Dungannon to refuel. I was mightily pissed off. What did TCG know that they weren't telling us? Our guys were still out there, so why had the Troop been pulled off?

Back at the Portakabin I fixed Matt and myself some tea and toast and continued to monitor the net, listening to the boys driving aimlessly around the area.

Three hours later Jack came up, sounding a bit fed-up. 'Zero Golf. Yellow two-one towards yellow two-four.' This was the signal that he was preparing to do an east-to-west drive-through of Cappagh High Street. Cappagh is a staunch Republican stronghold. None of the security forces go on the ground there, and even the police don't operate. It's a really hard area. Everyone in Cappagh, even the kiddies and the old grannies, is a terrorist, but Jack was determined to find the XR3i. It was his call.

He drove down the main drag without incident. Up at the far end by the church he did a circuit and prepared for another drive-through. He was taking a risk by making a second pass in such a short period of time, but it appeared to pay dividends.

'Zero Golf. Standby, standby.' There was a huge sense of relief in his voice – he'd spotted the XR3i in his rear-view mirror, the first time all day we'd had a result. Matt and I exchanged a smile at the good news, but within seconds Jack was back on the net, his voice raspy and clearly panicked. 'Stand . . .'

We didn't get the '. . . by for contact' part of the sentence. His finger had flicked off the pressle, and all we heard was silence. Fucking hell, was there a contact going down? Three or four seconds flashed past, and Jack didn't get back on the net. Something was happening out there. I grabbed my kit and we ran out of the door. The weather was still shite, but something big was happening and we needed to be on hand to supply top cover if necessary. There was no question that we wouldn't take the risk. It took all of five or six seconds to leave the ops room, dash to the heli and get myself plugged in.

Paul was on the net to Kurt, who was no more than a kilometre from Cappagh High Street. 'Papa Zero, can you do a drive-past?'

'Papa roger, doing that now,' said Kurt briskly.

As we lifted off I informed the ops room, 'Sierra mobile.' I chucked out the words as quickly as possible. This was the wrong moment to waste time on the net. We'd still heard nothing from Jack; he could have been malleted, we just didn't know. Sweat trickled down my forehead despite the cold as I tightened the helmet chinstrap. We didn't bother being covert. Matt lifted us 150 feet off the ground, just high enough to avoid the pylons. We raced along, skimming the ground, hoping for some visibility through the driving rain. There was a high risk of crashing into something. It was like pea soup out there, and Matt had no choice but to rely on the instruments as we were thrown sideways by the ferocious wind. Every now and then I glimpsed hedges and roads emerging beneath us through the fog. As we'd gone overt we also faced the risk of terrorist anti-aircraft rockets, but there was nothing we could do about that.

There was lots of confusion going on over the net. The ops room asked for reports, but no one could supply them. As we neared Cappagh I peered through the clouds, trying to see the high street. Kurt was doing a drive-past just as we arrived overhead. I could see three vehicles: Kurt entering the high street, Stephen 2 following him in, and, over on the right-hand side of the road, Jack's car on its side in a ditch. Jack must have seen Kurt at the same time, because Kurt came up screaming over the net, 'Stop firing, mate, stop firing! It's me, Kurt!' Then the window in the cloud closed up and we were unsighted.

Over the crackling transmission we could hear someone laying down 7.62 rounds. Although I couldn't see Jack, I knew he must be OK if he was up and firing at Kurt. I got another fleeting window through the cloud to the action. Cappagh High Street was deserted. No terrorist in their right mind would have approached the team when they were so obviously tooled up. Jack had stopped firing and Kurt had raced up and parked next to him. I could see them in conversation, and I waited for the sit rep over the net.

'Zero Whisky, sit rep mate,' said Stephen 2. 'Jack's been involved in a contact with the target vehicle. He's all right, no sign of any runners, although he thinks he's winged a couple of them.'

That was my cue. I fitted the round-catcher onto my HK53. Hanging out of the heli with the assault rifle, I searched the bushes and hedgerows for runners as Matt bobbed and weaved. I was pissed off that I could barely make out the rooftops, let alone any scurrying figures. So much for my airborne perspective. I scoured the ground for a couple of minutes, with Matt obligingly flying lower and lower, then updated the ops room, shouting to make myself heard over the rotors and the buffeting wind. 'Zero Sierra, that's a negative for three Ks out.' My eyes didn't leave the ground for a second.

'Zero roger.'

We flew in an increasing circle, being bashed about and thrown up and down. It was like being stuck in the spin cycle of a washing machine. We were four kilometres out when Matt spoke up: 'We're going to have to get some height here. It's too dangerous.'

I'd been waiting for this. He'd pushed it long enough. No regular heli-pilot would have dreamed of flying so low in these conditions, and Matt wasn't following any textbook procedures about caution. Although we were seventy feet above the rooftops, he was warning me that any minute now we were going to clip a pylon or radio mast, which would mean us going down like a sack of shit.

'OK,' I said. 'Let's get some height, but stay around.'

I gave the news over the net. 'Zero Sierra, it's hopeless with the heli. It's pea soup up here. We're gaining some height.' I felt severely frustrated. All tooled up and nowhere to go. Somewhere down on the ground were fleeing, possibly wounded terrorists, but they were out of reach.

'All call-signs, this is Zero,' said Paul. 'Get the kit sorted out, get Golf into Papa and make your way back to Castle Hill.'

Back at Castle Hill we piled into the Portakabin for an update. Jack was sitting in a corner looking very withdrawn and pale, nervously picking at his fingernails.

'All right, Jack?'

'Yeah,' he grunted.

'Wanna fag, mate?' I joked. He never smoked.

'No thanks, mate,' he whispered.

I put the kettle on to make him a brew, and patted him on the shoulder. He hadn't had a good day out.

Greg broke the ice with a sledgehammer. 'So what happened, mate?'

Jack sparked into frenzied life, gabbling a trillion words a minute. 'I don't really know. I just remember looking in my rear-view and seeing two humungous barrels pointing at me through the sunroof of the XR3i. It was right fucking behind me. They were wearing balaclavas and they were onto me. I tried to give "Standby for contact," but I was reaching for my gun. It happened so quickly. Then they started firing. I swerved to avoid the rounds, crashed the car and started firing back. I can't remember much more than that.'

He looked well out of it. His eyes were rolling, lines were furrowing his brow. He was hyper, not making a lot of sense, although he'd managed to paint the image we all saw in our worst nightmares.

'I couldn't get out of the car, so I just kept firing back. I know I winged a couple of them. I think I got one in the leg and one of the other bastards in the head.'

I was glad he'd dropped them. At least we had two injured. 'Can't wait to see the state of your car,' I said, trying to lighten the heavy atmosphere.

'I could feel the impact,' he gabbled. 'I don't know how many shots they fired from their AK47s. All my windows were out. Fuck, now I'll have to get a new car, and I'd just got that one nicely commed up. I managed to scramble out and just kept on firing at them with my pistol. When that ran out I grabbed my MP5K and the G3.'

A smile was curling over Stephen 2's lips. 'How many rounds did you use, Jack?'

'As many as they fucking hold,' he replied with a shake of his head.

'Well, that's a bit of a poor show, isn't it, lads?' joked Stephen. 'It's obvious you weren't on my training course. They'd never have let you pass with hits like that!' Stephen 2 liked to put the boot in.

'Fucking hell,' said Greg. 'Hope this doesn't mean we'll be up for more range practice.'

Halfway through our cups of tea Paul came on the net from the ops room. We all had to leave Dungannon and get ourselves back to the A-frame for a thorough debrief. But before we left the flying lawyers paid a visit. Forensics also turned up to examine Jack's guns and his empty magazines. It turned out that he'd used the thirty rounds from his MP5K, a full thirteen-round mag from his Browning, and most of the twenty-five clip from his G3 – some of which had been aimed at his own team. He'd obviously been well hyped up and, fearing for his life, thought the players had come back to finish him off. When he'd crashed into the ditch he'd just fired in panic through the rear window, liberally spraying the terrorists and their vehicle. It was the only strategy he could have adopted, since his brain was set into covering-fire mode. Then Kurt had turned up. In a fraught situation like that, your finger lives on the trigger, because it's the only defence you've got.

The contact said a lot about the players. When Jack, trapped upside down in a ditch, had started to return fire, the three courageous terrorists chose to scarper. Yet in *An Phobblacht*, the IRA free-sheet published for the cause and therefore notoriously unreliable, the contact was to take on a rather different complexion. The Provos claimed that their 'brave volunteers' had in fact killed two SAS men.

Jack's car resembled a colander, and there was a neat two-inch group of three rounds in the centre of his headrest. By rights, he should have been brown bread.

Back at the compound there was a tremendous atmosphere. We unloaded our rifles, pulling back the cocking handles powerfully enough to wrench out the bullets and send them flying up to whack the girders of the A-frame. Such bravado was part of the daily ritual of this macho environment. I was getting used to the rarefied atmosphere. We never saw elderly people, fat people or children. Instead I was always surrounded by sweaty young blokes who were constantly swearing, belching and farting.

By now Jack was a bit less flustered, and his recollection was sharper. The unanswered question was, why did TCG pull the Troop off? Presumably they had information from a tout or some other source that the job wasn't going to go down that day, but it was strange that the Troop had been pulled off and not us. Even so, Jack emerged from his nasty moment in the ditch a hero, and he was subsequently decorated. We later discovered from an SB tout that Jack had used up some of his generous allocation of ammo on Martin McCaughey's ear and Jack – aka Baldy – Quinn's leg.

After the full debrief we headed off to the bar for a drink. It was now 8 p.m., and the place had started filling up. It was always open, whether you felt like a drink at 5 a.m. or at midnight. We used bar chits and served ourselves from the heavily subsidised drinks. Whenever there was a success, the news flew round the agencies and other Dets quicker than a rat up a drainpipe. There was no better excuse for a piss-up. A few of the Untouchables came across, and a couple of lads from East and North also popped down. Anyone available would try to make a piss-up. As the evening wore on we were joined by the majority of the Troop, the pilots, the admin staff and all the compound dogs. There were always five or six mangy mongrels being fed by someone. The Troop had their own wonderdog, Benjy, an ex-sniffer who'd survived all sorts of contacts, including being run over by the operators on several occasions.

People were putting tapes and CDs on the hi-fi: Van Morrison, the Stones, David Bowie and the Beatles. My favourites were Irish folk music, country & western, and hits of the sixties and seventies

– real cheesy listening. The inevitable drinking competitions and bar games were going on, including one in which the guys competed to see who could piss furthest up the walls. Attitudes towards me had gone full circle. At first the boys hadn't wanted a big soft girly messing up their bravado and antics, but by now they realised I could kick, fight and drink like the next man. They accepted that I was a no-nonsense person, well able to look after myself, professional, hard-working and straightforward. I didn't let them get to me, and I gave as good as I got. But I never drank so much that I couldn't walk back to my basha, although sometimes it was one pace forward for every three to the sides.

Jed had decided that I was to be renamed 'the old trout', and one day I walked into the romper room to check the team names on the white-board and found that my name had been crossed out and replaced by a picture of a fish. In return I nicknamed Jed – already known as Alf (alien life form) – 'Fat Bastard'. Stephen was known as 'Spotty' because of the endless stream of zits that marched like an invading army across his forehead. Trev, from the Troop, stuffed dead animals in his spare time and liked younger women. After he'd trapped some infant up town one night newspaper cuttings appeared on the board showing an old man with a three-year-old child and the slogan, 'Watch out, watch out, there's a paedophile about.'

Two days later Jed and I were in the Cappagh area. Up ahead we saw an old stone wall at the side of the road. Big graffiti letters, punctuated with splodgy drips, had been specially prepared for us. They spelt out the words: 'SAS beware. The IRA are everywhere. You might have an eye in the sky, but we've got an XR3i.'

I roared with laughter. My role in the heli had been immortalised in white paint. Who'd ever have believed that the IRA had the same sense of humour as squaddies? It was the first time I'd seen any evidence of wit – usually IRA propaganda is very dour and militant. Significantly, once again they thought they'd been dealing with the SAS, not the Det.

The smiles didn't last long. When you're conducting surveillance you get to know all the nitty gritty of the terrorists' sad little lives.

You know their full names, their nicknames, what brand of beer they drink, how many children they have, where their wife shops, where she holds down her little cleaning job, where their kids go to school, who they're shagging on the side, all their vehicle details, and most crucially of all, where they go to socialise – that is, meet other known players. All this minutiae brings them right down to size. The general public, on hearing that a massive bomb has exploded, create a stereotype of tough men in a crack unit. In fact, the photofits tell the truth: these are ordinary-looking men. They don't have 'terrorist' tattooed on their foreheads.

One afternoon I had cause to get rather closer to one of the main men than I would have chosen. I was out on a surveillance in a Dungannon council estate, with my bag of shopping swinging under my arm. I was doing a walk-past of Baldy Quinn's house, trying to look nonchalant despite my racing heart. As I entered the estate a man was walking towards me. He was tall and good-looking, in his late twenties with a strong jawline and sandy-coloured hair. With a sickening feeling I realised that this was the OC of the Provisional IRA in East Tyrone, and the brother of a terrorist who had been killed in a Troop ambush some years earlier. He had been described in Belfast High Court as a 'very active' member of the IRA, and was supposedly one of the godfathers who ordered the murder of Tory MP Ian Gow, killed by a car bomb in 1990 at his home in East Sussex. He and I were fated to pass each other that day, on that cold grey tarmac under that lowering sky. In the split-second of recognition the thumbnail sketch of his life flashed like a reflex through my brain. Married with four children. His wife was another key player's sister.

He might not have looked like a scumbag, but I didn't let that deceive me. He was a little shit who usually got other people to do his dirty work. On one occasion he'd taken a Protestant man's family hostage and instructed him to drive a van loaded with explosives to an SF base if he wanted his children to survive. To make sure the terrified Prot didn't do a runner, he'd plasticuffed him to the seat of the van. That wasn't about the Irish cause, that was attempted murder. And only the previous year he and another

Provisional IRA suspect, from the Coalisland ASU, had been caught driving through the village of Ardboe in East Tyrone with a hysterical woman hidden under a coat in the back of the car. The woman was reputedly an SB tout, and it appeared that they were on their way to exact some revenge. With the OC East Tyrone facing a long stretch in the Maze, the IRA had put pressure on the woman's family to get her to do a deal. She withdrew her testimony against him and the case collapsed, leaving him free to carry on his terrorist career.

Now he was walking towards me. I tried to put my face into gear. I knew I had to make eye-contact; it would have looked odd not to have done so. When we were about six paces apart I looked up noncommittally. His blue eyes locked with mine for a second, he grunted in greeting and dipped his head back down again. I returned the guttural sound, which fortunately passed for 'Hello.' He hadn't registered me, and a smug satisfaction flooded through me: 'You haven't a clue who I am, Mr OC, but I know everything about you. What's more, I'm wearing a hidden radio earpiece and there's a Browning pistol stuck down my knickers.' By now my pistol had become an extension of my arm. I felt undressed without it – not wearing it was like not having my bra on. I wasn't particularly frightened by close proximity to terrorists, because I knew I had the skills to survive and I had confidence in my training. But you must never allow yourself to make the mistake of becoming complacent.

I was powerfully reminded of this when South Det was invited to a Special Branch debriefing on the murder of Derek Wood and David Howes, two Royal Signals corporals who were dragged from their unmarked car after they strayed into the path of an IRA funeral in March 1988. It was a disgusting double murder at the hands of a Republican mob, and two high-ranking IRA men, Henry Maguire and Alexander Murphy, had been banged up for life for their part in it. The lecture room was crammed full.

We were shown the uncut video of the murders which had been taken from an Army Air Corps Lynx helicopter equipped with a heli-tele surveillance camera. So sickening was the event that the television news reports had only carried the skimpiest edits from the film. There was nothing the pilot and the lance-corporal who was working the heli-tele could do to stop the murders. Their mission was to observe the funeral from one thousand feet. The cortège was that of IRA activist Kevin Brady, one of the men gunned down in Milltown cemetery at the funeral of the Gibraltar Three by Michael Stone, 'the mad Prod' as Special Forces had dubbed him. Feeling among Republicans was running high at Brady's funeral in the Andersonstown area of West Belfast.

We watched as the procession passed Roger Casement Park, adjacent to the local Sinn Fein HQ. The mourners were five hundred metres from Milltown cemetery when the two signallers drove into the middle of the fray.

David Howes had come out to Ulster to take over Derek Wood's job, and presumably as part of their 'handover-takeover' process, Wood had decided to take him on a trip round the hard areas of West Belfast, without realising that Brady's funeral was due to take place. In the first few seconds of the incident they could so easily have got out of the situation by reversing or throwing a handbrake turn, but before they could organise themselves they were surrounded by a crowd of angry Republicans, despite the fact that their car wasn't identifiable as a forces vehicle. Suddenly, as if someone had rung a bell, the crowd became a mob. Fuelled by hysteria, and led by a bold and violent Sinn Fein activist, they started smashing up the car's bodywork with iron bars and ripping off the wing mirrors. After a few seconds a single shot rang out from inside the car. The crowd instantly dispersed. It looked just like the parting of the Red Sea. I clenched my fists as I watched this perfect escape opportunity being passed by. The car didn't budge an inch.

With a sickening feeling I realised that the signaller must have pulled the pistol out from under his thigh without realising that he'd depressed the magazine-release button, which would mean that after one shot had been fired the magazine would have fallen out of the gun, making further shots impossible – a Browning can't be fired without a mag in place. The shot could also have been a panicky ND.

I didn't like to imagine the sheer terror the two young men must have felt as the bloodthirsty mob hemmed them in and they realised they were powerless to protect themselves. Being admin staff, they had only a passing familiarity with their pistols, and would rarely have had the chance to fire them. They wouldn't have been up to speed on the simple IA (immediate action) drill that gets the pistol working again: 'Tap. Rack' (tap the magazine back in, then rack back the slide to chamber another round). Second nature to anyone who regularly handles firearms, but meaningless to a signaller.

But it's pointless to speculate on what the outcome might have been if the two soldiers had been properly trained. The Sinn Fein member who led the initial attack would certainly have been recognised as the main threat by any operator trained in situational awareness, and eliminated accordingly. It's possible – if frightening – to imagine a good, aggressive operator engaging the crowd with an HK53 or a G3. The political fallout would have been horrendous, but at least the soldiers would have survived. As it was, after Corporal Wood's one shot there was no follow-up action. Their window of opportunity passed, and a few seconds later the crowd mobbed the car again. From above they looked like a swarm of bees massing round a hive, moving as one united invading force. The signallers were dragged from the car and subjected to a severe kicking and punching. At this stage the 'mourners' didn't know who they were. They could have been RUC, Protestant activists, regular army or SAS. Simply and cruelly by virtue of the fact that they didn't belong in West Belfast, they had become the objects of the crowd's pent-up fury.

We watched as the two men were viciously battered. The sight of blood seemed to spur the mob on. They dragged their prey through the wrought-iron gates of Roger Casement Park and dumped them on the grass next to a boundary wall, where more kickings followed. Great waves of nausea washed over me as I watched the clothes and shoes being dragged off the limp figures. Then a black taxi pulled up outside the wall, which had a nine-foot drop on the pavement side. The two signallers were picked up and lobbed over.

The blokes in the heli were powerless to act. They had no idea whose deaths they were witnessing, and even if they'd tried to land, it would have been impossible for them to have rescued the two men. The beatings continued, then the corporals were heaved into the taxi and driven off. The heli followed it to the Penny Lane wasteground two miles away. The terrorist grapevine works so quickly that when the taxi pulled up a few minutes later someone was already waiting for it with a pistol. The now naked corporals were dragged out into a shitty heap on the ground. Every time they tried to get up or crawl away they were kicked back down again. Even at this stage Howes made a desperate bid to escape, running a few yards before being battered to the ground.

There was total silence in the lecture theatre as we watched the last few seconds of their lives, just twelve minutes after they'd taken their wrong turning into the funeral procession. A gunman stood over Howes and cold-bloodedly executed him point-blank in the head. Wood was then shot by a second man. Bastards. Although both signallers were already dead, the gun was passed around the rest of the gang so they could all have a go.

My pulse was soaring, and my nausea had turned to anger. You wouldn't kill an animal that way, not even a rabid dog. It's one thing to kill an armed terrorist who's endangering the lives of innocent people, but this was ritualistic slaughter. These scumbags didn't even know who they'd murdered, but they gloried in the deaths. Even from the grainy video you could clearly see from the assassins' swaggering postures that their act had given them a buzz, that they'd got pleasure out of it. As the gunmen melted back into the cosy safety of the 'Nationalist community', a shocked and weeping Catholic priest knelt over the bodies and gave them the last rites.

As the video flickered to a halt my stomach was churning. I felt fired up against those fucking bastards out there. There was a dazed silence in the lecture hall. Jed and I were due on the ground for a routine surveillance job, so we made our apologies and left. For once there was no wheel-spinning or bravado as we drove off. Just each of us, deep in our own thoughts.

The video made a deep impression on me. Over the coming days my enduring memory was of the signallers' lamentable lack of basic training. They appeared to have had no quality firearms training, and no anti-ambush or vehicle drills. Their 'restraint' in not firing again after the first shot was praised by their commanding officer, Lieutenant Colonel Martin Roberts. I didn't see it as restraint; clearly their training hadn't provided them with the means to survive.

Although admin staff aren't required to go onto the ground operationally, they frequently have to travel between locations. The video brought home to me the fact that our own admin staff in South Det were going about their duties just as cluelessly as the two signallers. They had only the skimpiest knowledge of how to operate a gun, and would have been completely incapable of sorting out a stoppage or executing a hasty mag-change under pressure. They didn't have their own weapons, but had to sign out a Browning when leaving the compound. I decided to set up a little training schedule for them, to teach them how to use their weapons properly. I approached our three chefs, four bleeps, the mechanic and a couple of spooks, and asked if they'd like some basic firearms training with a pistol. Most of them were very keen. Their abilities proved to be as poor as I'd feared. They had a basic knowledge, but their reaction times were terrible. They couldn't draw the gun from the holster smoothly, couldn't execute a swift mag-change, and their shot placement was worse than a five-year-old's at a fairground. But they were anxious to learn, aware that it was a practical form of insurance policy. One of the chefs, Alan, even asked for some special training on multiple targets and fire and manoeuvre, which I gave him. I guess malleting targets made a refreshing change from beating eggs and chopping carrots. He was so grateful that he baked me a beautiful cake.

SEVEN

'ZERO SIERRA ROGER'

I'D INVESTED SOME time in making my basha more homely. On my bedside table I'd draped a King Billy tea towel, and on the wall above the bed I'd pinned a poster of a naked man flexing his muscles. It provided an inspirational backdrop to my hundreds of hours of dry-firing practice with the Browning to Gene Pitney classics in front of the mirror.

The incentive behind my hours of practice was to perfect my slick draw and improve my fastest time. I made sure my gun was well overhauled at all times. I would polish all the working parts – hammer and sear, trigger, slide, frame, mag well and magazines, and I became a familiar figure in the corner of the A-frame where Derek, the mechanic, hung out.

Good shooting is a combination of speed, power and accuracy, and I bought myself a shot timer as a start command. It made an intermittent beep which was my signal to react as speedily as possible.

I also cleaned, tested and oiled my other firearms frequently. I preferred the HK53 to the more powerful G3 because it was lighter, smaller and easier to handle. It also had a retractable stock, making it easier to conceal. An important element of using firearms is feeling comfortable with them. You have to feel that they fit you, and for that reason I loved the HK53. When I was out on ops I'd slot a forty-round mag onto it, and clip two spare mags for the Browning to my belt. Although the mags held thirteen rounds, I only ever used twelve, so as to cut down the risk of a stoppage by not stressing the spring tension. This gave me a total of seventy-seven rounds when I was mobile (in the car) and thirty-seven when going foxtrot.

The A-frame roof had started leaking, so we were all relocated while men with cranes carried out repairs. I was moved to a temporary basha about a mile down the road on the edge of the compound. I decided to clean up the filthy indoor range in the A-frame for live-firing practice. I spent two days scrubbing it out and got hold of some decent torso-shaped targets sent from Hereford. I had three of them ranged over ten metres. I would aim for two-shot groupings on the centre section of each target, then execute a speedy mag-change before burying two more shots in each target. I spent as much time as I could on the range, and got my time down to five or six seconds. These were nights of solitary intensity, with only the noise of the gunfire echoing around the range for company. On an average evening I'd get through three hundred rounds. Sometimes, after three hours of solid concentration, I'd get trigger-freeze, and have to take a break. The instant the mind becomes aware of the firing process it interferes with the subconscious signal, and you fluff the shot. It's like walking downstairs, suddenly concentrating on what your legs are doing, and finding that you start to stumble. Bruce Lee summed it up when he said: 'Conscious thought is the greatest hindrance to the proper execution of all physical action.'

The new basha wasn't much of a hardship, because I was scarcely ever there. My life consisted of hanging about at the compound, being on the range, out on ops, in the bar, or eyes-down in briefings. I kept up with my friends in the Troop, and on some occasions I saw more of them than we intended. The basha ten metres from mine had been dubbed 'the love shack', as the Troop used it to entertain the admin girls they sometimes managed to trap. They never brought civvies into camp; that would have been the equivalent of walking around Northern Ireland in combat boots. On a couple of occasions during the first night I moved in, I heard someone urgently turning my door-handle, followed by earnest rapping. I'd open the door a crack, stick my head round and tell a flustered-looking Troop bloke: 'Not tonight, thanks. You want to be over there.'

But the easy shagging was not to last. A few weeks after I moved in, Trev, one of the Troop lads, trapped a young army girl. He

nipped back to the love shack after midnight to make sure everything was in order, leaving her nursing her half-pint in the bar. He
walked inside and looked around, noticing the homely welcome
mat and the fragrant pine air-freshener. There were even some
photographs on the sideboard, although he turned these around so
as not to offend the evening's catch. He went into the bedroom
and made a quick check of the sheets. No problems there. Delighted
to find they were nice and fresh, he was impressed by the efforts
that had obviously been made to minister to the testosteronic urges
of the lads. With drunken delight he noticed there was scoff in the
fridge and several bottles of spirits in the bedside cupboard. As he
eagerly scuttled out to fetch his bird, in walked Patrick, a big Irish
fella from the Untouchables.

'What the fuck are you doing?' said Patrick with a scowl.

'Sorry, mate. It's my turn tonight. I'm on. It's all sorted. I'm just
going over to get her,' Trev replied.

'Oh no you're fucking not,' barked Patrick, who had to suffer a
few more disturbances of that kind until the penny slowly dropped.
The love shack was now permanently occupied!

Spring turned into summer, and in June 1990 there was a new
intake of operators, but no women had made it through the course
this time. Our four new blokes included Shane, a Rupert who was
destined to become head of South Det – all Ruperts did a short
stint on the ground before they became Det boss. Shane, a softly-
spoken jock, was a bit different to the rest of the lads in the compound: he was good-looking – jet black hair, dark eyes and good
skin. And there was James from Op Spice, who had been in the
Troop for many years. He was over six feet tall, well-built and
definitely one of the lads, although he was happily settled with a
woman in Hereford.

By now I was confidently doing the job. The only drawback was
that my once-lean, superbly fit body now had a layer of extra fat.
I was doing a lot of swimming in the camp pool, but not enough
to stop me getting porky. The trouble was that there's only one
method of dealing with the boredom of laying up when out on the
ground: food. It passes the time, and also serves to justify your

position in an LUP (laying-up point). We'd think nothing of chomping our way through several curries, bags of crisps, fish suppers and boxes of Wagon Wheels while on a surveillance job. After one particularly calorific session I turned to Jed, who was stuffing the last few crumbs from a box of biscuits into his mouth, and said, 'The things we do for this job. We're really sacrificing our bodies.'

The environment and the long hours meant that you didn't have the time, inclination or opportunity to eat sensible nutritious meals. In the cookhouse everything was deep-fried with sugar on top. One lunchtime as I tucked into a greasy plate of fish and chips, Jed told the other team-members that I'd scoffed six Wagon Wheels that morning in the five-minute stretch between blue nine and blue one-five; in fact I'd only eaten four, while Jed had managed to shovel in two whole ones at the same time as driving and speaking, pebbledashing the windscreen with flying debris as he nattered away.

There was an implicit rivalry in the cookhouse. The Troop would sit one side and the Det on the other, like the tribal hierarchy at a wedding. There weren't many serious arguments. We were a close-knit team, well aware that any day might see us trusting each other with our lives. But friendly banter was always being slung back and forth across the great cookhouse divide – especially after one of the guys had trapped the local gronk. The insults would multiply depending on just how aesthetically challenged the previous night's conquest had been. If she was low down on the ugliness scale, she might be a 'one-bagger' – meaning the blokes reckoned she'd need a single paper-bag on her head before they'd shag her. Further up the scale were the 'two-baggers' – just in case one bag broke. If she scored eleven out of ten she'd be a 'crocadilla-horrenda-pig'. This meant she automatically qualified as a 'one-armer' – meaning that if a bloke woke up next morning with his arm around her he'd rather chew it off than wake her up. A 'double-armer' is so ugly that you chew off the other arm as well, to stop it happening again.

Most of the lads in the compound were big, strong fellas with libidos to match. Some had girlfriends and wives at home, or in the Province, but that didn't dissuade a few of them from the nocturnal pursuit of other women. On one occasion, a couple of Troop blokes trapped a couple of girls who lived in the Republican stronghold of Toombridge. One of the girls' fathers was a Sinn Fein councillor, but the lads still overnighted at his house before escaping the following morning. If a bloke was out on the town he'd use any one of a million and one cover stories to explain why he was across the water, usually involving building work or spending time on the rigs.

One Wednesday morning in June we were eyes-down in the briefing room at nine o'clock. There was a big operation, code-named Op Craven, going down. The place was teeming with bodies – South Det, the Troop, TCG and E4A (surveillance division of Special Branch), and there was an air of anticipation. We only got a job of this size a couple of times a year. The intelligence was that the Provisional IRA had hidden a 4 × 4 vehicle in a barn not far from the border, and were intending to carry out an attack on one of the dozens of army bases situated along its 150-mile length. We had information that the 4 × 4 was stuffed with serious weaponry, including M60 machine guns, an M79 grenade-launcher, anti-tank weapons and several meaty bombs home-made from fertiliser mixed with diesel.

The Troop's task sounded simple: to arrest the IRA members connected with the vehicle before they could carry out a massacre. They decided to use a heli assault, rigging up four helicopters: two Wessex to carry the ground-assault troops, and two Lynx as gunships. Each Lynx would contain a .50mm Browning machine gun and a 40mm M19 high-explosive grenade-launcher. The Det task would be to supply heli surveillance, while E4A provided mobile surveillance. On the ground the RUC had already completed their CTR and were in a temporary OP, eyeballing the barn until the Troop could move in and take over. TCG had overall control of the whole operation.

After the briefing we all deployed to Bessbrook Mill, the HQ of the Armagh Roulement Battalion, an army base close to the border in South Armagh. Among our number was one willing South Det heli-operator – guess who?

It took Reg, the senior pilot in the compound, just thirty minutes to fly south. As we touched down I saw the converted four-storey stone mill which functioned as the accommodation block. Nearby was a helipad big enough for half a dozen helis and several Porta-kabins. In fact Bessbrook Mill is the busiest heliport in Europe, as the army presence in this dangerous area deploys by heli rather than on land.

We sussed out the most important areas: ops room, kitchen, toilet and bashas. The living conditions must have been in breach of the Geneva Convention. Two dim lightbulbs hung from bits of bare wire in the attic, and there were no windows. The floor was musty hardboard, and the loft space had minimal light. The standard army-issue camp beds were piled in a corner; we just had to wipe off the fungus and erect them. It was up to you to grab an area and make it your own. I put my maggot (sleeping bag) on my bed and stuffed my bergen underneath. This was to be our home for the next ten weeks – although of course we didn't know that yet. I slept in my kit, only taking my boots off before slipping into my maggot, in case there was a standby during the night.

We lived on permanent standby, hanging around the helipad hoping for the message from the Troop OP on the ground that the 4 × 4 was on the move. My Browning was always on my hip, the HK53 always stashed in the heli next to my helmet. We were ready to go, and would have been airborne within seconds. The one good thing about the waiting was the hot summer sunshine. As the days slowly dragged past, my hands and face became increasingly tanned.

Reg pilot, the Troop guys and I had formulated the plan that when we got the standby, Reg and I would go airborne as swiftly as possible, get sight of the target vehicle and relay its movements over the net to the Troop. The mobile surveillance role had actually been allocated to E4A, and we were only supposed to provide aerial surveillance, but we wanted to guard against any possibility of confusion. E4A were perfectly capable of providing the info, but they had their own techniques, communicated differently over the net and weren't used to working in tandem with the Troop. The plan was for me to give all the commentary, effectively blocking E4A from the net. It was vital that there was no confusion in getting the Troop the information they needed.

We wore our earpieces constantly, and several times during the first few weeks we heard 'Standby' over the net. But no sooner had we jumped in the heli than the Troop OP informed us that the 4 × 4 was returning to the barn. I'd flop down onto the tarmac and trudge wearily back to my sun-spot as the adrenaline dissipated.

After three weeks forward mounted at Bessbrook I was long overdue for a changeover, so Greg took over from me and I flew back to base. But I couldn't relax while I was killing time in the compound. Even though the conditions in the old mill were pretty shite and, once again, I'd been lumped with heli duty, I'd rather be on a good job in shite conditions than stuck in the compound without work. Fortunately Greg was soon bored, so I volunteered to change over with him again.

We passed the time chatting, getting a tan, and watching TV in the pilots' ops room. The lads always had the porn videos on – all heaving and pushing, with no storyline. Their favourite was a Scandinavian one which showed a bloke with a huge willy giving himself a blow-job with a vacuum cleaner. I stood and watched it for a few minutes until I got bored, and said, 'I suppose you'll all be volunteering for Hoover duties now, eh?' before walking out.

We all ate in the main cookhouse on a staggered rota. In the army you're rationed, and while two sausages, an egg and a couple of rashers of bacon was enough for me, some of the Troop lads were left starving. Massive Mark had already had a couple of tellings-off from the chef for taking too much food, and one lunchtime as he was leaning over to help himself to two meat pies, the chef whacked his fingertips with his fish slice. Instantly Mark grabbed his wrist and splayed his fingers onto the hotplate, where they made a nasty hissing sound. He didn't say a word, just glared into the cowering chef's eyes. Then he picked up his second pie and popped it on his plate. The chef didn't give anyone a hard time after that.

Resentment was gradually building. The Troop had asked if they could go in and do a CTR on the barn to find out what the score was, but Special Branch refused, on the grounds that the background intelligence was far too sensitive. This could only mean one thing – the information we'd received must have come from a source who was heavily involved. More and more, our suspicions grew that we were being wound up.

Ten weeks passed, and we were still living like rats in our hellhole, when we got another 'Standby, standby.' I was only yards from the heli, and I scrambled over and strapped myself in. There was a blur of activity as everyone else did likewise. Then there was a tremendous roar and a gusting wind created by the whirling of the rotors. It was like a scene from one of those Vietnam War movies as all the helis lifted off together. The Troop were hanging out of their tooled-up Lynx, and the two chunky Wessex were taking flight with the grace of swans. The net was crackling with a babble of commands.

'Sierra mobile.'

'Gunship one mobile.'

'Heli assault-team one mobile.'

'Gunship two mobile.'

'Heli assault-team two mobile.'

Reg and I cleared the compound fence and climbed rapidly, while the Wessex and Lynx stayed close to the compound. Our hearts were racing. This was it, the big one. We'd been waiting ten weeks for this, and finally we were geared up and on our way.

We soon reached a thousand feet, and were still gaining height when the OP team informed us that the 4 × 4 had arrived at the end of the track.

A few seconds later the Troop OP, sounding more than a bit pissed off, came up with, 'That's Charlie One doing a 180 and heading back towards the barn.'

'What the fuck's going on?' screamed Reg.

'You're fucking joking,' I cursed.

Here we were, all hyped up, supercharged into our roles, and it was just being snatched away from us. What was happening?

The answer came almost immediately from the Troop OP. 'Lima-Papa, one badly placed police VCP fifty metres from end of track.'

Brilliant. Another good job down the pan. It was obvious that the checkpoint must have been deliberately stuck out in full view so that the source, who was in the vehicle, would have a cast-iron excuse for pulling out. Who knew the reason? Maybe the tout was particularly valuable, and his handler hadn't wanted him to be put at risk, even if it meant aborting the whole operation. Or maybe the other players had guessed they had an informer in their midst. If the attack had gone ahead and our man had been the only sur-vivor, he might as well have been dead anyway, as the suspicions of the whole nationalist community would have been aroused, and he would have faced the ordeal of a savage interrogation and eventual execution.

The Troop deposited themselves back on the tarmac, and we followed them down. On the ground, with engines off and rotors cut, the team were angrily storming out of their aircraft, cursing and gesticulating. Everyone was incredibly pissed off. Speculation was rife. It was starting to look as if we'd been used, and the most popular explanation was that the whole of Op Craven had just been a source-handling exercise.

'Basically, we were just pawns in the game,' hissed Reg pilot angrily.

The thought didn't lift our mood. We wandered back to the mill to make a brew. A feeling of apathy sloshed over the troops. It was the closest to a sense of mutiny that I'd experienced. Every-body was slagging off the police, the politicians, the army head sheds and anyone else they could think of.

'They get up my fucking nose,' said Jock.

'Well, it's big enough,' Cuffy laughed.

'I'm serious,' said Jock. 'How do they expect all this shit over here ever to end, when they're so fucking spineless?'

'Don't kid yourself, Jock. A lot of those wankers who pull the strings don't want it to end,' said Reg.

There were a few suggestions about how we'd deal with the terrorists if it was left up to us. Someone had the idea of rounding them all up in the helis, flying across the water and dumping them and all their bombs on the Houses of Parliament, killing two birds with one stone.

We would probably never know why the operation had been aborted. But then, nothing is ever what it seems in Northern Ireland. It's not just the Prot versus the Catholic, the terrorist for the Cause, the army in aid of civil power and Special Forces gaining intelligence. There are always many more complex, tangled webs and sub-plots going on. We'd just spent ten weeks being moved around the chessboard of Northern Irish politics.

There was nothing for it but to get ourselves back from Bessbrook and ensconced in the compound bar to dissect the little game in which we'd been immersed. Reg and I flew back, showered, and joined the lads for the post-mortem of the previous ten weeks' events. The double vision came very rapidly, as we'd all been dry for ten weeks. We well and truly drowned our sorrows that night.

Within a few weeks we were back into the groove of normal Det life. I was in my new semi-detached basha just outside the A-frame, flicking through Luke's latest letter (he had to use a PO box number which would get mail to Lisburn before it was distributed to each Det), when I heard a gunshot. It came from the area of the range, but it was disturbingly loud. Had it been fired within the range it would have been muffled by the soundproof insulation. My first thought was that someone had had an ND. My second was to wonder if I'd mistaken the sound of a door slamming. Then my hackles rose. A single gunshot, even in the A-frame, is enough to make you sit up and take notice. What was going on? I had a horrible foreboding that something bad had happened. Recently there had been a tragedy at East when one of the bleeps had come in after a routine admin trip and unloaded his pistol. He'd accidentally pulled the trigger with a round chambered. The bullet had sliced through his left hand and gone straight into the heart of his mate, who was standing next to him.

I dashed over to the ops block. As I was running up the stairs I met a distraught, white-faced Aidan spook.

'Did you hear that shot?' I asked.

His normal jocularity had completely evaporated. 'Yes. That was Barry pronto. He's just shot himself.'

In horror, I followed him down the stairs. People clutching medical kits were racing towards the range. Bert, the DSM, was looking upset and bewildered. Heart pounding, I ran over to the area as the Troop guys – Jock, Marty, Rich and Cuffy – pulled up with drips. A pool of dark blood was seeping into the concrete. Barry's body was as still as a stone, and where the top of his skull should have been was a gaping wound. He was surrounded by seven or eight of the Troop guys urgently sticking lines into him. They tried everything they could to save his life, but finally had to admit defeat. At least they could get in a bit of training, and they practised searching for veins and plunging intravenous drips into his body.

I turned away. I knew what they were doing, but found it hard to stand by and watch their grisly efficiency. Had Barry committed suicide, or had it been an accident? I had a sinking feeling that it had been intentional. I wandered over to a couple of pilots who'd spilled out of the bar with undrunk pints in their hands. They looked washed out.

'He'd asked the army for time off work, you know,' said Taff. 'Despite the fact that he felt under such fucking pressure, they'd denied it him.'

Kiwi, Matt and Taff had been in the bar when Barry had wandered in and poured himself two double whiskies. He'd sauntered over to sign his chit and written, 'Hole in the Head Barry'. He'd thrown the measures down his neck, left the bar, signed out his pistol and taken it to his basha, near the range on the opposite side of the A-frame to mine. Bert had seen him wandering through the compound staring at his gun and had run after him. They'd gone back to Barry's basha, where he'd told Bert he was contemplating suicide. Bert thought he'd talked him out of it, and the two of them had been walking back to the A-frame when he'd heard the single shot behind him.

'Fucking awful news,' said Kiwi, downing his pint. 'All he wanted was some time to sort out things with his missus.'

But that's the system. The military machine can only accommodate individual needs up to a certain point; the whole philosophy is about sacrificing the individual for the majority. We soon brightened up again. The running joke became the rule: 'Never go into the bar if there are more than two pilots in there quaffing ale.'

When no ops were on, you were free to get up when you wanted. One blustery morning I didn't emerge until 10.30 a.m., due to the fact the beer hadn't run out until seven hours earlier. I showered and wandered out to find some breakfast in the cookhouse. As I passed the Troop guys on my way into the A-frame I casually observed lots of good-looking bods slumming around in flip-flops and towels, standard early-morning attire between the accommodation and shower blocks. They had an ongoing competition called the 200 Club, which required them to bench-press two hundred pounds. It wasn't that they loved themselves; they were simply fit because that's what their job required.

Breakfast – the full monte of fried eggs and bacon dripping in oil – was usually a raucous occasion, fuelled by hangovers. To save on washing up, you'd have your own diggers (knife, fork, spoon), plate and mug with you. Afterwards you'd slop them out in the sink outside. As I wandered into the cookhouse I sensed that all eyes were on me, so I nonchalantly scanned the walls. Glaring out at me was a new picture. Jed's face and mine had been superimposed onto kids' bodies, with the words 'I love Jed' and 'I love Sarah' in thought-bubbles. We were the only working couple, so that made us fair game.

Big Marty, one of the Troop team leaders, bellowed across from his table, 'Look, hen, I told them not to put it up there. I knew you'd go mad. It's got nothing to do with me,' he added sheepishly, knowing full well that I knew it was him.

I laughed. 'You're all jealous 'cos Jed's got me and you haven't.'

I'd gradually become a sort of Troop mascot. The SAS blokes never gave me a problem. They were big enough to see you for what you were, irrespective of gender or colour, and they welcomed a woman's presence on camp because they were aware of the advantages it brought. Later that day I wandered up to the Troop's ops room to get the keys for the range. As I went down the corridor I spied a large sheet of paper with the names and positions for an upcoming rugby match between the RUC and Troop lads on camp. There I was. Prop forward: Sarah. Obviously I wouldn't be playing, but I was touched to have been remembered.

Before scoff, I trained. Most days when I didn't have work on, I'd run the mile and a half through the compound to the indoor swimming pool, swim between half a mile and a mile, then run back. The run to the camp would take me a week, the swim about an hour, and it would take me another week to make it back.

One morning Rich sauntered over at breakfast. He was a Troop guy, nearly six feet tall, with lots of luscious unruly black hair. He had a soft Welsh accent, and was one of the founders of the 200 Club. 'How you doing mate?' he mumbled.

'Oh, bit of a baggy head, but I'm all right.'

'We've got a job on tonight down in Newry and we want to use you. What do you reckon?'

'Yeah, of course. What does it involve?' I was flattered that the Troop had asked me to help them out. I knew it would piss off Paul, the Det ops officer, that the world's most élite soldiers had requested me.

The Troop were doing recces on various locations in Newry, on the Down–Armagh border, with a view to making them future OP positions. They needed 'a couple' to hang around street corners, check out entrances and exits, mark the positions of installations, and develop a feel for the layout of the area. A guy on his own would have drawn attention.

Marty, who was mopping up the last of a humungous breakfast with slabs of Mother's Pride, saw us chatting and yelled out: 'Leave her alone, leave her alone.'

Rich laughed. 'It's all right, mate, I'm briefing her on tonight.'

Marty, his voice all sausage sandwich and mock caution, replied, 'Where you taking her? Don't you be flexing your muscles at her.'

He rolled up his sleeve. 'I've been down at the 200 Club as well, you know!'

Rich told me to wear the normal kit, meaning that I should look like an ordinary girl from Newry. With that, he wandered off to fetch himself a sea of tea and a mountain of breakfast.

My outfit had to tell the world that I was going out for an evening stroll with my boyfriend, so 1830 hours saw me pulling on American tan tights, a pair of court shoes with a tiny heel, a knee-length blue skirt, a pale cotton blouse and a slightly more trendy jacket than I'd have worn on my normal ops. I wouldn't be commed up, so I wouldn't be wearing the scruffy cotton jacket with the hidden wires. All I had to conceal was my Browning.

Once I was tooled up, I strode over to the Troop ops room. Stephen and Kurt were wandering back from the cookhouse to their bashas.

'Where are you going, you old trout?' Stephen called out.

'Mind your own business, Spotty,' I said gruffly. If he wanted to find out what I was up to, he could ask Paul. I wasn't going to tell him.

As I entered the ops room, my three team-mates looked up and acknowledged me. The white-board up at the front was daubed with essential info about the op. There would be four of us on the ground: Rich and me in one car, Lenny and Big Marty in the other. Rich and I would go foxtrot around Newry using doorways for cover, as ardent young lovers do. The other guys would stay mobile until we'd gathered all the info we needed. They would be on hand just in case anything happened. You'd never go out on an op only two up.

We drove out and got on with the job. Newry is a staunchly Republican town, and we had to be careful not to arouse suspicion. We got on with the task using all the resources we had, including my gender and my kissable lips. Rich and I must have cuddled in every doorway in Newry. Our task was to look as if we were immersed in each other, while focusing our minds elsewhere, scrutinising locks and hinges on the other side of the street, watching traffic flow, memorising cut-throughs and alleyways, and storing

189

all this visual information onto an internal log. When we got back, after two hours on the ground, we had an extensive debrief, jotting down our observations and talking them through.

An hour later, the debrief completed, Rich looked up. 'Thanks very much, Sarah. Excellent job.'

'No probs. Give us a shout anytime. If I'm not working I'll come along.'

It was 11 p.m. when I wandered back across the A-frame and into the bar for a quick nightcap, to be told that Iraq had just invaded Kuwait. There was a handful of admin staff, as well as Frank, Stephen, Paul and Greg, who'd become inseparable from a stray Alsatian he'd befriended. 'Back, are we?' Stephen sniggered. 'Finished our tour of duty with the SAS, have we?' The rumour had got around, and the fact that I'd been out with the Troop had left the sexist Det blokes a bit miffed. 'Must have been scraping the barrel if they need you to work with them,' he added.

I gave him an I-can't-be-bothered-with-your-pathetic-remarks look. 'Ooh, harsh words. Has your boyfriend dumped you?'

He made a face and mumbled into his pint as I pushed past him.

'Move out of the way, luvvy. This woman needs a drink,' I said merrily.

Stephen's attitude was symptomatic of the Det geeks' close proximity to the Troop. Having a woman there with them did horrible things to their macho image. Lots of Det guys go for SAS selection after their tour, more from South than any other Det. Living in close confines with the Regiment leads them to view it as the ultimate occupation. While I was across the water four ex-South Det blokes went for selection. Only one failed, and that was due to injury. For a woman to enter their little pack and be able to hold her own made them feel less than manly.

The following morning I was doing a little domestic car-maintenance, wiping off the grime of ages and excavating Jed's six-month-old toffee wrappers while chatting to Derek, South Det's mechanic. He was a quiet man, always shrouded in grease, and he wasn't the world's best conversationalist, probably because he was the hardest-working bloke in the A-frame. Due to the number of handbrake turns, Derek was constantly changing tyres and clutches. You don't want a blow-out on a motorway, or to overheat in the middle of a bad-arse estate because the radiator hasn't been flushed through effectively, or has a hole in it.

I was reaching the bottom of the archaeological dig that was Jed's sweetie graveyard when I saw Jock, from the Troop, rushing in from the helipad. He was wearing civvies under his DPM jacket and carrying a Hasselblad camera.

'Hey, big nose, how's it going?' I shouted. 'Where've you been?'

He ran over. 'We've just had an op come in that we're going to start tomorrow, so I've got mega recces and plans to sort out.' When you're given a job there's always tons of recces and briefings to sort out from scratch. There may be other agencies to detail off, options to decide upon, and masses of procedural planning. Jock charged off like a headless chicken to sort it all out. Later I managed to pull him aside for a quick rundown. He told me that Op Samurai would involve the Troop, HMSU (Headquarters Mobile Support Unit, part of TCG), E4A and possibly South Det.

'The info we've got from the SB boys is that some baddies are gonna be up to no good in the area of a barn adjacent to Lislasie Road, Loughgall.' They'd also had a tip that Dessie Grew, an experienced and committed Republican paramilitary and a member of the IRA since the early 1970s, wanted to show an INLA splinter group how to carry out an assassination in style. This followed their disastrous attempt in April to hit a seventy-eight-year-old ex-UDR man who was also a member of the Orange Order. The Troop had been tasked to babysit the old man, who we suspected could be a target. Two terrorists had pulled up in front of his house and started firing at him through the windows. The Troop, positioned in the house and outside in the bushes, had had no option but to try to slot the aggressors. One was killed, the other arrested.

Dessie Grew, who was also thought to have been involved with the Provisional IRA's arch Republican rival, the smaller, less disciplined but equally fanatical INLA, had been boasting that he would have been a more effective assassin. Grew was a low-life scumbag, known amongst his fellow Republicans as 'the widow-maker'. He would strut arrogantly around his home town of Loughgall, a charming, almost entirely Protestant village which, but for the Troubles, would undoubtedly feature on tourist itineraries for its elegant Georgian houses. It had been dubbed 'the IRA graveyard' by security forces after the Provos lost eight gunmen and bombers there in an SAS operation three years before.

There was good reason to believe that Grew had been involved in at least sixteen killings, including the murder of RAF Corporal Mick Islania and his six-month-old daughter in Germany the year before. His ASU was made up of corrupted fresh blood – 'lilywhites' in IRA parlance – whom he had trained up to carry out a murder campaign on the Continent. The gang had been scouting for victims in Holland when they spotted a British-registered Citroën. Believing that its occupants were British servicemen, they gunned them down. In fact, they were Stephen Melrose and Nick Spanos, two twenty-four-year-old Australian lawyers based in London who were visiting Holland as tourists. Grew's brother Seamus had been slotted by the RUC in one of the so-called 'shoot-to-kill' incidents in 1982. In revenge, Dessie had promised to 'drench' Armagh in police blood. Another brother, Aidan, was pushing a fourteen-year stretch in the Maze. If there was any scumbag we would have liked to see boxed and despatched, it was Dessie Grew.

Jock wound up by asking when I'd be back from leave. He was spotting me for doing a drop-off.

'After the weekend. If you can hang on till Monday, I'll come and give you a hand.' I hadn't got much on, so I was fired up by the prospect of getting involved on a Troop operation.

Next day I went on leave. Luke met me at Heathrow. It was great to see him. He drove me back to his pad, and the next morning we headed up to Lancashire. Melissa was getting engaged to Dave, her boyfriend of two years, who she'd met in the NAAFI. By now I'd decided that he was all right, although we'd got off to a rough start. I'd given him a hard time because he was unemployed, had no money and no home. I was only protecting Melissa, and suggested to Dave that he'd better come up with some solutions before he met our Mam. Things had got a bit out of control and I'd ended up holding him by the neck in a vice-like grip.

When he did eventually meet our Mam he was terrified of her, and he also reckoned I was a real ogre. But we'd gradually come around to the idea of each other. At the engagement party Melissa and I danced the night away, while Luke was left chatting to Katherine. All Melissa's friends were tittering and asking if Luke was her dad. I told him later that I loved him just the way he was. I've never been one for young whippersnappers!

On Sunday morning we drove back to Hereford, and on Monday Luke drove me to Heathrow and I flew back to the compound. Back to the job. Jed met me at Aldergrove and gave me a rundown on recent Det activities. Op Samurai was still happening. South Det were doing drop-offs; he'd done one the previous evening. He told me that East Det had had a weapons find, locating a big arms cache and arresting four key players.

'North Det are still boring bastards. The boys next door are still watching reruns of *The Untouchables* to try and perfect the accent and the swagger. I've had no one to give a hard time, so I'm glad you're back,' said Jed, giving me a slap on the back. 'Oh yes, and the car needs another clean-out. I spilled my curry the other night. I had to drive, do surveillance and scoff a vindaloo all by myself. Where are you when I need you, you old trout?'

I always approached my basha cautiously when I got back from leave. Once, when Al was away at his family's cottage in Wales, the lads reckoned they'd make his basha a touch more homely. He'd arrived back to find a sheep munching on a 'lawn' of mustard and cress, in place of his cherished furniture. But I was lucky this time.

After sorting out my gear, I met up with Jock, who gave me more of a brief about Op Samurai and told me I was down to do a drop-off the following evening. Jock was looking distinctly haggard, having had very little sleep in the past few days. He shook his head wearily. Although it was 3 p.m., he'd only just got up. He'd been out all night and was now preparing to head back out again.

He gave me a run-through. At last light the Det driver would drop off the OP team of five Troop members near the barn in Loughgall. They would walk a pre-planned route into the OP area, passing quietly along the edge of fields, past bushes and hedges. Halfway to their OP position they would meet up with the daytime OP, which consisted of one Troop guy, who would join them, and an HMSU bloke, who would make his way back to the pick-up point. The six Troop blokes would move off to their positions in the area of the barn, ready to react to any activity. The source had stated that the hit would take place at night, hence the extra activity after sundown. The Troop had mobile intercept vehicles laying up in the area should the terrorists decide to scarper, and E4A were on hand to offer surveillance. A second Troop team was on standby one and a half kilometres away protecting the old ex-UDR man, just in case he was to be the target again. There were also a number of Op Sinai guys in the area from the SAS Special Projects team. On big jobs Op Sinai personnel are called in from Hereford to boost numbers. You can't be too careful.

At five each morning the Troop team would pull off. On the way out they'd meet up with the HMSU bloke, and one of the Troop would stay with him for the daytime OP. Five weary men would walk out to the pick-up which would take them back to the A-frame. This had been the routine for the past four days. Jock glanced at his watch, and went off to prepare his kit.

The next afternoon saw me checking over and cleaning the drop-off vehicle, in this case an innocuous-looking white Transit van. I pushed my duvet jacket onto the passenger seat along with some packets of crisps and some big fat sweeties to see me through the night. Before heading off I'd prepare a couple of flasks of sugary coffee, some dry biscuits and a packet of moist babywipes. I felt like our Mam, coping with the tender needs of all these boys! When they lifted off at 5 a.m. they'd be gagging. It was the least I could do for them after they'd been stuck in a bush for ten hours.

At 1800 hours I went into the Troop ops room for a fifteen-minute mini-brief. This was important. Despite the major brief at the beginning of the job, we all needed to be refreshed about the plan and kept up to speed on any additional info. As well as the standard drop-off procedure we ran through several other options, just in case. I also needed to know who else was on the job, so there would be no surprises. Every possible scenario had to be examined. Across the water carelessness costs lives.

After the brief we headed down to the vehicle. There was lots of activity going on. Jock, Jake, Big Marty, Rich and Al were tooled up with G3s and spare magazines. Their faces, hands and necks were covered in dirty brown cam (camouflage) cream. Wearing DPM jackets and trousers and black boots they looked lethally efficient. They jumped into the back of the van and slammed the door. I turned on the ignition, did a 180, and headed out of the A-frame as all the other vehicles were revving up and preparing to leave.

It was a blustery, dark night, threatening rain. I turned right out of the compound and headed south to blue nine. My monster maps were stashed in the well of the passenger seat. Everyone was quietly focused and contemplative as I drove south along main roads, then turned south-west along a maze of country roads and narrow tracks. The lads were sitting silently on the floor. They weren't belted in, so I drove carefully and safely. You want to make the ride as smooth as possible for them, but at the same time you don't want to attract any attention through over-caution. I continually gave my location over the net, and I could hear other people coming up with their positions. The guys in the daytime position had to keep eyes-on until the lads were in, but they would know we were on our way.

When you're nearing a target to do a drop-off you have a sequence of countdown markers, distinguishing features such as an old oak tree or a bridge which allow you to count down – three . . . two . . . one – as you approach them. This gives the ops room your precise location relative to the drop-off position. As I approached the first marker, a telephone box, I could hear the blokes in the back doing their last-minute organisation and positioning themselves ready to exit the vehicle.

'Alpha Sierra, at three towards two,' I said.

'Alpha roger,' came the Troop ops room. The lads in the daytime OP also acknowledged our proximity.

I passed the elm tree, then my last marker, a five-bar gate on my right-hand side. The drop-off. I flicked the cut-off switch to kill the brake light. As I slowed down, the guys already had the sliding side door open. The second we were stationary they exited swiftly and dived into cover. The last man out silently slid the door shut before vanishing into the bushes. I eased away gently.

'Alpha Sierra, drop-off complete.'

It was a tension-soaked moment. There was always the risk of an ambush, and as I pulled away, completely alone, it was with quiet, nervous excitement. This became a shiver of relief as I picked up speed, heading for the LUP three hundred metres away, where I went static. Two HMSU guys were already stationed there. As drop-off driver it was my task to stay in the vicinity. If the boys needed out, I'd provide the means. While they were on the ground, so was I.

Then I settled down to a long night, munching my way through packets of crisps, slurping coffee, filing my nails, picking my nose. The usual stuff. I was on my period, so I had to keep nipping into the bushes to change my Tampax, sticking them in a plastic bag to take away. I had to move to a different bush after I spotted the HMSU watching me, dirty bastards. At 2100 hours I joined them in their car. They were good blokes, swapping war stories and tales of bombings. The hours ticked by. It was looking pretty much the same as the previous five nights, i.e. nothing doing.

Then, at 2354 hours, the net crackled into life with a whispered 'Standby' from Jock. My adrenaline started surging. I dashed back to my van, locked the doors and wound down the driver's window. After nearly five hours of radio checks we faced the prospect of some activity. I was alert and ready to do a pick-up.

Three minutes later, word came over the net: 'Standby for contact,' said Jock, a touch of dry-throatedness in his voice.

Suddenly the inky black of the evening was shattered by the sound of heavy fire being laid down four hundred metres to my left. The noise of the 7.62 mm rounds was stunning in the quiet of the Armagh night. If you've only ever heard gunfire on TV and in films, the real thing is a damn sight louder and more frightening.

The firing stopped, and Jock came up on the net, panting out a quick sit-rep. 'Alpha Delta One, two armed and masked gunmen dead. Three unknowns apprehended. My call-sign no casualties.'

After the area had been made secure and Jock had handed over to the HMSU, I was called in for the PU (pick-up). Now there was no need to be covert: the place was filled with police, SAS and dead terrorists. I pulled up and the lads jumped in.

'All right, lassie?' Jock asked.

'I'm fine. Here, have some coffee.'

I was glad Jock was OK. I wouldn't actually have said so, as it would have sounded a bit naff, but we had an implicit under-standing.

I drove to the barracks in Armagh town, where the lads would RV with the flying lawyer and hand over their weapons, ammo and magazines to forensics. After a short debrief we headed back to the compound. I screamed to a halt in the A-frame. The lads jumped out and went straight to the bar. It was the usual routine; everyone who could make it turned up to offer congratulations.

It was 2 a.m., but the chefs had really surpassed themselves. There were loads of thick sandwiches, pies, pasties, chicken drum-sticks, even a big tureen of onion soup. The lads were looking tired, haggard and very warlike – most of them had used their sweat to rub off the cam cream. The beer was free, as the other Dets had put money behind the bar. I fished out a six-pack of Tennants, tearing one off and handing it to Jock, patting him on the arm as he was mobbed by the head sheds. It was a good half-hour be-fore the unofficial debrief was over and I was finally able to grab hold of him and get the details. He was probably sick of talking by this stage, but he ran through the events of the evening with me.

At 11.54 p.m., nearly four hours after the drop-off, Jock had seen movement to his front. On looking through his night-sight he saw two men opening the door of the barn and going inside. It was the first time on the OP that any targets had been spotted. Jock had given the 'Standby.'

Another man came down the track and into the barn. Shortly

afterwards the original two men appeared at the door, both carrying AK47s. The third man re-emerged, walked back up the track and out of sight. The two armed men moved in Jock's direction, weapons at the ready. One of them was wearing a balaclava.

Jock was in an unenviable position, squatting in his OP with five team-members, with two armed players pointing rifles at him just fifteen metres away. 'I gave standby for contact and then initiated contact by shooting the nearest one,' he said without ceremony. 'He went down and I turned on the other one. By this time four of us were firing, and I watched the second man fall. I called for a ceasefire and we moved forward to clear the barn. Inside, we found a white Vauxhall Astra containing two walkie-talkies, some firelighters and, on the front passenger seat, another AK47. This obviously belonged to the guy walking up the track.'

By now one of the mobile intercept drivers had arrived. Jock tasked him to look for the runner in the nearest outbuilding. The Troop moved to the house and apprehended three suspects. The SOCO (scene of crime officer) carried out a forensic search and took away evidence including a video. Outside the house he'd found a car containing fresh clothes and a bottle of whiskey. 'The clean get-away car,' said Jock. These items and the three apprehended players were handed over to the RUC. The video showed all five terrorists having a slap-up meal and in high spirits just hours before they were planning to carry out their kill.

The two men who had been killed were Dessie Grew and Martin McCaughey, who had once been a Sinn Fein councillor. Although we don't celebrate the death of players – in this case we were just thankful that our boys had survived – to say that I didn't mourn Grew's passing would be the world's biggest understatement. McCaughey, who was said by the police to be 'involved in serious terrorist activity in County Tyrone and County Armagh', was the guy who'd shot at Jack through the sunroof of the XR3i, and lost part of his ear in the firefight that followed. Needless to say, Jack had a few extra beers that night. We were also pleased because, following the shootings, the Home Secretary, David Waddington, announced plans to redouble the all-out offensive against the IRA.

A month before, Mrs Thatcher had promised tougher action and more anti-terror squads. It looked as if things were coming to a head.

We later heard that Dessie Grew's funeral cortège in Knocka-coney was attended by hundreds of Republican supporters. His seven sisters had carried his body into the church for the funeral before a paramilitary burial – complete with Provisional IRA firing party – at St Patrick's cemetery in Armagh alongside his brother Seamus. I suppose it's a mark of the sick morality of terrorist organisations like the Provisional IRA that a murderous, psychopathic gangster like Grew can be described as 'a patriot and a fine, upstanding Irish citizen', as Sinn Fein leader Gerry Adams called him. Dessie slaughtered innocent people. If Mr Adams thinks that is 'decent', he's off his head.

Graves are well-tended in Northern Ireland: being dead is a really big deal across the water. A Nazi spy sent over in the Second World War said of the IRA: 'They know how to die for Ireland; of how to fight for it, they have no idea whatsoever.'

Lately Jed and I had been taking it in turns to drive and do surveillance – but I wanted more. Because of the rule barring women from driving solo, I'd never been one up on a surveillance serial. This was a source of some irritation, and I was determined to show the detractors that it made no difference whether I was driving two up or one up.

When Paul, the ops officer, was on his annual leave, Niall, a more progressive thinker, stood in for him. A routine surveillance job cropped up, and as usual I was down for heli duty. Jed was to be part of the four-car team, and I asked Niall if Jed and I could swap. He agreed – he could see no reason for the rule in the first place.

For four tense hours that afternoon I was one up in Dungannon keeping tabs on the players while Jed took over from me in the heli. Everything went like clockwork, but although I really enjoyed it, I didn't see it as a big deal. I couldn't understand why I shouldn't be driving one up in the first place. Over the next fortnight I went one up as much as possible. None of the lads in the A-frame raised an eyebrow. By now they were fully aware of how competent I was, and viewed me as their professional equal. The only person who wasn't happy about the new arrangement was Jed – freezing his nadgers off and starving in the heli. When Paul returned from leave, Niall and a couple of the other experienced operators tried to make him see the light. He wavered a bit, and for the rest of my tour he sometimes let me drive one up. It felt like a small victory for womankind.

One evening at 11 p.m., four weeks after Grew's funeral, I sauntered out of the range pleased with myself because I'd done my quickest ever draw and first shot, within 0.78 seconds. Thousands of repetitions of a particular action ensure that your motor responses are sharpened. This 'muscle-memory' also applies to other activities, such as typing or playing the piano. I was urgently in need of a brew and some toast, to wash down the lead that gets up your nose and stuck in your throat on the range. As I bimbled across the A-frame one of the Troop Cavaliers executed a nifty handbrake turn, leaving black tyremarks on the concrete. We were always getting bollocked for wheel-spinning, but on this occasion no one shouted at the driver, Rich, to make a voluntary contribution. He spilled out of the car along with the Troop team leader Big Marty, Will and Trev. They looked well pleased with themselves.

'Join us in the bar in a few minutes, Sarah. We've had a success!' shouted Rich.

Minutes later I was grabbing my usual can of Tennants and awaiting Marty's flamboyant retelling of the evening's events. The Troop had been briefed that afternoon and teamed up with North Det to do a job against INLA. The intelligence was that INLA were planning to slot a UDR man who lived by Victoria Bridge, Belfast. They planned to drive past his cottage and open fire with a monumental nine rounds from a Second World War M3 sub-machine gun, also known as a 'grease gun' because it's very nasty and rough-looking.

The Troop had deployed into the target house, with cut-offs (a secondary line of defence) outside. North Det were carrying out surveillance, and they'd picked up two terrorist vehicles approaching the target. When they arrived at the UDR man's house the front vehicle pulled off. The rear one, which had the shooter in it, opened fire, and the Troop leaped into action, pumping round after round into the gun car, which zigzagged across the road and crashed into a tree. All the occupants did a runner except one, who was shot in the head by Trev. He was Alex Patterson, a convicted armed robber and father of four from Strabane, and he died before he knew what had hit him.

It was later alleged in the press that Patterson was an SB tout. If that was the case, what was he doing in the rear car, containing the shooter? He should have let the terrorists get on with the business and buggered off. Hadn't he realised that when the INLA men opened fire he'd be at risk?

These things happen, but you can't get emotionally involved: most informers are terrorists who have turned tout because they're greedy for money or want to evade a prison sentence. They're happy to live a double life, playing both sides off against each other. But despite their two-faced personalities they're hard to get hold of, and it seems a waste when one of them dies.

As the evening wore on the beer was flowing freely, as was the vodka and Coke, the wine and the Southern Comfort. I wobbled off to the toilet, almost crashing into the chimney-breast, which was covered with tell-tale chalk marks and scrawled names. I didn't notice the stench of stale urine because of the stink of drink and fags. When I returned, Beast had just beaten his long-standing record of pissing seven and a half feet up the wall. The drunkest lads were busily trying to snatch his record away from him. Trev had his willy in his hand and was staggering backwards in a vain attempt to direct it at the ceiling. He could barely coax a drop out, let alone reach the target.

I peered over his shoulder. 'Is that it, Trev? Where's the rest of it then?' I laughed.

Beast was looking on from the sidelines, making sure no one

beat his record. He turned to me. 'Well, go on then, Trouty. See if you can do any better.'

The gauntlet had been thrown down. Suddenly there was silence. Everyone wanted to see how I'd respond. I was no longer being tested, I was one of the lads, so it was even more imperative that I didn't back down. I was wearing one of my knee-length numbers, which made things a bit tricky, but I didn't let it put me off.

I assumed my best British-bomber accent: 'Stand by, I'm coming through,' and selected a dry patch on the floor. I planted my palms in the middle of it and did a handstand, trying to retain as much dignity as is possible when you're upside down, your skirt over your head, with a lot of drunken SAS men looking on to see if you can beat the Beast mark. Fortunately the handstand was enough for them. I certainly wasn't going to actually wee. But my feeble effort went down very well indeed, and I got a nice bit of cheering and backslapping when I eventually planted my feet back on terra firma.

EIGHT

ON PERMANENT STANDBY

IN DECEMBER 1990 WE were preparing to receive the new intake. The Camp Three grapevine had told us that five female Ruperts had passed the course: four army, one RAF. This was a high female pass-rate, and was apparently motivated by political reasons. No girls had been getting through, and with only three females in the province – two of whom, including me, were due to leave in the next six months – something had to be done.

Charlotte and Helen, both army, were heading to South. I wasn't against having some female company, so long as they weren't going to try to swap make-up tips and clothes. I wouldn't have had anything to say to a girly girl.

Of course the lads were busy going through their 'We don't need old slappers here' routine. I felt for these girls – they were up for a tough time. Forget the fact that anyone who passed that course was worthy of a place in any Det; not only were they female, they were officers, and as such faced a double dose of discrimination. I reckoned I'd gone some way in shifting the boys' attitudes towards women, but I could already hear them gobbing off in the cookhouse, the bars and the cars that they'd dipped out again.

'Two Rupert tarts,' huffed Jack into his beer. It wasn't said nastily, just matter-of-factly. But remarks like that were always cropping up in my presence, and I was aware that my reaction was being assessed. The overt sexism didn't bother me – I found most of it quite funny. It was the closet sexists I had to watch out for, and Dippy was one. He was forever pretending to be my mate, but when he smiled, his eyes didn't. There was no one incident I could nail him on. It was just a feeling. He used to speak to me as if I was a child, a patronising note creeping into his voice. And he did it in such a way that no one else would have been aware of it. I had no doubt that he was with Paul in the sexist closet.

Things died down a bit until evening scoff a week before the new ops were due to arrive. I was eating a lasagne in the company of Shane, Greg, Frank, Adrian and Chris, the new DSM. There were two main topics of conversation: the new Prime Minister, John Major, and his likely stance on Northern Ireland; and the progress of the new ops. Jed walked in and overheard us.

'I'll have 'em,' he swaggered. 'They can come in the car with me. One of them can be massaging my head, the other can do the map-reading, and if I'm a really good boy, I might even get a blow-job.'

I fixed him with a wicked look. 'Don't flatter yourself, big boy. You're just lucky to have me, because I've got a soft spot for puppy-dog eyes.'

Kurt leaned across me and hissed at Jed: 'You're welcome to 'em, mate. I'm not having no tart in the car with me.' This gave me the perfect opportunity to elbow him in the jaw.

These comments weren't jokes, but neither were they meant seriously. They were driven by testosterone, male bravado just fulfilling expectations – like a comedian telling a racist joke in Brixton. They knew it would look really weird if they hadn't given the new ops a slagging. The biggest insult for these lads would be being considered a 'new man'.

The new ops arrived one cold winter's day just before Christmas. Charlotte had the Rupert-issue blonde bob and the accent to accompany it. Helen was taller, with a mop of unruly black hair and the same plummy accent. First impressions were good. They both seemed keen to learn, switched on and not wimpish. Charlotte moved into the other half of my double Portakabin – which automatically earned it the nickname 'The Chicken Ranch – The Biggest Whorehouse in the West' – while Helen took up residence in a basha near the rest of the lads. I decided to take them under my wing a bit; I didn't want them to face the gruelling time I'd undergone the year before, when I'd wished there was someone in

South Det to speak up for me. A bonus was Donald, the third new arrival and an Op Spice lad. One of the world's nicest men, he had a big Garfield grin and was a real darling, with no obvious hang-ups.

During the pre-Christmas incarceration, Helen and Charlotte navigated the minefields of sexist remarks with cautious efficiency. They'd been forewarned and had me on their side, speaking up for them as innuendoes were lobbed like grenades around the cookhouse and bar. Being Ruperts put the girls at an unfair disadvantage: they didn't feel able to swear back. I even dropped my customary Rupert jokes in a display of solidarity.

Christmas 1990 was a non-event. I was forward mounted at Dungannon, and one by one we were going down with the usual bubonic plague because of the horrendous conditions. New Year saw me back in Hereford with Luke. One lunchtime we went out drinking and he suddenly flipped when I mentioned that a couple of the Troop boys and I had been windsurfing on Lough Neagh. His eyes filling with venom, he publicly did his nut at me. I refused to be drawn into his rant, which had him practically foaming at the mouth. He stormed off, and I decided to sit in the pub all day to let him calm down. At midnight I got a taxi home, hoping we'd be able to talk it over. A single table-light was on, and Luke was sitting solemnly in an armchair.

'Where've you been?' he demanded aggressively.

'I thought we needed time apart so you could cool down a bit.'

He refused to talk, and sat silently festering in his anger. I'd never seen him like this, and it scared me. It reminded me of what our Mam had gone through. I looked at Luke in disbelief. I thought this man loved me, yet he could suddenly flip like this. Two days later I went back to the Det, feeling distant and uncertain.

Back across the water, the ops officer briefed us on a new surveillance job called Op Travallion. Background info came courtesy of Aidan spook. The CTR team had located a weapons hide in the cellar of a pub in a town in South Armagh. There was a shedful of HME, yards of ammo and a 5.56 calibre M60, which the technical bods had bugged. Bugs are always growing more sophisticated, but fitting them is still a long, laborious task. At every stage of the operation a sequence of infra-red photographs of the hide was taken so the team could check that nothing looked as if it had been disturbed.

I would have loved to have had a place in a CTR team involved in this work, but being female I was confined to either acting as cover or doing the drop-off. Apparently boobies get in the way of the camera lens. So I sat in the car twiddling my thumbs while the boys went in and used the skills we'd all learned.

Op Travallion turned into one of our longer, semi-permanent surveillance ops. For the four months that it ran there was a team on constant standby in Bessbrook Mill, near Newry. As usual the job consisted of sitting it out and waiting for the beep box to go off, indicating that the weapons were on the move. At least this time conditions were a bit better at the Mill. There were just five of us at a time, living in semi-decent rooms with almost acceptable washroom facilities. But it was as frigging boring as ever – hence the need for two teams. We changed over every four or five days, which stopped us from degenerating too badly, and kept the boredom levels down.

16 January was a red-letter day, as we crowded around Kurt's tiny TV to watch the latest on Operation 'Desert Storm'. Baghdad had been blitzed by bombs and missiles the night before, and we watched news footage of Scuds hurtling across the sky. I knew some of my mates from the Troop would end up out there, but I couldn't muster any fear on their behalf. That's just the job, and the reason why they signed up.

On days that we were stood down in the compound we'd be part of other ongoing ops, but Op Travallion always took precedence. If the South Armagh job kicked off, everyone was on standby. Over the next few months the kit in the hide moved a couple of times. The first time it was shifted to one of the town's bad-arse estates and stashed in a wash house. Of course we were aware who the active players were at this point, but if ops were always wound up at an early stage, you'd never build up a bigger picture. There was a temporary distraction on 7 February when the IRA launched a mortar attack on 10 Downing Street, shattering windows a few metres from where the Cabinet was meeting in full session.

A few weeks later the kit shifted from the wash house to a nearby backyard, where it was stuffed inside a shed. Fortunately the next day, Saturday, was changeover day, and I drove Jed back to the compound. With our normal stupid sense of humour, he was pretending to be a straightfaced driving instructor. As I reached 110 miles an hour he pretended to have a coronary and collapsed slobbering in his seat. Then he changed tack, wound down his window and started shouting for help. 'I'm being kidnapped by a female fishmonger!' he screamed as he rattled the door in mock desperation. A hundred metres from the camp was a white marker post, and we'd always see how fast we could go as we passed it, while still managing to hang a left into the camp. My personal best was 105 miles an hour, but 110 was the target to beat. Two weeks later Jed took it at 120. We had to drive carefully back to the compound after that one, as there was no rubber left on the tyres.

Once inside, the emphasis was on stepping into your trapping kit and getting downtown. But first I warily phoned Luke and our Mam for the first time in a week. They were both fine. Luke had calmed down, and said he was missing me like hell, and was aching for me to be by his side. At 7.30 p.m. I was in my basha and popping the kettle on when the buzz box above my bed went off and its red light flashed on.

It was Stephen, on urgent business. 'Are you coming out tonight, you old trout?'

'I'm not too bothered. Where you going?'

'The Rooftops,' he replied, referring to a nightclub near Belfast. Four bars and two dance-floors were spread over two levels; downstairs was chart-hit territory, upstairs was more cheesy-listening.

'We're celebrating Kuwait's liberation by the Allies,' he said. This was excellent news after six months and twenty-five days of occupation by Iraqi forces. So much was going on in the world: the Berlin Wall had come down, Nelson Mandela had been freed, and now we'd triumphed in the Gulf. It seemed that for once some wrongs were being put right, and the news had something good to say, rather than the usual diet of constant death and destruction.

'Brills. Who else is going?'

'Kurt, Jed, a couple of the Troop lads, and I've even managed to drag Frank out.'

I laughed. 'No, I'm not coming. You'll all trap and leave me sitting alone like a spare part!'

'You know we only do that to make you jealous 'cos you won't snog us!'

'Oh, all right, then. But only if you put your good-looking head on. I'm not looking at that spotty one all night.'

Stephen laughed. 'Right, see you in an hour after you've been down to stores to sign your legs out. Oh, and don't get those fat stumpy ones you got last week!'

Things had changed a lot in the past eleven months. Even the young lads – Stephen, Kurt and Jack – had grudgingly accepted me as an equal. I'd also reappraised them. They were the blokes who'd got South Det its misogynistic reputation, and at first I'd viewed them as pathetic, immature sexists. But they'd soon realised that I could outdrink, outshoot and outwit them, and I saw that if you didn't let them get to you, they weren't so bad. They were just good, keen operators, always ready for a laugh. The key was to give an equally cheeky rejoinder to their remarks, or to brush them aside with lofty disdain as being too irrelevant to acknowledge.

A metamorphosis occurred when I went out. I reached into my wardrobe for my little black Top Shop dress, sheer black stockings and three-inch heels. On went loads of make-up and I scrunch-dried my hair before backcombing it and blasting it with hairspray. Into my River Island handbag I popped my Browning Hi-Power. All the best-looking operators were carrying a 9mm that season; but it meant we couldn't get shitfaced. If you're tooled up you always stay sober. At 8.45 p.m. we met up by the ops block. As the lads were standing there in their bulging chinos, the comment 'Is that a gun in your pocket, or are you just pleased to see me?' was well overdue. On nights out the lads would stash their Brownings down their underpants. They tended to wear brown brogues, crisp shirts and pints of aftershave. They smelt like a whore's handbag.

Eight of us, including three Troop guys, got a drop-off at The Rooftops. Music spilled out onto the street, where a queue waited impatiently. Two bouncers were conducting handbag searches on the girls and frisking the blokes. I sneaked my way through the crush and evaded their amateur efforts. We split up so that we wouldn't look like the Gestapo arriving and headed towards the bar at the far side of the club. Kurt bought the first round as the lads scanned the dance-floor for talent. Big Marty popped upstairs with two other Troop lads, Phil and Beast. Moments later he reappeared.

'You want to be upstairs, Sarah,' he said. 'No use scanning around here. You want to be where the real talent is. We've just seen an old boy about five foot two doing a crack Elvis impression.'

I sucked on my shandy. 'What sort of music are they playing up there?'

'You know, all that old crap you like.'

I threw down the dregs. 'You coming with me, then?'

'Aye. But remember, don't ask me to dance!'

None of the lads would have dared to do something as unmacho as dancing before they'd had at least six pints of Ireland's finest. And I was hardly ever asked to dance by civvy men: the presence of seven burly guys must have been a bit offputting. Instead, on nights out like this I always resorted to asking men who caught my eye. At least that way I had a chance to swing my Browning in time to the beat of 'A Little Time' by the Beautiful South, 'Nothing Compares 2 U' by Sinead O'Connor and 'Itsy Bitsy Teeny Weeny Yellow Polkadot Bikini' by Jimmy Mallet. Just after 1 a.m. we got a pick-up and headed for some big fat scoff in Belfast centre. Belfast at night has the buzzy atmosphere of London's West End. Bright lights, neon signs, and crowds of young people milling around in their nightclub finery. I'd always found Belfast to be a glitzy, upwardly mobile city rather than the downcast, depressed place you usually see on the TV news. Despite – or perhaps because of – the paramilitary activity, there's much less street violence and petty crime than in other cities.

One slack day we headed for the Ballykinler shooting range about an hour's drive away. We planned to do fire and manoeuvre, advance-to-contact, retreat-from-contact, embussing and debussing drills using our longs (rifles) and shorts (pistols).

Jed and I would have driven down together, but the car was having a clutch-and-tyre change due to one too many handbrake turns in the compound. So I jumped into James's grey Cavalier GLS and we headed south, driving too fast as usual, in macho fashion. We were at the front of the team and passing through Dromore in County Down as we took a blind bend on the wrong side of the road at about eighty-five miles an hour. Suddenly it appeared. I glimpsed the shiny cab of a vast tanker with a blue cylindrical trailer powering towards us. Instinctively, I made myself into the tiniest ball possible and covered my head with my arms as I anticipated the impact, just nanoseconds away. Time slowed down, and I was aware of the tension in every sinew of my body. James was trying to swing the car back over to the left-hand side of the road, but we didn't make it in time. There was a massive impact. The sound of ripping metal, breaking glass, screeching tyres, and the smell of burning rubber overpowered my senses. I felt the car being propelled through the air, then the impact.

My hands were still clamped over my head when we landed. Cautiously I sat upright, so winded that I couldn't force out any words. I appeared to be intact. I reached out my hand in slow time to touch James, who was sprawled across the steering wheel. I tried to ask him if he was OK, but my words were no more than a whisper. Completely dazed, he could only grunt in response. My first reaction was to get onto the net and tell the team we'd just had an RTA. Nothing doing. I no longer had an earpiece, and the comms had been ripped out of the car by the force of the impact. I was unable to open my door, which had caved in like a cardboard box. Nor could I unhook my seatbelt. My hands weren't working properly and there was no sensation or strength in my arms.

In less than a minute we were surrounded by distressed civvies peering into the wreckage with characteristic Ulster care and concern. They asked if we were all right, so I gave a thumbs-up, which was all I could manage. Someone unfastened James's seatbelt. His door had been ripped òff in the impact. I knew that our first priority was to get him out and assess the extent of his injuries. Two men prepared to ease him out of the vehicle, and as they pulled him out his pistol fell onto the grass verge. I couldn't fucking believe it. My body tensed and blood rushed to my face. This wasn't a Republican area, so the threat wasn't too great, but you couldn't be too cautious. It was a tense moment. Our English accents must have made it obvious to the locals that we were army, but fortunately they either didn't see the Browning or chose to ignore it.

I edged across the seat and wriggled out, then shoved James's gun down my jeans. No one appeared to have noticed. James was being laid out on the ground, and all attention was on him. His face and chest were covered in blood from where he'd split his mouth and nose on the steering wheel, and he was mumbling incoherently. Thank God he'd been wearing a seatbelt.

I leaned down. 'James? James? Are you all right? It's Sarah.'

Groaning, he pointed to his right hip. 'My back, my back.'

I quickly examined him. At least he was conscious and breathing, and his injuries appeared to be superficial. A nurse who had been driving past rushed forward to tend to him, but now I had to take control. The other guys in the team would be stuck in the traffic jam caused by the accident, but wouldn't know what was happening. I was on my own. I needed to sort out the kit on the back seat and conceal it from the gathering crowd. I turned around slowly, every muscle in my body aching, and took in the car's wreckage. Where the back seat should have been, all I could see was the exhaust box and the grass underneath. There was no boot, so I didn't bother looking inside that. When the tanker had struck our rear driver's side the car had unpeeled like a tin of sardines. We'd ended up fifty metres from the site of the impact, and the tanker had come to a halt a hundred metres further down the road. Fortunately the driver was fine.

Traffic was building up in both directions, and I saw with a sense of creeping horror that all our kit was strewn over the road. Seconds later Adrian – who'd been driving the first car in the team behind us – screamed to a halt and ran up to us. I gave him a quick report on James's condition, and stayed with him while Adrian ran back down the road to tell the rest of the team, and to try and reclaim the kit. Because I tended to be overzealous on my range days there was quite a lot to track down: two thousand rounds of 9mm, a thousand rounds of 5.56mm, six hundred rounds of 7.62, two G3s, an HK53, two MP5Ks, four Brownings, one Walther PPK, twenty spare mags of varying sizes, and the video kit from the boot. It was all lying somewhere out on the tarmac.

Up until now I hadn't really thought about myself, but once Adrian had taken charge I felt myself becoming nauseous, and realised I was going down with a bit of shock. I decided my best course of action was to sit with James until the ambulance arrived, leaving the other boys to find all our bits and pieces. As I sat talking to him and reassuring him, I looked across the verge and into the bushes. My eyes focused on a metal night-viewing aid for the G3 which had been cleanly split in half.

Everything went smoothly from then on. The RUC arrived, and one officer said it was the worst non-fatal road accident he'd ever seen. Fortunately the lads were able to find most of the kit – although it took them half an hour to track down one of the G3s in a field two hundred metres away. They found the car's door and door-armour in the bushes, thirty metres apart.

The ambulance rushed James and me to Royal Victoria Hospital in Belfast. I had emerged remarkably unscathed, with just one small cut on my right thumb. But poor old James had smashed his face in, broken a few ribs and done severe, possibly irreparable damage to his right hip, which was shattered and horrendously bruised. He was laid up for several months and out of regular duties for eighteen. It turned out that the tanker driver was the brother of a UVF member who'd recently topped a Provisional IRA volunteer.

After a nice nurse had stuck a plaster on my thumb, I got a lift back to the compound. Chris, the new DSM who'd taken over from Bert, ordered me to my bed for rest. Every time I tried to fall asleep I saw bloody images of what might have been. Six fretful hours later I dragged myself out of bed and headed for the shower.

For no particular reason, other than that there hadn't been one for a while, the Untouchables had planned a piss-up, so I headed over to the bar. The mood was merry, the place was throbbing and everyone was happily drinking. News of our accident had spread, and Stephen 2, who'd recently been promoted to Det boss, wandered over.

'Hey, Sarah, I've just had Volvo on the phone. They want to know what you're made of so they can use it in their cars.'

I was forced to drink six pints of beer before moving onto the vodka for medicinal purposes. Out of the corner of one drunken eye I got the feeling that Vic and Sean were up to some devious mission. I was vaguely aware of them wandering furtively in and out of the bar. Suddenly a streak of fire flew past us and jumped onto the table. It was Joe, entertaining the troops with his version of the dance of the flaming arseholes. He'd rolled up part of the *Sun*, shoved it up his arse and lit the end. The idea was to see how far it could burn towards your – in Joe's case – peachy bottom before you had to put it out. There have been many singed Armed Forces botties because the lads have been too pissed to pull the flaming paper out in time. I didn't take much interest. I'd seen it all before, having worked with the Marines for two years.

By 2 a.m. I was extremely merry. Some of the lightweights (people who don't drink much) had headed back to the bashas, and the bar was now only half full. I watched as Vic and Sean crept through the doorway together, and sidled silently up behind Sparky, who was deep in conversation with David, one of the admin staff, about his days in military college. David just managed to grab his pint as Vic planted his hand over Sparky's eyes and gagged him with a cloth over his mouth. Sean put him in an armlock and dragged him outside. Sparky was kicking and screaming like a big girlie. He'd turned thirty-six two days earlier, and had nervously spent the whole day with eyes in the back of his head. The lads had bided their time until he'd dropped his guard. We all wondered what delights lay in store for the poor old git as we merrily followed the hijackers out of the bar.

Some work was being done on the drains, and there was a large crater in the floor. It had now acquired a crucifix made from two scaffolding poles. Sammy the chef was standing by, armed with a hosepipe. Sparky was unceremoniously stripped of his attire and plasticuffed to the scaffolding, still kicking and screaming like a tart. Some of the boys started hosing him down while the rest of us stood around in a semi-circle, beers in hand, gloating at the free show. Freezing cold, Sparky's willy certainly wasn't what I'd expected! For once there was a part of him that was introverted.

Worse was to come. Several stray dogs were always scavenging for free scoff around the base, and now Vic emerged from his basha with a tin of Pedigree Chum, a rare treat for the compound dogs. He leaned over and started slapping handfuls of it all over Sparky's shrivelled bits. Sparky's yelps went unheeded, and his willy retracted so much that it looked like a Walnut Whip.

Luckily for Sparky, Rebel was a gentle dog. He didn't bite into his food, but ate his Chum like a gentleman sampling ice cream. Sparky hung there shivering, silent, white with fear, eyes bulging, as Rebel delicately licked the last remaining morsels off his bollocks. Vic and Sean then cut him loose and did a runner. Purple-faced, Sparky dashed towards the shower in his basha, swearing revenge on everyone in the compound. Even the dog.

Wiping the tears from our eyes, we piled back into the bar for a final vodka before bed. I was certainly feeling a lot more cheerful than earlier in the day.

Next morning we learned of yet another casualty from the night before. Reg, the chief pilot, was a heavy off-duty drinker. One of the last out of the bar, he'd attempted to stagger back to his basha, a journey which involved negotiating the building works. Cut into the concrete floor twenty metres from Sparky's crucifix was a six-foot trench half-full of dirty water. Reg had splash-landed in the hole, cut himself up, twisted his ankle and bashed his face. He tried to get out but the sides were concave, and in his stupor he couldn't get a grip. There'd been no one else around as he stood in the cesspit shouting for help and slowly going down with hypothermia. After fifteen minutes Jock had heard his increasingly desperate cries and had rescued him in the nick of time.

The general consensus at breakfast was to stay away from vehicles and anything to do with shooting or alcohol, and to feed the dogs regularly.

My Op Travallion duty came round again. For the first two days at Bessbrook things were much the same, i.e. nothing was happening. Our Mam was never far from my thoughts, and I wrote her a long poem. Words were always swilling around inside, just waiting for me to find the time to write them down.

I also wrote a long letter to Luke. I was still amazed by his emotional honesty, but now I had also experienced the dark side to his nature. He had put me on a pedestal, as a wonderful creature who could do no wrong – so where did that leave him? It felt like an imbalance. He seemed to be debasing himself by putting himself in a position of relative humility compared to me, rather than seeing us as equals.

More flaws had begun emerging in our relationship. I'd just spent four days watching Luke compete in a joint service shooting competition in England. After several hours of socialising with mutual friends, most of them competition shooters from the army, I noticed that Luke had drifted to the edge of the group. As the evening had worn on he'd withdrawn further. This had resulted in another severe flare-up. He couldn't understand why I was having such a good time and seemed happily independent of him. He said he'd felt he wasn't wanted, as if he was dispensable to me. I tried to tell him that I wanted to be with him, but I also wanted to have a good time with friends. He refused to understand, seeing only what he wanted to see.

After this, we started to have increasing numbers of petty arguments. The more I pulled away from Luke, the more he poured out his love for me, which further heightened my instinct to back off. I suppose that deep inside I had emotional barriers that stopped me growing closer to Luke. Perhaps that was what the perceptive part of him had sensed. I began to worry that maybe we'd shown each other too much too soon, that we'd become enveloped with one another too early. No doubt because of our family backgrounds, we'd both been keen to rush into our love. Spending time with Luke on leave had sometimes been a bit difficult because he couldn't wait to have me in his arms, while initially I always felt more distant. Working flat out in a pressured macho environment, where physical contact consisted of nothing more intimate than a slap on the back, my physical feelings became deeply buried. But as soon as we were reunited Luke would smother me, before I'd had time to adjust. These issues were creating a vague sense of discomfort within me, but from the point of view of letter-writing, things carried on pretty much as normal. I simply blocked the problems out and concentrated on the positive aspects.

Jock, my mate from the Troop, and I were spending a lot of time together, either on the piss or up the hills. We got on really well, and he'd recently admitted to harbouring a soft spot for me ever since the course. One afternoon he blurted out that he'd fallen in love with me, but because he was less articulate than Luke, it was harder for him to tell me how he felt. Jock had married too young, after a shitty childhood from which he'd escaped by signing up at fifteen. He was a good soldier and a solid, trustworthy man, but when he spoke of his love for me I told him that my heart and soul lay with Luke. He tried hard to accept this, but when he'd had one too many he would still pour out his love to me, telling me I was everything he wanted. At times his passion bubbled up and we'd end up having big fights. He'd storm out of my basha and creep back early the following morning to apologise. The fact that he'd woken me at 7.30 a.m. to do so pissed me off even more.

I just had time to spray some Chanel No. 5 on Luke's letter when the buzz box gave us the signal: the machine gun had gone mobile. The sleepy stupor of all the bodies in the room was immediately shaken off as we were galvanised into action. We raced out and jumped into our cars. All our gear was already stashed in them, and my Browning never left my side. Within minutes we were entering the town and picking up the signal. At first it was barely audible, but over the next minute or so it strengthened in intensity.

As we headed in the direction of the council estate where the arms had been stashed in the garden shed, it grew stronger and louder. Then a white Ford Fiesta pulled out of a sidestreet and accelerated towards us. As it passed us the signal was at full strength, and it began to weaken immediately afterwards. We had our target. The M60 was in that vehicle, and was heading into town.

'Zero Oscar. Standby, standby,' I said briskly over the net. In those brief seconds we'd got a good look at the driver, who was one up. He was in his early twenties, with a fat, oafish face and straggly blond hair. None other than Francis Murphy, a well-known player.

The adrenaline was pumping now. We'd got a mobile M60 which could be pressed into service at any moment. As soon as Murphy was out of sight we did a neat 180, while informing the other team members of the target's location.

'Zero Oscar, that's Charlie One in on red.' Murphy was heading north towards the centre of town. We were eyes-on, so the beacon was now redundant. The other call-signs acknowledged, picked him up and followed him covertly to the church carpark.

Then we heard, 'Zero Hotel, that's Charlie One into carpark and unsighted.' The next car picked him up again. From their vantage point on a small road behind the carpark they watched Murphy jump out and fish a bin liner out of the boot. Jed and I didn't need to tell each other what to do. We had to keep tabs on Murphy at all costs. We pulled over on the main road thirty metres from the church. By going foxtrot I could cover the front.

I stepped out of the car and began to cross the deserted road, heading for an alleyway which led towards the church. When I was just a few yards from the alley, Murphy suddenly emerged from it. I focused on making sure my face registered no emotion as he strode past. He was looking very nervous and furtive. In his hand was a black bin liner containing a long, heavy object. After he'd passed I whispered 'Zero Sierra' into my mike.

The ops room came back with 'Send.'

'Zero Sierra, that's Bravo One foxtrot with heavy bin liner out of alley towards high street.'

'Zero roger that,' came the response.

I'd been within inches of the weapon we'd focused on for nearly four months, but it was vital that I kept walking down my pre-planned route without looking back. Murphy must not be alerted to the presence of Special Forces. Within moments I felt the adrenaline hit back with its rich mix of exhilaration and terror. The fact that Murphy didn't pose much of a personal threat didn't stop my physiological fight-or-flight response from kicking in. Murphy was just a young lad who'd been tasked by someone further up the chain to move the weapon to yet another location without being seen. They were simple instructions, but enough to create the beads of sweat on his forehead. He knew that he couldn't afford to fuck up. He just wanted to do the job and go home.

I legged it down the alleyway and into the carpark, where Jed picked me up. Murphy continued down a maze of roads, the gun weighing heavily in his hand. The team sat on his tail, following him both mobile and foxtrot while keeping each other constantly informed so another op could take over at any time.

Minutes later Jed and I were heading east through the town when Frank decided it was time he dropped the target. Jed pulled over and I jumped out. Murphy was fifty metres ahead of me on the other side of the road. He must have been a fit lad – an M60 is a heavy piece of kit, but he was hoofing it. I followed him for one minute and dropped him at the next available junction, where Shane took over. You only have the target for a short period before dropping him so someone walking towards him can take over. It was like a sort of synchronised dance. By now our surveillance abilities had been so finely tuned that we should have been able to follow a target indefinitely. Swapping over was just a way of making doubly certain he didn't spot that he was being followed.

Murphy turned left at a T-junction and into the sidestreet where Jed was parked a hundred metres on the left. This was good. There was no need for anyone to go foxtrot. Jed could observe Murphy in the mirrors, and he gave bursts of information over the net. Murphy stopped just behind Jed's car and talked briefly to an unknown man, then stashed the gun in bushes at the side of the road.

In order not to walk past the new hide on my way to Jed, I navigated through some grubby backstreets and approached him from the other direction while the rest of the team headed back to their cars. Shane and Adrian followed Murphy and his unknown companion back to Murphy's car. The two then drove back to Murphy's house, clearly believing that no one had seen them.

Jed and I stayed put eighty-five metres from the new hide. We expected something big to happen at any moment, and every nerve was straining as we tried to guess what it might be. In such situations you find yourself fantasising about the contents of the players' warped minds. Were they planning to commit an atrocity now – possibly by shooting up an SF base? Or would they rehouse the weapon overnight so that it would be ready to take out on business the following morning? After so many covert moves, for the gun to end up stuck in a hedge by the side of a road implied only a temporary placement.

The minutes passed slowly as we kept our eyes peeled for any activity along the road. There was no street lighting, and we were relying on our night vision to pick out the shady figure we expected to sneak up and grab the goods. The net was dead quiet. Everyone was waiting in taut expectation. The odd vehicle swept past.

At 2207 hours Zero came on the net. The words broke into the tense silence, and we jolted as he said: 'All call-signs, this is Zero, radio check.' A radio check is Det housekeeping, a way of keeping tabs on us if we hadn't had cause to give our location for a while. Paul breezed through the call-signs in order. As each name was called the operator would reply 'OK.' We heard the words only as background noise. Our attention remained focused on the bushes. Back in the compound we knew that since the standby Paul would have lived on the landline to TCG. We were always eager for any additional scraps of information.

An unmarked police car slid slowly towards us, a red Ford Sierra cunningly disguised as – a red Sierra. Anyone in the know could tell it was armoured: bulletproof glass has a giveaway green-tinted gleam, there was an extra antenna sticking out of the roof, and I could see a flash of green shirt – RUC uniform. We stayed motionless, making sure our heads and shoulders were perfectly aligned with the headrests. That way, the dark and the police car's dipped headlights meant it was unlikely that the coppers would see that our car was occupied.

The police appeared to slow down near the weapons hide. Paul came back up on the net: 'All call-signs, this is Zero. Lift off.' There was a note of leaden sarcasm in his voice. Jed and I looked at each other, gobsmacked.

Adrian came on the net. 'Zero November. What's going on, mate?'

Paul spoke briskly. 'Basically, TCG want an overt pick-up. Get yourselves back and I'll give you a full debrief.' We were all hyped up, and now this. It was the world's biggest letdown. For a moment we couldn't move. With a rising sense of nausea, we saw the police car pull over and cut its lights. Seconds later, a Royal Engineers search team arrived with a sniffer dog and walked straight up to the hide, covering their arcs. One young lad coolly reached into the bushes and fished out the M60. Four months' hard work disappeared into an army bergen. The job had gone down the drain. What was going on?

Jed voiced all our feelings into the chill night air. 'Fucking hell, you're having a laugh, aren't you? Just let us work our arses off for the last four months on permanent standby. Why don't we just sacrifice our social lives for sixteen weeks to do some really good surveillance on these players, and how about we just watch some Engineer lift it all out of the bushes for us?'

He turned on the engine, and in silence we headed back to the compound. Everyone was dejected. It seemed like such a waste of time. If that was TCG's intention, why didn't they just lift out the kit on day one? But all the time we knew that it was up to the blokes at the top to decide how to conclude an operation. We're not there to dictate the outcome, just to carry out the legwork. In one sense we'd got a result. For four months we'd carried out covert surveillance properly, gleaning more info about the players and their associates. It just seemed like an extravagant way to go about getting a few facts. We might have got a fuller picture of who was involved, but we'd have liked to see a different end result.

This was fairly typical. About 70 per cent of all surveillance ops finish with a disappointing anticlimax. We'd been hand-picked for Det work because of our ability to spend our lives watching, watching, watching, and then being able to switch off when necessary. But it didn't stop us feeling pissed off about it.

Next morning at breakfast, still wiping the sleep from my eyes, I watched as the Troop lads queued up for their greasy fry-up on the other side of the great cookhouse divide. Marty was in a particularly wicked mood. He looked at Rich, who was standing behind me in the queue. Rich had been cultivating a short goatee for a few weeks, but now it was gone, and his face was so clean-shaven that it was glowing red like a traffic light. Marty nudged his mates then shouted out, 'Hey Sarah, there you go, hen. See what he's done for you? All soft and shiny like a baby's bum. He must fancy you.'

Aidan spook sat back in his chair and like an umpire cried out: 'Troop fifteen, Det love.' Folding his arms, he turned pointedly towards me. My stomach was churning. People obviously thought Rich and I were an item. Rich was a sweetie, but I didn't fancy him. Still, I knew I needed to produce a sufficiently eloquent retort to throw the spotlight back onto Marty.

'About bloody time,' I shouted at him. 'All that designer stubble plays havoc with your inner thighs.'

Aidan clapped politely. 'Fifteen all.'

Rich, this strapping SAS man, was blushing beneath his shaving pimples on my behalf! Marty had it in his power to make anyone blush.

The embarrassing thing was that Rich and I had been getting closer recently. He often came around to my basha for tea and a chat. He was a modest bloke, and he said he found it easy to talk to me about his divorce. Being one of only three women in the compound meant that I was an automatic focal point. If the lads saw me with anyone they would start making innuendoes.

Meanwhile, things with Luke were going downhill big time. His letters were as amorous and caring as ever, but I was continuing to lose my respect for him because of his self-abasing attitude. When Rich enquired how things were going with Luke I told him the truth, and talked through some of the rougher moments with him.

NINE

FINAL FLIGHT

IN MID-APRIL Northern Ireland was blanketed in heavy clouds dumping sleet in diagonal lines over the countryside, and the roads were covered in a lethal coating of black ice. 80 per cent of the Det were recovering from a severe bout of compounditis. The four months on standby for Op Travallion had messed up our collective health and mental attitude. Compounditis renders you unable to sleep at night, while systematically pocking your skin. The craters which opened up in our faces made it look as if we'd fallen prey to some terrible virus.

It was hardly surprising, as we'd been confined indoors beneath the same roof, eating crap, drinking too much and seeing everything under the blue glare of fluorescent lighting for weeks on end. It was a uniformly grey and bleak environment, surreal for its lack of colour. When your life consists of waiting for a job that never comes, your brain slowly degenerates into braised cabbage. You are completely confined: can't work out in the gym; can't go down to the main camp; can't do anything but wait – just in case. The less you do, the less you want to do. Being on standby is the emotional equivalent of being strapped into a long-haul flight to Karachi, unable to move and living on stale air.

Compounditis is one reason why Det tours across the water are set at a maximum eighteen months. After that you head back to your parent unit to get normal. Det life is an intense existence of unrelenting pressure, the military equivalent of air-traffic control. One fuck-up and you know you could be dead.

One Tuesday morning while I was upside down with a plastic bag over my head, bleaching my hair to get rid of the black roots,

Jock wandered into my basha, shouting, 'Hey, big nose, where are you?' He had details of a Troop operation, named Op Jedda. They'd been tasked to protect a member of the local UDR battalion who lived in a farm complex near Cappagh. The intelligence received was that the Provisional IRA were planning to mallet him. Did I want to be drop-off driver? Yeah, sure.

The history behind the planned op was that a month earlier, in March, a pub in Cappagh High Street had been shot up. At the time it was filled with members of the Provisional IRA, including the evil OC of East Tyrone, who survived the attack because he was in a shithouse out the back. But Baldy Quinn and three of his associates were shot dead. Although Baldy and I weren't exactly best mates, I couldn't condone his killing – wherever your sympathies lie, a terrorist murder is a terrorist murder. The UVF claimed they hadn't made a sectarian attack on the Catholic community, instead they viewed it as an operation directed at the roots of the Provisional IRA command structure in the Armagh–Tyrone region.

On the night of the shootings South Det had been operating in the area. The attack was mounted just thirty-five minutes after we'd lifted off. Now the IRA wanted to hit back, and they had chosen the UDR man as their target for no other reason than that he worked for the security forces and lived nearby.

The Troop briefing took place on Tuesday at 9 a.m. It was as informal as usual. Jock, the team leader, gave a brief rundown. I'd be driving a one-tonne Renault Trafic van with eight Troop guys crouched in the back. The lads were already rigged up in DPM kit and cam cream, and faced the prospect of being *in situ* for a number of days. Some of them would lurk inside the UDR man's house, while others would hide out in the barn and surrounding fields. The van would wear East Tyrone plates on this occasion.

We finished our mugs of tea, extinguished our fags and left the ops room. Downstairs we piled into the van and pulled out into the chilly spring air, heading south towards blue nine, then west until the motorway ended, then up the Ballygawley Road. After a few miles we turned north towards the Cappagh mountain region, a barren, sparsely populated area covered in uninviting scrub. The further north we headed, the more the countryside looked like the North Yorkshire moors on a bad night. It was a spooky, bleak environment.

The UDR man's stone farmhouse was off a small country lane. A cobblestone courtyard contained three or four outhouses and a barn. As we approached it I gave the countdown markers over the net to the Troop ops room, and felt the familiar tension rising inside my ribcage. There was no specific threat; just a sense of heightened awareness. As we rattled towards the drop-off I caught a glimpse in my rear-view of the lads preparing to exit the van. Hell, what did I have to worry about? I had a truckload of the world's most élite fighting force tooled up and ready to go. I pulled swiftly into the courtyard and out of sight of the road. The lads jumped out of the sliding door and moved to their pre-planned positions. One duo nipped into the house while two other pairs made their way to the hedges on either side of the road. Jock was one of the last pair to exit. He'd been sitting immediately behind my seat, and as he jumped out of the van he muttered, 'Cheerio, see you later, mate.'

'Yeah, see ya. Be good,' I replied.

He quietly slid the door shut and hurried off to his position inside the outhouse that overlooked the farmhouse. Thoughts of my mates' mortality never occurred to me. It seemed inconceivable that any of them would be hurt, and you couldn't afford to waste time on morbid thoughts.

Immediately I went mobile, driving out of the courtyard and turning right into the lane as I informed the ops room that drop-off was complete. I didn't race: once the boys exit the van they need to establish comms with the desk before the drop-off vehicle disappears from the area. As I drove I scanned about, my fingers instinctively pressed on the Browning nestling against my hip.

It wasn't completely unknown for fuck-ups to occur on the drop-off. A few weeks earlier North Det had been doing a drop for an OP out in the cuds. This was a rare task for them, as they were normally city-bound. Mike, the driver, had approached the target area, remembered to trip the brake-light cut-off switch, and his lads had debussed. As they were shutting the door, Mike pulled the boot-release lever. A few seconds later he heard some light tapping on the boot lid. Assuming that the boys had hauled out their kit and were signalling that he should move off, he pulled away, informing the desk that the drop-off was complete. After about twenty seconds the desk came up over the net. They hadn't heard from the OP team, and Mike was asked to do a drive-past to ensure that everything was OK. He did a 180 and headed back around the bend, where he was confronted by a very pissed-off-looking operator standing in the middle of the road, hands on hips, flagging him down. Only then did he realise that he'd pulled the petrol-cap release-lever instead of the boot-spring, leaving the lads twiddling their thumbs in the bushes without comms. Not only did Mike receive a slagging from his own Det and have to buy in the beers that night, but it gave us some great ammo in the ongoing war between South and North.

With my lads installed I headed back to the compound. Five days later they lifted off. Nothing had happened. TCG had made the decision that the threat had passed and had given the order to move. The Troop boys were wearing five days' growth of beard, and were in need of a hot bath.

Three weeks later the Troop was suddenly redeployed. The briefing was identical. It was a grey, overcast day, and everything was going smoothly until we were about twenty minutes from the drop-off point, when suddenly the Troop ops room came over the net with an urgent message. I had the comms coming over the loudspeaker at the time, so everyone heard the clipped voice of Marvin, Troop boss. 'Call-sign One Delta. This is Alpha.'

'One Delta, send.' I replied, wondering what was up.

'One Delta, do not, repeat do not, go for drop-off.'

There was a rustle of interest in the back of the van. What was all this about?

'One Delta roger,' I said.

Jock spoke up. 'Ask him whether he wants us to return to base or hang slack for a while.'

I asked the question, and got an abrupt answer: 'RTB [return to base].'

'Roger that. Towards you.'

I did a 180 and headed back. The frustration from the lads in the back was tangible. Back at the compound we headed straight to the ops room, where Marvin was waiting for us. He told us that when we were about twenty minutes from the drop-off a contact had gone down three hundred metres from the target farm on our route in. A terrorist squad had come across a UDR patrol in our out-of-bounds area, and a contact had occurred. Lots of fire had been exchanged, but there had been no casualties. This raised a number of interesting queries. Who were the Provisional IRA waiting for? And why was a UDR patrol in our out-of-bounds area?

Jock had a hunch: the Provisional IRA had been waiting for us. He was certain that the players had switched on to the fact that the Troop were operating in the area, because the farm and its outbuildings were overlooked by nearby buildings.

I had only one thought – thank fuck. If we'd been twenty minutes earlier, it could have been us. The guys in the back were tooled up with G3s all right, but it would have been little old me – trying to juggle steering wheel and Browning – who'd have copped it. If I'd seen a gang of armed and masked terrorists up ahead, I would have had several pretty raw options. After changing my knickers, I could have shouted to the guys to standby for contact, at which point they would have jumped out and headed left and right. I would also have debussed – the van would function as the focal point for incoming fire, so it would be vital to evacuate – and we would have dealt with the situation.

Alternatively I could have attempted a handbrake turn simultaneously with the world's fastest draw. There was another, more stomach-curdling option: I could have driven straight past the terrorist roadblock, hoping like fuck that my gender would help me pass off as an innocent driver. Retreating was never really an option. It would have taken an eighteen-point turn to get us out of there.

A week passed without event and Saturday rolled around. For once we weren't on standby, and there were no ops on, which meant we were free to enjoy the luxury of going out and into town and able to live a little. It was a bright spring morning, and I drove one of the admin cars, equipped with County Antrim plates that wouldn't draw attention, into central Belfast for some retail therapy. I went through the cursory security check at the Victoria multi-storey carpark in the city centre. A couple of bored-looking, over-weight security men asked me to pop open my boot. They had a quick peer inside. 'Have you recently left your vehicle unattended?' the plumper of the two half-heartedly asked me. I shook my head and was waved on. It was so pathetic they might as well not have bothered. These guys were supposed to ensure that no vehicles containing explosive devices entered the carpark, but like most people doing a mundane job with few prospects, they were slacking.

Once I'd parked on the third floor I went foxtrot with a wad of cash and a pair of comfortable shoes on, fully prepared to shop until I dropped. Belfast is a girlie Det geek's paradise. There's a massive pedestrianised shopping precinct in the centre of town, with all the high street shops like M&S, River Island and Top Shop, several shopping arcades, and a number of market areas where the distinctive sharp smell of Irish soda and tatty bread wafts from the bakeries and out between the stalls.

It was wonderful to be among normal people doing normal things. I savoured the taste and aroma of freshly-ground coffee at Bewley's, my favourite coffee shop, automatically checking my inside-the-waistband holster when I stood up. I was smarter than usual, in crisply ironed canvas trousers and a satin blouse, but I wore my blazer at all times to hide the Browning. As I paced around town I was still switched on. It was a reflex action to scan the buildings above eye-level. If there was going to be sniper fire it would come from above. I was ever alert to vehicle checkpoints and instinctively aware of patrolling policemen. I kept a covert eye out for anyone paying the plods more attention than they should. I wasn't looking to invite trouble, but if it had happened I wouldn't have ignored it. Keeping up general observation at all times had become second nature. In reality, I faced no more threat than any other shopper, but Belfast is the sort of unpredictable environment where an incident could spark up at any moment. My subconscious wasn't going to let me make the mistake of being unprepared.

Money wasn't a problem: I was being paid well. While I was across the water my basic WRNS pay was supplemented with Special Forces pay, Northern Ireland pay and technical pay one rank above my own. Halfway through my tour I was promoted to Leading Wren, so I was on Petty Officer pay. I also received an additional £100 ops pay every month, which was supposed to cover expenses incurred while out on the ground. Most of it went into the beer fund and the chip-butty-and-curries fund. As I had no food or accommodation charges, I was taking home about £1500 a month after tax. That might not sound a lot to some people, but to me it was mega money. If I died in action our Mam would have been in line to receive £3000 immediately, plus a pension, plus any top-up provided by SASA and the Navy.

I bought *The Best of the Chieftains* to add to my boggy music collection (so called because Ireland is mostly peat bog); I ordered our Mam some flowers for Mother's Day and chose a nice sentimental card for her, and another for Grandma; on impulse I bought a new suede handbag, a trendy jacket and a skirt from River Island.

I had a delicious sense of freedom and solitude. For once I was on my own. Another symptom of compounditis is going slightly crazy because you're always surrounded by other people. Everything is lived out under the close scrutiny of everyone else. It's a bit like eating, drinking, working and sleeping in an open-plan office. On days off when I desperately needed some space I'd drive like a madwoman to Bangor or Donaghadee by the sea, urgently needing to get back to myself. Once there I'd stand on the sea wall by the fishing boats, close my eyes, and breathe in deep lungfuls of the sea air. Such solitude was heavenly bliss. I would do a bit of mind cleaning, discarding all thoughts in a sort of meditative trance. I could just be, for hours, no matter how bad the weather. Afterwards I would feel cleansed, relaxed, and able to look at life from a more healthy perspective. Sometimes I contemplated so deeply I wondered if I might be metamorphosing into a closet Buddhist!

I popped into Boots just before closing time and stocked up with facial wash, cotton buds and shower gel, then headed back to the carpark and climbed the concrete steps to the third floor, well aware that this was a potentially dangerous moment. If I'd been followed it was here, rather than out in the street, where I'd face the threat – either from someone on foot or from a bomb attached to my car. I had a swift and nonchalant look around: there was no activity on this level of the concrete sandwich. The bleeps had recently fitted the admin cars with a new-fangled gizmo called a device-detector, a panel of three LEDs next to the dashboard. If the green light was on, it meant the car hadn't been tampered with in the driver's absence. Amber showed that the car had been touched in some way, while red indicated serious interference.

When I reached the car I looked in through the driver's window. And froze. The red light was illuminated. I swallowed hard and thought for a second. Oh shit!

I looked around. No one. Just in case, I opened my handbag and fiddled around until I'd knocked out my keys. They fell with a metallic clatter onto the concrete, and with a swift kick they were under the car. This was my usual routine on admin runs, irrespective of the state of the device-detector. I'd follow up with a quick crouch on the ground to retrieve the keys while swiftly scanning for any devices. It had to look natural. Too obvious a search would immediately give me away as a member of the police or security forces. This time was different, though. I didn't care who was watching as I peered under the wheel arches and craned to see into the crevice where the exhaust meets the chassis. I couldn't afford to touch the car, even fleetingly. The lightest brush could activate a device.

I felt remarkably calm, probably because I knew that if a device was rigged to the car it would probably be on a mercury tilt switch. Movement was the threat – proximity wouldn't be enough to set a bomb off. There was a risk that a device might be hooked up to a timer, but this was fairly unlikely. I spent a minute on my knees peering around. I knew I was vulnerable, but I tried not to think about that. I couldn't see anything, but I was still wary about getting into the car, so I decided to ring the ops room from a public phonebox on the street outside. Dicky bleep answered the phone.

'Hi, Dicky. It's Sarah. I've just come back to my car in the Belfast multi-storey and I've got a red light. I've looked all around but I can't see anything. What's the score on these device-detectors?'

Dicky was calm and measured. 'If you've got a red it means the car's been tampered with.'

'I know that, but could it be a malfunction? I've had a scan around and can't see anything.'

'To be honest with you, the device is too new on the market to comment. Hang on a sec and I'll get hold of the Pronto [head bleep].'

I heard him calling up Graham, the new Pronto, on the buzz box, but he wasn't there. Instead Jed, who was downstairs in the bleeps' office, answered. He came straight to the phone when Dicky told him about my little problem.

'You've got two options. The first is to stay put until I get the Royal Engineers over with the sniffer dogs' – this was worse than waiting for the AA; it'd take them three hours minimum to show up – 'or you have a bloody good scout under the car and take the risk.'

We both knew what I was going to do. 'If I'm not back in an hour, phone up me mam and tell her I love her,' I said.

'What size boots are ya?' he joked.

'Too small for you, you fat bastard.'

'Take care. See you soon. Good luck.' His voice had taken on a serious tone.

I was sweating now. I knew I had no option but to get into the car and switch on the ignition. I walked briskly back up the steps. I didn't bother chucking the keys onto the floor this time; I didn't care if anyone saw me. I just took a deep breath and got down into the press-up position, rolling onto my back like a mechanic. I lay there for three weeks going over every inch of the bodywork. Everywhere I looked I followed up with touch, gingerly pushing my fingers into each dirty hollow. Black road gunge soon coated my hands. As I was wriggling my way down the chassis I heard footsteps coming across the concrete floor. My body tightened, but

I kept working away. The steps came closer. Between the front wheels I could see two bags of shopping and a pair of jeans moving towards me at a fair old pace. I froze, but they kept on walking. I moved on to the transmission, pushing my fingers around the bodywork, working my way meticulously and slowly, then looking and feeling along the length of the exhaust.

Eight minutes later I'd checked every little nook and cranny, finishing off with a careful feel inside the front bumper. I was as sure as dammit that the car was clean. I took the key out of my pocket, gently placed it in the lock and turned it with a click. Cautiously I opened the door, placed my bags of shopping on the passenger seat, carefully sat down and pulled the door shut. There were no attractive options, but I couldn't sit here for the rest of my life. I slid the key into the ignition, aware of my heightened heart-rate. The key moved around to the first click without incident. On the second, the dashboard lights came on and I nearly shat myself as the radio screamed to life with a cannon blast from Tchaikovsky's *1812 Overture*. I fumbled with the dial and shut off Classic Hour, then moved my sweaty fingers back to the key and prepared to bring the engine to life. My fingers took up the pressure, the key turned, and with a jolt the car roared into life. I felt a flood of relief – so far so good. But there was still a risk in moving off. The mercury tilt switch – if one had been attached somewhere inaccessible beneath me – might yet register movement.

I slid the gearstick into first, touched the accelerator and drove cautiously towards the ramp, expecting at any moment to end up as pizza on the concrete ceiling. By the time I'd reached the bottom of the ramp I knew for certain that I was in the clear. I'd had my quota of adrenaline for the day. As I drove back to the compound my mind drifted to the days I'd spent over here with the Marines in 1986. I'd been told the story of Sergeant Mick Willets of 3 Para, who gave up his life when a bomb was discovered in the lobby of Springfield Road RUC station. He dived on top of it, muffling the blast with his own body and saving the lives of many innocent bystanders. That is the meaning of courage.

When I got back to the compound Dicky bleep was still on the desk. 'So you made it, then?' he laughed. I went upstairs to the ops room to drop off the keys and to sign myself and the car back in. I unloaded my pistol in the romper room, then headed back downstairs and beat a hasty retreat to my basha for a shower. Jed was down below, messing about with our car. A look of relief lit up his dirty face. Without a word he loped across to the foot of the stairs and tenderly placed his arms around me.

'I'm glad you're back safely, you old trout. I haven't had a cup of tea for hours, and I've had to clean out the car all by myself.'

'Well, actually it's quite nice to see you as well, fat boy. I suppose I'd better stick the kettle on then.'

Jed glanced at the Mickey Mouse watch adorning his hairy wrist. 'At nine o'clock we're going down to Pantiles,' he said. 'So you've only got two hours to make yourself look like a chick worthy of hanging off my arm.'

'Right, better get a move on then,' I smiled. I left him cleaning up the latest strata of sweetie wrappers from the car, and dived into a much-needed shower.

Two hours later I'd transformed myself from Det geek to girl-about-town. I was wearing a clinging, backless blue velvet dress, sheer black stockings and high heels. The works. My hair was all done up and tumbling off the top of my head. There were lots of wolf whistles when I emerged from my basha and met up with the gaggle of five Troop and four Det guys by the ops room stairs. It had been months since the last fancy-dress party!

The Troop guys got a drop-off in central Belfast from their admin staff, while we cadged a lift in the people-carrier from young Craig, one of the Det boys who preferred nights in. The radio was blasting out the Saw Doctors as we drove along the winding country lanes. I was next to Jed, my hands resting on my knees. He put on his most censorious Mary Whitehouse voice: 'Close your legs, young lady. There's men who haven't had a shag for a couple of months in this van.' I obediently did so, but my dress rode up a couple of inches to reveal the lacy stocking-top on my left thigh. Jed's eyes were glued to the half-inch of bare flesh. Briskly, he said: 'Cover yourself up, lass. As you were before.'

I gave him a look. 'For Christ's sake. Legs crossed, legs together. Why don't I just wrap them round your neck and get it over and done with?'

Jed put on the prim and proper voice again. 'Pass me your hand,' he commanded.

I girlishly gave it to him. I knew what was coming next; this was one of his preferred ways of interacting with me, and I duly received the expected little slap. 'Naughty girl,' he whispered.

'If that's what marriage is like, forget it,' grunted Craig as he dropped us off outside the Europa, Belfast's biggest – and the world's most bombed – hotel. The Europa has become a symbol of business-as-usual defiance of the terrorists, and it's always teeming with journalists and television men, creating a wonderful spirit of camaraderie and friendship. We jumped out, Jed theatrically holding out his hand to help me, and made our way to Pantiles and straight upstairs to the disco. We'd just got a drink when the Troop boys arrived. Their number included Massive Mick, who was six foot three, Big Rob, a vast Welshman, and Lenny, rippling with muscles. As they strode in, a young local lad exclaimed: 'Fuck me, the SAS are in.' And he thought he was just being witty!

For two and a half hours we propped up the bar, sinking vodka and Cokes. I wasn't wearing my pistol tonight, as I wanted to get drunk. All of us were relaxed, happy and having a good time. Jed and I had a dance or two as usual before leaving at 11 p.m. in search of taxis to take us to East Det for a piss-up. There was no minicab to be got for love nor money. On the horizon we saw a black cab and took the decision to hail it. Black cabs are usually a no-no. They're one of many Ulster organisations that fund the IRA. At one stage the Falls Road Taxi Drivers' Association was handing over a straight 15 per cent of their takings to the Provos, for the privilege of operating without competition. I jumped in with three of the Troop lads, and Sammy said, 'Can you take us to North Park Barracks, mate.' The taxi driver wasn't too happy about the destination, but before he had a chance to object Sammy drew his Browning, put it next to his head and added, by way of encouragement: 'And if you take us down the Falls Road I'll fucking slot you.' I tried to keep a straight face. The taxi driver looked well rattled, and nodded earnestly. 'Sure, no problems mate,' he spluttered. He dropped us right outside the main gates, and didn't even charge us.

In the East Det bar, the games were already well under way. Some people were drinking their way through the optics left to right, knocking back the alphabet of shots, from Bourbon to whiskey. Others were on a coloured drinks run, swallowing down a pint of snakebite and blue Curacao – a nice greeny blue – followed by a pint of lager and black – an inky purple – topped off with a pint of Guinness and any other drink they were sober enough to pour themselves.

Joe was back off leave, and told me he was planning his revenge on Davey and Mike, fellow Det operators who had cut out a tin-foil template in the shape of a pistol and placed it in his hold-all. When he'd passed through security at Aldergrove all the lights and bleepers had rung out. He'd been dragged to the security room to explain himself, with the result that he'd missed his flight and a night out with a girl. Near the end of the evening Davey staggered off, comatose, and headed for his basha. With a wicked look in his eye, Joe followed. For the next half-hour, with the help of a couple of mates, some mortar and a trowel, he stealthily bricked up Davey's door, and even filled in the window for good measure.

It was 2.30 when Jed and I decided to phone for a pick-up for us and some other smashed Det guys. We practically fell into the van, and after a few minutes Jed planted his hand on my thigh. 'If you put your hand on my leg once more, boyo, you're going to get it,' I slurred.

With a naughty look on his face he said, 'I hope so.'

'What's wrong with you tonight? Haven't you had your dose of bromide this week?'

Jed was smiling broadly. 'That's right, go on, get angry with me. I love it when you're angry.'

As I looked at his cheeky, animated face and slightly podgy six-foot body, a great wave of affection hit me. Jed was my mate, he'd supported me through thick and thin; we knew so much about each other and he was always cheering me up. Now he was gazing at me with puppy-dog eyes, and for the first time I found myself attracted to him. It had been a heavy day, with the device-detector scare, and I couldn't forget the look of relief on his face when I'd arrived back in the compound safe and sound. As we sat in the vehicle he gently started stroking my leg. I found myself relaxing for the first time in weeks as a result of this rare dose of physical affection.

A couple of Jocks were trying to sing 'Flower of Scotland', and most of the others were snoring loudly with their mouths open. No one was watching us. When the van pulled up at the A-frame they all staggered off towards their bashas. Jed said, 'Thanks for the lift, Craig, I'll sign us in.'

He grabbed my hand and pulled me up the stairs behind him. We stumbled into the secondary ops room, filled in the board, said goodnight to the bleeps and headed back down the corridor towards the stairs. We were holding hands, swinging our arms back and forth and skipping like a couple of kids. Just before we reached the stairs we passed the Det boss's office. Jed stopped, turned to face me and with a wicked grin said: 'Do you know what would be really funny?'

'Go on, what?' I knew it was going to be a sexual suggestion, and I also knew that I would go along with it.

'If we went into Shane's office and . . .' he paused like a naughty schoolboy, his eyes flashing. 'Done it on his desk.' This last was delivered in a furtive whisper.

'What if someone hears us?'

'It's all right, you can put your hand over my mouth!'

I opened the office door, and we slunk in like two teenagers. I hissed, 'Close the curtains,' and Jed crept towards the window on tiptoe. He looked like a cartoon character, peering back at me for approval as he gently tugged them across.

We could just make out each other's silhouettes from the trickle of light filtering around the edges of the door. The joking stopped as we met in the middle of the room, tenderly embraced and started kissing. Jed had a lovely, soft, kissable mouth. Minutes passed, and he led me over to the boss's desk, covered in a neat layer of paper-work. We stayed clothed, apart from the essential bits, and did it on the documents. It was great fun, heightened by the illicit nature of the venue. We were overcome with the giggles and pressed our hands over each other's mouths to try and muffle them. Half an hour later we embraced for a last passionate time and before doing a bit of hopeless drunken rearranging of the paperwork and our clothing. Then we tiptoed out. The A-frame was silent as the grave as we crept down the stairs and back to our bashas.

Next morning Jed came bustling over to me as I was eating breakfast and whispered, 'I've just heard Shane mentioning to Dicky that his curtains were drawn this morning, and he can't work out why.'

'Perhaps he's been sniffing the metal polish again, or overdoing the paperwork,' I smiled. Things between us were back to normal. He was still a fat bastard and I was still an old trout. I wasn't racked with guilt over the encounter. I didn't cheat on Luke because I didn't love him, or anything like that. It was symptomatic of the environ-ment, the surreal way things were in the compound. It didn't feel like real life. It didn't feel like real cheating. The compound was a world all of its own, far removed from my life with Luke.

A week later, any guilt I might have felt was wiped away when I discovered some shocking news. One of the Troop guys, Danny, who'd known Luke for many years and served with him in Belize, came back to my basha one night after we'd been drinking in the bar with Phil and a couple of other Troop blokes. Phil had been teaching me to play his guitar while the others sang along. We'd all seen the bottom of our pint glass a few times when Phil and his backing group finally left. Danny and I were sitting on my floor, quietly finishing our last beers, when we got onto the subject of Luke. I didn't say much. I wasn't one for confiding in anyone but my closest mates. As far as Danny was concerned Luke and I were still Cupid's best invention, so he looked a shade embarrassed as he asked, 'Have you met Luke's son?'

I nodded, thinking nothing of it. 'Yeah, a couple of times. Nice young lad. Being his only child, Luke dotes on him now that he's around again.' Luke's son had lived in South Africa for many years.

Danny hesitated. 'Luke also has a daughter, Sarah. When he was in Belize about eighteen years ago he was going out with a young local woman who he got pregnant. She had a baby girl.'

I was gutted. And embarrassed. Here was Danny telling me something that I should have been able to tell him. Luke and I were supposed to tell each other everything. For him to have something in his life as significant as an eighteen-year-old daughter, and to have 'forgotten' to tell me, was very hurtful and confusing.

'Are you sure? It was a long time ago,' I said quietly. 'I'm certain that if it was true Luke would have told me.' The news was taking time to sink in. I was very perplexed, and had run out of words. I sat pensively sipping my beer. The whole of our relationship was flashing past as I raked through the memories, trying desperately to pick up on any clues that I'd missed. After a while I spoke up. 'I don't believe you.'

'I'm sorry you had to hear it from me, but it's true. I've got no axe to grind,' said Danny gently. He moved a bit closer and put his arm around my shoulders. 'Sarah, you know I've always had a soft spot for you.' He was a good-looking guy, with a nice body and a lovely Highlands accent, but my mind was elsewhere, still running through the chapters of my relationship with Luke. When I snapped back into real time Danny was kissing me. I pulled away, showed him the door and finished his beer off for him. I didn't sleep well that night.

After breakfast next morning I was washing up my bowl when Danny wandered over.

'Hi, how are you feeling today?' he asked.

'I've got a hangover that would kill a battalion of Gurkhas. Apart from that I'm all right,' I said.

'Sarah, I'm sorry about coming on to you last night.'

'That's OK. A little boost to the ego every now and then doesn't do a woman any harm.'

He smiled and relaxed a bit. 'Look, in all seriousness, I wasn't lying when I told you about Luke.'

'Thanks, Danny. See you at the next singalong-a-Phil.' I was in no mood to discuss it. I had started to question my entire relationship with Luke, and to wonder what else he'd 'forgotten' to tell me. I didn't want to risk speaking to him on the phone. It was only two weeks until my annual fortnight's leave. I would confront him then.

Sparky and Joe had planned a skiing trip to Bavaria at the tail end of the season, and ten of us were going, a mix of Troop and Det, including Luke. Danny's revelation had cast a shadow on the trip for me. We flew to London and spent the night with Sparky's wife, where Luke met us. I couldn't confront him there, so I pretended everything was fine. For the next four days I gave him ample opportunity to tell me the truth. I kept talking about his life, quizzing him about past relationships and chattering away about his son. One evening, in the bar near our chalet, I tried a more direct approach: 'Would you have liked to have had more children, Luke? Perhaps a little girl?'

'It's just the way things turned out,' he sighed. I didn't know whether to hit him or hug him in gratitude. But why would Danny lie? I dropped the subject.

The following evening after a shedload of beer and a couple of arguments over stupid things, I couldn't resist hitting him with it. 'Luke, I've been informed by a reliable source, who has no reason to lie to me, that you've got a daughter. She'd be about eighteen now, and her mother was your girlfriend in Belize. I've given you plenty of chances to admit it during the past few days, and you haven't. So there it is. The cards are on the table.'

His eyes looked as if they were going to pop out of his head. Come on, you lying bastard, I thought. Are you concocting another lie, or are you innocent? Luke's expression was unfathomable, but when he eventually got his breath back he was seething with anger. He denied everything, which left me even more confused than before. He'd always been so honest. Had it all been lies? In that moment I knew things would never be good again. I couldn't trust him any more. My feelings for Luke were dying.

For the next few days we got by, surrounded as we were by all the other blokes having a great time. But one night I was in the bar, mulling things over and feeling a bit down, when I started talking things over with Janet, Sparky's wife. Soon we were swapping stories. It turned out that things between her and Sparky had been bad for several years now. After my fourth pint and third vodka I looked at her. 'You know, Janet, if I don't trust him and can't believe anything he says, then I guess I don't love him any more.'

I felt so downcast that I left the bar and skulked off to bed. Two hours later Luke erupted into the bedroom, virtually kicking down the door and calling me all the bitches under the sun for telling strangers that I didn't love him. He'd got his angry head back on, the one I'd first seen back in the New Year. 'Haven't you got the guts to tell me yourself, you fucking bitch?' he screamed.

'Look, you arsehole, the issue is not me telling Janet that I don't love you. The issue is your deceit. I don't trust you any more. How could you lie about something like that?' My tone was cold and accusatory.

'What do I have to do to make you believe me? I haven't got a fucking daughter,' he shouted in response. 'Tell me who told you.'

Luke's eyes were crazed; he looked like a schizo. Eventually he passed out, but the rest of the holiday was a disaster. There was an icy atmosphere that you could have cut with a butter knife. Luke even gave away all the Easter eggs he'd bought for me. Many of the other blokes had been Luke's students, and they knew better than to speak out of line. When we arrived at Heathrow Luke grabbed his backpack off the carousel and headed for the Hereford train. We were both too angry to say goodbye to each other.

The rest of us flew back across the water, and life continued as normal. There wasn't much happening in the way of ops, so we did quite a bit of hare and hounds, and I also got in some shooting practice with my personal Browning competition 9mm pistol. Luke had one too, and I'd bought mine to compete in military shooting competitions. Before the skiing trip Luke had entered me in my first one, which would take place in May at Bisley.

On days off, which cropped up pretty frequently, the operators were able to get out and about. Jed went off to the local golf courses, Greg went running in Glenshae forest with his compound hound, Dippy and Paul could be spotted on Lough Neagh practising their windsurfing, while Jock would head off to Londonderry to skydive with a civvy club. On days like this compounditis was a distant nightmare, and life in the Det was more like summer camp. Jock had been going on about me parachuting for a while, and he eventually persuaded me to tag along one Saturday morning for my first jump, from three thousand feet. It was pretty scary sitting on the edge waiting to hurtle out of the aircraft, and the three seconds before the canopy unfurled were terrifying. But the gentle floating-down part was brills. I did four more jumps after that.

The first time I heard from Luke after the ill-fated skiing trip was when he wrote me a letter saying we needed to talk. He claimed his feelings were as strong as ever, and that he wanted to sort things out. We spoke on the phone a couple of times, which didn't help much, but at least we were communicating again.

One afternoon I asked Rich, from the Troop, if I could borrow his camcorder to film myself dry and live firing to perfect my technique. Maybe it was because things with Luke were ebbing away, but over the past few weeks I'd started to pay more attention to Rich. He was every bit as gentle as I'd initially thought, and almost a carbon copy of Luke: rough SAS man to his peers, with a sensitive nature hiding inside. Halfway through my practice session with the video, Rich opened the door to the range, under the pretext of checking up on his camera.

My finely-tuned new Browning with its competition modifications was unfamiliar to him. He wanted a go, and I helped him position his hands correctly. As I placed my hands over his, I couldn't resist the temptation to glance at his rippling forearms. My thoughts were wicked. Marks out of ten? I'd give him one!

The next morning I was scoffing breakfast in the cookhouse. Jock and I had planned to go walking in the Mourne Mountains that day. We'd done this several times before, and it was always wonderful to escape from the compound and breathe in the fresh country air. After the first trip I'd grown used to his pace. I'd expected a simple walk, but Jock was so mega-fit that we'd ended up running over the mountains. On the way down I'd lost my footing and fallen into an icy stream. Although I was all Gore-texed up I was drenched down to my bra and knicks. So much for its waterproof properties! Jock and I had also been shooting together; he was developing an interest in competition shooting.

Jock wandered over, clutching his tea and toast, and told me he wouldn't be able to make it to the mountains as he had to do a recce for a job. Just then Rich came in, wearing PT kit of tight shorts and white vest, with an ocean of rippling muscles sticking out all over the place. He sat down opposite Jock and me, his plate piled high with sausages and beans.

'Fancy a trip up the Mournes, Rich?' I asked.

He nodded. 'Sure. Just you and me, is it?'

'Yeah, Jock here's just bugged out. Leave in about half an hour, OK?'

It took us an hour to drive to the Mournes, and we chatted as we jogged up the hills with day-packs on. Rich was a good listener, and easy to talk to. I didn't feel the need to censor myself, and I told him about the problems Luke and I were having. After a couple of hours we reached our first pit-stop. We sheltered by the side of a rock, huddled together because the wind was picking up. His arm slid around me, and I thought how nice it felt. I was warm, comfortable and very relaxed.

We made it back to the compound at about six o'clock and headed down to the local Chinese in Antrim, where we quaffed a couple of bottles of red wine and demolished a big fat scoff. I invited him into my basha for a coffee to end the day. As we perched on the edge of my bed listening to 'Orinoco Flow' by Enya, he leaned over and, cupping my chin in his hand, gently kissed me. I fell into it. I felt no desire to pull away, although I hadn't planned for this at all, and we drifted into a lovely intimate evening.

A couple of hours later, before he started to fall asleep, I nudged him and suggested he should leave, so we wouldn't face any embarrassment the following day when sneaking out of my basha. I slept well, and when next morning I caught his eye in the compound, our brief look said it all: we both sensed that this would probably happen again. Equally, we both knew we'd keep mum. I didn't want to create gossip: I was aware that in an all-male environment the hormones could get out of control. The rest of the boys might be jealous, or they might start to think of me as a free-for-all. There was also the sticky issue of Luke. They all knew him – he'd trained most of them. But it wasn't difficult to hide what was going on between Rich and me. There were no fireworks going off, and I had no desire to do a Glenn Close on him and boil his rabbit. Over the next couple of months we had a number of pleasant evenings together. If everything had been fine with Luke perhaps it would never have happened, but at the time it served a purpose.

A few weeks later Jed and I were involved in a monotonous surveillance op around Coalisland, East Tyrone. One important element of driving around an area is to pay attention to the locals' tribal peculiarities. In a Republican area, passing motorists flick an index finger off the steering wheel to acknowledge one another. It would look odd if we didn't do the same, but we had to take care: in Loyalist areas, people raise a flat palm, symbolising the red hand of Ulster.

We'd been working eighteen hours a day for a week, and were seriously knackered. At midnight on the Wednesday we decided to drive into a layby for a while. The target car had been unsighted for an hour, so we pushed back the seats, and while one of us kept an ear on the net, the other kipped for ten minutes at a stretch. As soon as we stopped I was out. When you're that seriously shattered, even five minutes of gonk can really make a difference.

After about half an hour we decided to leave and have another drive around. As we moved towards the layby exit we almost smashed into the back of another car sitting in the gloom. With a sense of dull horror we realised that it was our target. It had been parked forty metres in front of us, but we'd been too tired to notice. We drove out and informed everyone where the target was, then carried on with the job.

When we got back to the compound, obviously keeping *schtumm* about our little embarrassment, I unloaded my Browning. The procedure is that you point the pistol in a safe direction and release the mag. The only round is then the one in the chamber. You pull the slide to the rear and it pops out, the slide glides forward and you simply pull the trigger to release the spring tension. That's the process, but on this occasion I was practically hallucinating. I pulled the slide to the rear and watched the round pop up its shiny brass nose. Then I let the slide move forward and took up the first pressure on the trigger. At that moment some aspect of my programming flew out of my brain and said to my fingertips, 'Don't do it.' I hadn't released the magazine. By releasing the slide, I'd chambered a live round and was about to pull the trigger. Mentally I was already in the sack.

Two months after the skiing trip, I agreed to meet up with Luke to have a chat. I went up to Lancashire to visit our Melissa and her fiancé, Dave. Katherine was coming up for the weekend from Middlesbrough, and Luke was staying in the area with his friend Windsor. The atmosphere was frosty. I still cared for Luke, but couldn't shift the thought that he'd betrayed my trust by not owning up about his daughter. He remained adamant that it wasn't true, and was just as keen that nothing between us should change. I stayed wary, despite his efforts to make me believe that everything was all right.

On Saturday night, Melissa, Katherine and I decided on a night out in Blackburn. It was the first time we'd all been out together in ages, and it was brills. We ended up in a nightclub, but Luke and Windsor lightweighted because they were tired and not feeling in the party spirit. As I was gyrating on the dance-floor I saw a fat slag – straight out of *Viz* magazine – pick up my handbag from my chair and start tottering off with it. I strode across and reclaimed it. Then it started. She stood her ground and started jabbing me in the chest with a red-taloned finger, pretending she'd thought it was her mate's bag. She was a real slapper. You know the type – white high heels, blue eyeliner and badly applied bottled permatan. I'd soon had enough of her frosty-pink lipsticked mouth yelling at me, so I decked her. Tribal warfare immediately broke out between our two groups. Within moments we were down on the floor, cat-fighting.

I saw a flash of blue polkadots as someone leaned over me. I thought it was one of her mates about to kick me in the head so I rolled over into a half-crouched position and swiped with all my might. As my fist connected with a tender little mouth I realised I'd clouted our Katherine, who gasped in pain. I felt terrible. It was only her second ever fight, and both times she'd only weighed in to help me. The bouncers pushed us outside, and although we knew the police would soon arrive, the fight continued. I felt the two gold necklaces Luke had given me being wrenched off my neck. That was the last straw: no more Ms Nice Guy. I straddled the slapper and started bashing her head up and down on the tarmac, intermittently smacking her in the face. I was completely out of control. Something inside me had flipped. Dave attempted to pull me off her, and when I didn't respond he practically stood on the girl's head and levered me off.

We managed to find a taxi back to Windsor's place, where he and Luke were waiting. Luke was shocked when he saw the state of me. Half my hair was ripped out, I had a black eye brewing, and my neck was fingernail-deep in gouges. All the tassels had been yanked out of my gypsy top and one sleeve was missing. Katherine had a bust lip and was still trembling, and Melissa was bruised. I felt terrible. Luke boiled up some water with TCP in it to disinfect our wide assortment of scratches.

The next morning Luke and I drove down to Hereford. Things weren't right between us, but at least we were communicating on some level. There'd been nothing going on when I left the compound for the weekend, so I rang Paul in the ops room to see if I could get an extra day's leave. Everyone routinely does that, it's just part of the ritual of being on leave. But this time the answer was a big fat no.

'Get back here as soon as you can, Sarah. There's a briefing tonight for a job early tomorrow,' said Paul. I didn't ask for details. There was no point, he couldn't brief me on the phone. Instead I chucked my gear into my bag and Luke ran me down to Heathrow.

Before I'd even got to the ops room the word was that this

job was almost certainly going to go down. There was a sense of anticipation right across the board, from the boss down to the collators. My absence had coincided with an exceptionally violent weekend as the Provisional IRA increased its activity in an attempt to destabilise the faltering Brooke initiative. The Northern Ireland Secretary Peter Brooke had been trying in vain to get the various factions around the negotiating table. In an interview, he'd made the remark that Britain had 'no selfish interest in remaining in control of Northern Ireland'. This was intended as a signal to the paramilitaries that it was worthwhile laying down the guns to talk. Instead, the daft bastards in the IRA had seen it as a sign of weakness, and stepped up the violence. A lorry containing bombs and mortars had exploded near the St Angelo army base just north of Enniskillen in County Fermanagh, but nobody was hurt. There was also an explosion at a lumberyard in County Antrim, and a senior civil servant with the Industrial Development Board had been injured in a car bombing at Drumbeg.

I checked the board to see the team. Surprise, surprise, I was in the heli. I didn't feel particularly pissed off about this, though. I knew I'd been put up there because they rated me as the eye in the sky. I'd had lots of practice and was exhaustively versed in the use of the GOA (ground observation apparatus), well able to keep a vehicle or a house, seven thousand feet below, in its sights. With my map in one hand, the joystick that controls the GOA in the other, and my face pressed up against the lens, I was very efficient at transmitting to the team, telling them where the target was while keeping the pilot briefed on what to do next. Consequently, on jobs that needed someone in the heli, I was the automatic first choice. Even so, I often wished someone else would get up to speed in the air, so that when a big job went down I wouldn't automatically be stuck in the clouds.

By 7.30 p.m. the Det and most of the Troop were eyes-down in the briefing room awaiting orders for Op Fountain. The atmosphere was solid with tension. As I took my place I saw that Paul had pinned two maps to the board. The first was a 1:25,000 of the general area; the second was a detailed plan of a village in County

Armagh, where a sectarian hit was expected to take place just two hundred metres from the spot where two Protestants had been maimed by an IRA bomb six months before. The intelligence was that the Provos planned to take out a police reservist as he went about his daily routine.

We were told that at 1.30 every afternoon the target always picked up a friend on the way to work, pulling up in a layby opposite a church on the high street to wait for him. This was the obvious location for the hit.

The plan was for the Det team to pick up the terrorists, keeping them under surveillance as they headed for the village. One of the Troop guys, Jake, who roughly matched the description of the Provos' target, would take his place in the target's red Escort. The bleeps had got hold of an identical car and fitted it up with the same plates, and with the addition of armour in the bodywork. Jake would also be kitted out in body armour, and would be fully tooled and commed up.

To say that he would also have a fair amount of back-up would be an understatement. Four members of the Troop were to be hidden in an unmarked Transit van with one-way glass around the corner. Jed and Daniel, one of the Op Spice guys, would be positioned nearby to give the final movements of the Provos' vehicle as it pulled into the layby where Jake would be waiting. In the bushes at the back of a nearby house would be the main assault group of four more Troop men. There were Troop cut-offs at the top of the village and at the bridge over a disused railway line at the other end of the high street, and three OPs on the roads into the village. It was their task to take over from the mobile surveillance team, giving the Provos' movements as they drove into town. In addition to all this manpower there would be a solitary Troop guy positioned inside a garage six feet from Jake and his red Escort in the layby. You could never be too careful! There would also be aerial surveillance – me.

The HMSU boys would also be waiting on the sidelines just outside the village. Should we manage to apprehend the terrorists they would come in and formally arrest them. Soldiers can arrest terrorists, but it's a real hassle – better by far to detain them and await the RUC.

If Jake was nervous about being the sitting duck, he didn't show it. He just focused on the briefing, running through the details in his mind, getting on with the job like the pro he was. After the ninety-minute tactics and technical briefing we were joined by eight members of HMSU, for their briefing. When we'd run through the plan we grabbed an early night.

Preparation for the job the next morning followed the normal routine: comms checks, weapons checks and a quick run-through with Kiwi, who would be my pilot. The mobile surveillance team drove to the east of the village, to the area through which the Provos would pass as they travelled towards the hit. All the OPs were in position before first light.

At 1250 hours, Kiwi and I flew to an SF base seven kilometres – three minutes' flying time – west of the target, where we would remain forward mounted until we got the standby. I removed the door of the heli to clear my fields of fire, and fitted the round-catcher over the ejection port, ready for action.

Everyone had given their positions over the net. Now we just had to wait. Dead on 1326 hours Adrian came up with a hasty 'Standby, standby.' This was excellent news, and exactly on time. He'd picked up the Provo team heading west towards the village in two cars, a red Nissan Sunny and a blue Renault 21. Everyone sparked into life as the mobile surveillance team carried on with the commentary. By now I was strapped into the heli with my helmet on, and the second we got the word we went airborne, dipping our nose and heading due east. The team were continuing their commentary on the location of the Provos' cars. When they were within five hundred metres of their target, the Nissan pulled off, and the surveillance team went to their lay-up position as planned. The Renault passed two rural OPs in quick succession, and they gave a commentary on its progress as planned. This had all gone down inside a minute. Meanwhile Kiwi and I were powering along at two thousand feet, just minutes away from the area.

What should have happened next was that the rural OP would go silent as the Provos cruised into town, then Jed would take over the commentary. But as the car entered the village, Dippy, positioned at the far end of the high street, started gobbing off on the net. Jed should have been controlling everything by now, but there was no way he could get onto the net with this jabbering idiot blocking everyone else out. This was insanity. What was Dippy thinking? Only Jed, from his position opposite the Escort, could observe everything that was going on. There was no way Dippy had a clear picture.

Kiwi and I could see the village now, but all I was getting on the net was Dippy, jabbering away like a maniac. The Provos had crossed the railway bridge and were approaching the layby where Jake was sitting in his red Escort dressed in overalls and flicking through the *Sun*. I had no way of communicating with the team, but I knew we were all thinking the same: Get off the fucking net. Vital seconds were slipping past, and the operation had to be carried out as planned if we were to have a chance of a success. It was only as the Provos were actually pulling into the layby that Dippy decided to give his vocal chords a rest and Jed could finally come up with a desperate and powerful 'Standby, standby.' He flung out the words as fast as possible as the Provos' Renault swung round to face the entrance in preparation for a swift getaway.

The Provos came to a stop, and one of them jumped out of the Renault, slowly brought up an AK47 and pointed it at Jake. As he did so, Jed gave 'Go! Go! Go!' Within moments the Troop team were out of the van. There was no chance for them to make an arrest without putting Jake in serious danger, so they initiated the contact with their G3s. In the meantime, Jake had obviously thought, 'Fuck this for a game of soldiers.' He jumped out of the car, raced across the gravel and leapt like a gazelle down the eighteen-foot railway embankment, despite his heavy body armour.

The 7.62 round is a big, powerful bullet, and at close range it will slice through car bodywork like a knife through butter. The Provo driver started to pull away, even though he must already have been dying from the bullets raking his car. After a few seconds he lost control, and the Renault slewed across the road and smashed into a parked car. The reaction team had moved into position, and they continued to fire. Two bodies were left hanging half out of the shredded Renault. Despite the massive roar of gunfire, the street remained deserted.

Moments later, Kiwi and I arrived on the scene. We swooped and circled low, watching the bloody aftermath of the ambush. The wind buffeted me through the heli's open door. At a hundred metres from the ground I caught the unmistakable whiff of cordite. I was hanging out of the heli, HK53 at the ready, but it was obvious there weren't going to be any runners. Big Marty raced across from the unmarked van and down the embankment to see if Jake was OK.

The ambush had lasted just a few seconds: four dead terrorists, no security forces casualties. It was a classic result. The Det and Troop guys all emerged from their nooks and crannies, filling up the previously deserted street. The HMSU cordons on standby moved in, and a Wessex was called up to evacuate the Troop. As the Det moved out, we veered off to the right and headed back to the compound.

There was great relief that we were all OK, back-slapping, relieved faces and manic chatter. In the debrief everyone talked in detail through their role and what they'd seen. Jake, the stand-in target, had some scary news. At the point when the Renault had crossed the railway bridge, his comms had gone down. For all he knew, no one else had comms either. It must have been terrifying for him sitting there, not knowing what was happening. He also told us that as the Provo had aimed the AK47 at him he'd given him an evil smile down the length of the barrel. Without comms Jake had had to use native wit, hence his incredible leap down the embankment at the earliest opportunity. Part of the debrief involved the luxury of a second assault on our eardrums from Dippy.

The RUC later announced that the AK47 recovered from the terrorists had previously been used to murder seven people. We found out that the gang we'd taken out included one of the Pro-visional IRA's leading gunmen and close-quarter specialists. Sinn

Fein named the other three bodies. They all had bloody pedigrees. One of them had taken part in the mass escape from the Maze in September 1983 after being convicted of the murder of an army major. He was a big fish, and had been one of the IRA's top terrorists for years. He'd also led the bombing at Warrenpoint, in which eighteen British soldiers were murdered, and was suspected of killing a police officer in 1984. The driver of the Renault was an explosives expert who was responsible for a series of bombings. The other terrorist had murdered four police officers, and was said to have been involved in the killing of a senior Northern Ireland politician.

Lisburn HQ, the other Dets, the RUC and the SB all rang up to offer congratulations on our success and to buy us barrels of beer. Nobody needed any further encouragement. We were straight down to the bar, fired up and ready to go. With the beer flowing, the real debrief started: Dippy was getting a well-deserved slagging for clogging up the net with his crap, but he was OK because Jake hadn't come to any harm. If he had, it would have been a different story.

After a few beers, Marty told us that as the contact was going down an old woman walking a dog had wandered along the pavement, passing by the side of the unmarked van. The dog was going bananas, but she was stone deaf and hadn't heard a whimper.

It was one hell of a party, with much joviality and good-humoured slaggings, and it was well into the next day before the bar showed any sign of emptying. When it did, Rich and I got it together again in my basha. Afterwards we spoke at length about the situation between us. I was realistic. 'In a couple of weeks my tour here will be over and I'll be moving back with Luke. Things aren't wonderful, but I'm determined to make the best of it.'

He nodded sadly. We'd enjoyed each other's company, but there were no strings binding us.

EPILOGUE

CLOSE PROTECTION

BY JUNE 1991, AFTER eighteen months immersed in the pressure-cooker environment of the Det, I was more than ready to leave. My basha might have been the place where I lived, but its functional interior had never felt like home. I'd been an enthusiastic and efficient cog in a piece of sophisticated military machinery, but now I was gagging to come down to earth. I was always on my guard, never able to fully relax.

I thought back over my tour with a sense of achievement. I'd done well. I'd overcome many problems, gained respect and pro-voked some of the misogynists into reassessing their attitudes. But I was more than ready to leave, and I was already making plans for my new life in the outside world. I'd been cocooned in an institution where there were no bills to pay, no meals to prepare, no domestic hassles. I'd lived every day as if it were my last, in a place where long-term decisions were irrelevant. Now I was facing the prospect of having to fend for myself in an environment which didn't carry the daily potential of a bullet through the brain.

Shane and the head sheds at Lisburn had said nothing about where I would be going. I still had twelve months of my nine-year commitment to the military to serve, and I believed that my future career didn't lie in the greasy world of aircraft maintenance. My case was unusual because I was both female and a rating, not an officer. Ruperts would go back to their units after a tour across the water, while male 'other ranks' tended to gravitate to Hereford and a spell as instructors. I took it for granted that I would join them.

There was a job going at Stirling Lines in the CRW (counter-revolutionary warfare) wing. This would have been a rare slot for a woman, but I knew I was a natural for the work: house assaults, recces, range-work – I was ideal. Then I found out that I wouldn't be able to join CRW until I'd served two tours over the water. My disappointment was nothing compared to the hammer-blow of discovering that I was being sent back to the Wrens. I couldn't believe I was being wasted; I had so much to offer. A year later I realised that it was a class issue when Charlotte, a Rupert, was posted to CRW after a single tour with South. I felt a sense of loss at the prospect of going back to the Navy, but I knew better than to complain. There was nothing I could do about it.

There wasn't much to do during the last week in the compound. I concentrated on drinking as much as possible, and started packing. I had to consider Kieran and Mary's future: Kieran was a black fantailed goldfish, Mary a normal carrot-coloured job. I gave them to Charlotte, but within weeks they were dead.

I was demob-happy. One evening we drove into Dungannon, and as we neared the market square Jed flashed his headlights and beeped the horn, acting like a joyrider. His mood infected me and I said, 'Let's come back tonight in one of the admin cars. I'll go into the Venue Bar, order a pint of Guinness in my best English accent, and if the barman gives me a look I'll pull open my jacket and say: "You do take 9mm, don't you?" You'll be waiting outside, and I'll come tearing out and we can drive away.' Jed thought this wasn't such a good idea, as he was staying in South Det a while longer.

On my last night I went into town with the seven other girls from the Dets. Sally went up to the DJ at Pantiles and told him it was my hen night, so the jazz foursome played 'Here Comes the Bride'. A squaddie was standing by the bar. He was trying not to look like a squaddie, but in their jeans, T-shirts and desert wellies you can always spot them at a thousand paces. He swaggered over and began to make conversation. 'Who are you getting married to? Lad over here?' I nodded. 'Where's he from?'

'From a small place. You've probably never heard of it,' I said, deadpan.

'Go on, try me.'

'It's called Cappagh.'

His face registered complete horror.

'Yeah, it's a nice little place,' I continued. 'I've known him for a while now, at least a couple of months.'

He collected himself and asked cautiously, 'What's his name?'

'Seamus O'Hanlan,' I said, naming a notorious player.

'Are you sure you really *know* him?' asked the squaddie, genuine consternation seeping out of every pore. He tried gently to talk me out of it. 'People are often not what they seem,' he said.

'Oh, Seamus is lovely,' I said cheerfully. 'He's got lots of brothers, and they're all really protective of one another.'

The squaddie turned a shade of green and wandered off to get another drink. The night wore on and I consumed shedloads of vodka and Coke. My gang and I fell down the road by the Europa. It was a busy, buzzy night, and APVs were cruising up and down. We lined up along the pavement, and there was a partial eclipse of the moon as we flashed our botties. We got a pick-up from Jed, who pretended to be an oppressed male with all these drunken, scantily-clad women pawing him. We mooned through the windows all the way back to camp.

It was midnight by the time we arrived, and body parts were sticking out everywhere. We were shouting and singing 'I Will Survive' by Gloria Gaynor. The new operators had just arrived, and they looked a bit intimidated at the sight of these scary, raucous women. As I poked my bum out of the sunroof I looked at the new blokes standing by their bergens, and remembered my own sense of disorientation eighteen months before. That night the bar saw another severe drinking session.

Troop handovers are staggered. Everyone serves twelve months, with half the Troop changing over every six months. But because of the Gulf War, our lot had been over the water for eighteen months. In the bar that night everyone raised a toast to Vince Phillips, who'd died four months earlier in the failed Bravo Two Zero patrol in the Gulf made famous by Andy McNab's book. Vince was a good bloke, and was sorely missed. He'd been a professional soldier for many years, and a solid, dependable character.

Big Marty had had some black T-shirts made up with a modified SAS emblem screen-printed on them. Instead of the winged dagger pointing downwards, a fist was grasping it and holding it angled up, as if ready for use. There were only enough T-shirts made for the members of the Troop. Vince had died before he got his, and Marty told me that he wanted me to have it.

I was sticking to vodka and Coke, but as it was my last night everyone was plying me with so many shorts that I had to tip them all into a pint glass and quaff from that. I was well tanked up, and I shouted to Jed, in earshot of Shane and Frank, the new ops officer, 'I'm gonna shag all the head sheds before I leave.' It was a case of role reversal as they looked embarrassed and soon wriggled out of the bar. The girls gradually buggered off, until only Charlotte was left. A few hours later Gerry, who would soon be replacing Marty as team leader of the Troop, lurched over. We clambered onto the large central table and started drunkenly falling about in an excuse for a dance. 'Let's take off an item of clothing for an item of clothing,' he dared me.

'Yeah, all right. You first,' I mumbled. I was barely able to stand up, but I'm pathologically unable to refuse a dare. The clothes started to tumble off – dress, bra, pants and stockings all followed in quick succession. The floor soon looked like a Chinese laundry. Minutes later I was standing at the bar swigging from my pint without a stitch on. I noticed Gerry staring at my bulgy abdomen. 'Stop looking at my belly!' I shouted. 'We're not looking at your belly,' he replied lasciviously.

I can't remember much else, but Jed must have looked after me and returned me safe and sound to my basha, because the next morning that was where I was when I came to and realised that two hippos were fighting in my brain. I looked at my watch: 7 a.m. Me and my baggy head were due to leave the Det. Half an hour later I wandered into the cookhouse, looked around at the blokes and said simply, 'See you around, mateys.' Then I walked out, loaded up one of the ops cars and drove out of the A-frame and through the compound. It was a bit of an anticlimax.

I drove from Antrim to Larne, took the car ferry to Stranraer, then drove to Luke's house in Hereford. A few days later we dropped the car off at a garage in Gloucestershire where it would have all its armour removed before being recycled as a training vehicle.

I had about a month's leave before I was drafted back to Yeovil. Things weren't the same between Luke and me; the spark had gone out, and I could feel myself falling out of love with him. It all came to a head after a few days. Luke had gone off to work, and Jock, who'd left the Det some months earlier and was now working at Hereford in the NI cell, had popped in for a cup of tea. At about 11.30 a.m. Luke popped back to pick something up. He wandered into the kitchen, took one look at Jock and started frothing at the mouth. 'What the fuck are you doing here?'

I couldn't believe his aggression. 'What's up, Luke?' I asked.

He was barely coherent. He pointed at Jock and screamed, 'You're having it off together. Don't fucking deny it, I've read the letters.'

He marched towards Jock, who was backtracking across the kitchen. 'You'd better fucking leave. Now.'

Jock didn't need any further encouragement. He stormed out and slammed the door.

'What the fuck's got into you?' I demanded. Luke's eyes worried me. They were wild. He'd flipped, and his whole face was contorted with jealous rage.

'I found letters from him this morning. Now I know why our love is fucking slipping away. You're fucking in love with him.' He was quivering with a desperate mix of rage and dejection.

It took me thirty minutes to calm him down and get to the truth. All my gear was stashed in his living room, including a bundle of his love letters. I'd been asleep that morning when he'd got up to go to camp. On the way out he'd absent-mindedly flicked through the cards, notes and pieces of torn-out exercise-book paper he'd sent me over the past eighteen months. In amongst his *billets-doux* were a couple of letters from Jock, who'd been infatuated by me ever since we'd met at Camp Two. He'd sent me Valentine's cards and the odd badly written poem. I liked him very much, and we'd become the best of friends. He often told me of his love for me, but Luke had always been my man. Despite our ups and downs he was everything to me. I'd never told him that Jock had written to me, certain that jealousy would colour his view of an innocent matter. My instinct had been right.

'You only read what you wanted to read,' I reasoned with him. 'It's not a two-way thing.' But the damage was done. Luke had alienated me with his possessiveness and his explosive temper. I didn't want a man who could metamorphose like that. What would happen if we got married? He'd never hit me or damaged me in any way, but we were only living together. If we were married I feared he might become violent. Looking back now, I realise that I might have judged him harshly. He realised he'd lost me, and needed a focus for his despair. Despite my assurances, he wouldn't accept that Jock and I weren't having an affair. He needed to believe it, because he needed a reason why I didn't love him any more.

Two days later Luke bumped into Jock in the training area. He stood rooted to the spot, anger oozing from every pore, and snarled: 'I'm gonna fucking get you. It might not be this week or next month. It might not be for a long time, but I swear to God I'll get you.' From then on whenever they saw each other Luke would look daggers at Jock, then stride off. Jock told me he'd even thought about keeping a pistol in his desk, just in case.

Two weeks later, Luke had calmed down a bit. I was even able to tell him that Jock and I were going for a tab up the Brecon Beacons, and he appeared to accept it. It was a fearsome tab, and a blizzard soon blew up, leading to a complete white-out. We covered a lot of ground, and didn't see a soul on top of Pen-y-fan. After nine hours' hard workout I got back to Luke's house absolutely knackered, needing a hot bath and some big fat scoff. Luke was upstairs ironing, and as I clumped wearily towards the bathroom he said, 'Hello, darling. We're going out to meet Tommy and Brenda at the Green Dragon. Do you want anything ironed?'

'Oh. I don't really fancy going out. I'm knackered.'

I heard the iron banging on the ironing board, and thought 'Here we go again,' with a sense of dread.

Luke appeared on the landing, his face grey and ready to explode. 'You're too fucking tired, eh? A good shag, is he?'

'What are you talking about?'

'Oh, come on, Sarah, just admit what's going on. How do you think I feel, sitting here while you're out with him? We haven't had sex for ages. You must be doing it with someone else.'

I didn't have the heart to tell him that the truth was I just didn't want to do it with him.

He put on his old schizo head again, shouting, going completely over the top and cursing Jock for destroying our beautiful relationship. It didn't matter how many times I told him he was wrong. He was back in his own lunatic little world. Suddenly he stopped ranting. 'I want you to leave,' he said coldly.

I stared back, dazed. 'What . . . When?'

'Tomorrow. As soon as you can get your kit together.'

I was filthy and knackered, my car was off the road and I was starving. It would have been better to wait until morning, but my pride was telling me to get out now. 'Are you sure?' I said icily. 'Because if you tell me to leave, I'll never come back. When you've calmed down and changed your mind, it will be too late.'

He'd turned away, and was leaning on the ironing board for support. 'Yes, I'm sure,' he said in a quiet, choked voice.

'Right, fine. I'm out of here now.' I knew I would never go back. I also knew that Luke would have second thoughts and apologise. But it was too late. I turned around and walked in a trance down the stairs, picked up my purse and slammed the door. In a daze I marched down the lane, phoned Jock from the box on the corner and gave him a run-down. He drove down to pick me up and put me up for the night.

Next morning, after I knew Luke had gone out to work, I drove up to his house in Jock's car and went in to collect my stuff. On the kitchen floor a white envelope awaited me. My hands were shaking as I opened it. 'Darling, I'm so sorry. Please don't leave me . . .' I couldn't read on – and I couldn't leave fast enough. I ran into the front room and started grabbing boxes and bags. I heaved them into Jock's car, my throat choked. I'm a bit of a Joan of Arc in these situations: I'd rather mutilate myself than return to a man who has ordered me out. Once the car was loaded I slammed the door and drove away for ever.

I had three weeks' leave left before I was due at Yeovilton. I phoned up Kimberley, a Northern Irish girl I vaguely knew who was living about twenty miles away with a Regiment bloke called Matt. Six months earlier he'd had a motorbike crash and lost his arm, but the SAS had kept him on, as they always do in such situations. He was a well-respected, experienced soldier, and not having an arm didn't make him less of one. Kimberley had said that if ever I was passing I should drop in. Her generosity was a godsend, and I remain eternally grateful to them. She welcomed me in, and I got my life back together again. The day I left to return to the Navy I gave them a blank cheque for bills, but it was never cashed.

After the informality of the Det, Yeovilton was a huge culture shock. People were parading around in uniforms, saluting and saying 'Yes, sir' and 'No, sir.' I couldn't bear the thought of living on-camp, so I rented a room in a house nearby. On my first morning I dragged myself to the regulating office to find out what fate awaited me. The chief petty officer scanned his lists. 'Leading Wren Ford? You're down for AED [Aircraft Engineering Department].'

I was horrified. AED was an administration block. 'There must be some mistake,' I said. 'That's temporary, isn't it?'

He checked his file. 'No, that's your draft for the next twelve months. That's where you're down to go.'

I stormed out. I couldn't believe I was going from the Det to a poxy office job. It was a horrendous waste.

AED was a single-storey brick building. I went in and knocked on the DO's door. 'Good morning, sir. I'm Leading Wren Ford. Is this for real? Am I really doing this job?' My documents were laid out on the desk in front of him. He nodded regretfully. Clearly he too thought it was madness, given my experience.

'In that case, can I have October off?' I'd been selected for the armed forces pistol team for the Commonwealth Championships in Canada. The DO was great about it, and wished me luck. Just as well, because I'd already booked my ticket!

A team of eight of us flew out early for the Alaska Championships. I came top female and seventh overall – 'Not bad for a girlie,' said Graham, our team Rupert from Sandhurst. Our week in Canada was equally brilliant, and I collected a heap of medals, despite the fact it was my first overseas competition and I'd only been shooting competitively for eighteen months. After a week of competition I became the Ladies' Commonwealth Champion.

While I was in Canada the Guildford Four's conviction for the pub bombing in 1975 was overturned, and they were set free. My first reaction was surprise; after all, there's usually no smoke without fire. But when a couple of years later I saw the film about the case, *In the Name of the Father*, my opinion changed, and I came to see them as the victims of an enormous miscarriage of justice.

After the championships I returned home a local heroine, with many interviews and publicity in naval magazines. Back at AED I did the minimum amount of work necessary to get by, and took part in joint service shooting competitions as often as possible. So did Luke, apparently, although we never met. I heard on the grapevine that he'd scan the contestant lists to see when I was shooting, and would stay away on those days. Eventually he gave up shooting altogether. Stories drifted back to me of his heavy drinking and his desolation at our breakdown. At first I felt terrible about this, but if he was so devastated, why had it taken him only six weeks to find another girlfriend? So much for him loving me! I didn't have another relationship for ages. I missed him terribly. I was hurting badly, but I didn't let it show.

As the months ticked past, I considered my future. If I signed on again it would be for another three-year stint which would include a second tour across the water. Things in NI were really hotting up: in 1991 there'd been almost three hundred bombs and four hundred incendiaries planted by terrorists. If I served another tour I'd then be eligible to become an instructor at Hereford. I knew my decision would influence the rest of my career. Returning to the Det was an attractive prospect, but I had a nagging thought within me: I'd already conquered that mountain. I needed a new challenge. I wanted the lure of something different, perhaps working for myself. I told our Mam of my confusion. 'Sarah, you're forever looking over the next horizon,' she said pointedly.

After much heart-searching, I decided on a career as a surveillance specialist and BG (bodyguard). Going on the close-protection circuit is a fairly typical route for SAS and Det personnel to make. Liz had done just that, and was able to furnish me with a number of contacts. Although we call it BG-ing, the term 'bodyguarding' is rarely used. It's considered rather naff and very Hollywood.

There are half a dozen or so big companies who specialise in security services in Britain. When they secure a contract they supply freelances to make up the required teams. There are many freelances specialising in close-protection and security work: people just out of the police or the regular forces, civilians who fancy the life, as well as Special Forces personnel. It's a fascinating twilight world where reputations can be made, or destroyed, within hours. Ex-Special Forces personnel are obviously a valuable commodity in the private sector. Not surprisingly, there are more members of the 'SAS' sloshing around than the infantry. There must have been at least six thousand men on that Iranian Embassy job!

Being female was a rarity, and made me even more valuable to employers, for the same reasons as across the water. Employers are aware of what being in the Det entails, so CVs are not always required. The money is good, if sporadic. On a typical job you can expect to earn between £100 and £200 a day, often paid cash in hand, plus expenses. But the work is hard. A typical shift lasts twelve hours, and I often work 6 a.m. to 11 p.m. Frequently you're overnighting miles from home, in posh hotels if you're on a BG job, or in shitty little dives on surveillance. Either way, it soon gets a bit draining, so the dosh is hard-earned.

Before signing up with the agencies I went to a shooting academy in Germany for a two-week firearms instructor course. I wanted to be able to supplement my career as a BG and surveillance specialist by teaching.

My new life is arranged in an essentially hand-to-mouth manner. Work rolls in, and it's always for tomorrow – there's scarcely ever a job with more notice than that. The most common BG job is close-protection of Middle Eastern clients while they're in the UK. These contracts tend to be London-based, and can last anything from a couple of days to six months. And there's always the prospect of being signed up for a permanent job. Surveillance serials also tend to be London-based, but can roam anywhere. There's a lot of marital work. Often the client requires you to follow their spouse and find out who they meet, where and when. Video evidence can be obtained, and it's now admissible in court. I also branch out and mount investigations allied to surveillance, uncovering info using a variety of techniques, including using computer networks to tap into various organisations, or getting access to bank details. It's a fascinating grey area.

Having served in Special Forces, I've absorbed the techniques needed to remove a client from a threat. I've also become skilled in the art of observation, able to look at a situation and anticipate events. I can protect my client and eradicate a threat.

There's also security work. Static security consists of looking after a house in the owner's absence, or covering AGMs by acting as a steward and removing troublemakers if necessary. Technical work is less common, but there have been a number of occasions when I've been required to insert a device somewhere in a work-place. On one job I was tasked to hide a stash of recording equipment under false ceiling tiles in an office, and to hide a camera in a wall clock. The company manager was convinced that he was being diddled, and had arranged the spy system so he could eaves-drop on his employees.

There have been times when I've rejected work because I didn't like the client. On one occasion I went for an interview with a famous and wealthy businessman at his offices in Kensington. He was seeking security personnel to look after his children at his country retreat. While I was waiting for my appointment, a scruffy middle-aged man slouched into the room. He looked like a house boy, in old grey flannels, a scruffy shirt and a pair of battered slippers. I also noticed that his flies were undone. When he started asking questions, I realised that this was the man himself! I had no hesitation in turning the job down when I heard rumours from people who'd worked for him before. Apparently he expected BGs to be on standby twenty-seven hours a day. He'd ordered a previous incumbent to patrol the perimeter fence of his Oxfordshire mansion all night in the pissing rain, despite the high-octane security cameras that were continually scanning the grounds.

Another job sounded much more appealing. I'd be required to work as a BG for an American family based in the UK, with plenty of international jet-setting thrown in. The wages were £40,000 a year, plus lots of enticing benefits. The client, one of the world's richest men, had specified that he only wanted ex-Regiment men on the two eleven-strong teams, but he also needed two women. Each team would consist of a mobile reaction force of eight men and a domestic team of three, who would be in charge of residential security at the family's Kensington house. Liz was my double on the other mobile team. A swift calculation showed me that the client would be spending nearly a million pounds a year in close protection alone. But as he was personally worth £900 million, I didn't lose any sleep on his behalf.

At my interview I learned that the perceived threat to the family was posed by the client's brother, who apparently harboured a grudge because their father hadn't apportioned his wealth equally between his sons. In June 1994 I flew out to America with the rest of the team to the family's thirty-acre country estate, where the client's wife was staying with her young son and daughter. Chris Ryan, author of *The One Who Got Away*, about the failed Bravo Two Zero mission in the Gulf War, was another of the specialists on the team. We were accommodated in a pretty wooden chalet by a lake. We never saw the client himself, who spent his whole life flying around the world in private jets and staying in mediocre hotels. He didn't believe in wasting his fortune.

We were required to hang around the lake all day with our

charges, playing with them, taking them out, eating dinner with them. Every day was much the same, waterskiing on the lake, getting scoffed by the mozzies. The worst thing about it was the old bag of a grandmother, an old, fat, two-faced dragon who viewed the security personnel as her personal slaves. She had us taking the rubbish out and running errands. If she wanted something done, protecting the kids came a distant second.

I'd been there two weeks when the team leader, Russ, strolled over to me and another member of the team. He looked grim-faced.

'I've got a bit of bad news for you both,' he said soberly. 'You've got the sack. They're putting you on the next plane home.'

I was pole-axed. 'What the fuck are you talking about? Only yesterday the client's wife was telling us what a great team we were. What's going on?'

He shook his head slowly. 'Beats me.'

I sensed that the grandmother had something to do with it, but I didn't have a chance to find out. Later that afternoon I was sitting on a plane at 36,000 feet, analysing my lack of a life. I was on the way back to Britain with no fixed abode and no job, but my biggest concern was to figure out why I'd been sacked. It had never happened to me before, and I needed to know if I'd done something wrong.

Within a few days of arriving back in Britain I decided that I needed somewhere to live. I took the plunge and bought a one-bedroom flat in Surrey. At least now I had somewhere to call home.

Over the next few months I kept in touch with the team over in the States. One by one, the rest of them were ditched without notice. I couldn't understand it. The team was made up of ex-members of the world's most élite regiment. Surely there couldn't be problems on a professional level? Eventually the truth came out. Apparently the real reason the team had been formed was not because of any threat posed by the client's brother, but to keep his wife sweet until the divorce papers he was secretly serving on her came through. He was planning to make his move after his wife and children had lived in Britain for a year, so avoiding a massive pay-out in the US divorce courts.

We'd got the sack because one of the team had started getting more than friendly with the client's wife. They'd soon become inseparable, and the guy's new-found power went to his head. He started inventing stories about other members of the team. Liz got the sack when he falsely told the client's wife that he'd overheard her call the grandmother a fat old bag. Although the client didn't like seeing all these good men and women sacked, he felt powerless to intervene. In fact he was probably delighted at what was going on between the team-member and his wife, as it would give him more fuel for his divorce petition.

Several months later I heard that the divorce had gone through the London courts. The client's wife was awarded £9 million, plus £5000 a month for the rest of her life, the thirty-acre American estate and custody of the children. Her lawyers described the settlement as 'excessively mean'. I didn't waste much sympathy there.

Most of my close-protection work is with Middle Eastern clients. When they go shopping in Knightsbridge or Bond Street they travel with an entourage of anything from half a dozen people to a busload of friends, nannies, children, and servants to order food in restaurants, carry spare clothing, wipe their arses and carry their designer handbags crammed with thousands of pounds' worth of £50 notes. I keep my eyes trained on my principal, but always make sure I know where the money carrier is. Every gang in London is aware that a crowd of Arabs will be carrying a stash of cash. They make the easiest target imaginable.

People sometimes think I lead a glamorous life, jetting about doing undercover surveillance and mixing with the rich and famous. That's not quite the whole story. Once I was on a job with two ex-Marines, Paul and Dave, and Irwin, who was ex-Det. We found ourselves in Belgrave Square, standing in deep snow and attempting to do surveillance on a target despite the fact we had no flat number, no photograph, basically fuck-all. The target had been sacked because his boss suspected him of being an informer who had facilitated a takeover bid. We were tasked to follow him, watching him stuff his face in plush restaurants. This is one genuine perk of such a job: we were at liberty to scoff expensive food while covertly videoing the target. And the client gets to pick up the tab.

One afternoon we watched the target buying a Christmas tree. At that point I really began to hate him. We'd been on him for ten hours that day, and he was returning home to dress his tree while quaffing vintage port and scoffing Stilton. At times like that you're tempted to pack in the job. You can never arrange a night out, or make a doctor's appointment, let alone consider organising holidays – a job will always spoil your plans. Yet, when a task is complete and paid for, and I'm basking in a few days off, I always forget the hard graft. I'd be bored shitless in a normal job.

A couple of days later the target and his wife came out of their building with a set of luggage, and a taxi drew up. I followed it out of London and along the A4 to Heathrow, and shadowed the couple as they made their way to the international check-in. Unfortunately it was a general desk, with no indication of either flight time or destination. I rang the client, who was quite clear: I should stick with the target. It was 5 p.m. on a Friday, and the first of the four flights the target could have been catching was due to leave at 6.15. I got on the phone to Mick, my boyfriend at the time, who lived twenty miles away.

'Hi, Mick. Look, I need you to meet me at the roundabout on the M3/M25. Bring my passport, crash helmet and a few bits of summer clothing. Meet you in half an hour.'

I drove like a loony and made it to the roundabout in thirty-four minutes, spending most of the time on the hard shoulder because the motorway was jammed solid with traffic. Mick was waiting for me. He quickly handed over a helmet and a holdall that he'd packed for me. Paul screamed up on his motorbike, and twenty minutes later I ran into Departures. Dave thrust a wad of pesetas and a ticket into my hand, having found out that the target's destination was Minorca. I got through check-in in the nick of time.

It wasn't until I was installed in my seat that I began to formulate a plan. I checked my money. The tight gits had only got me about £17-worth of pesetas. Great. I ran through possible scenarios. What if the target and his wife stepped off the plane into a waiting car, and I lost them? What if they got a pick-up? What if there were no taxis? I'd never been to Minorca before, and didn't know the score at the airport. Oh well, I'd soon find out.

The plane landed, and after scooping his luggage off the carousel in the terminal, the target and his wife headed for the taxi rank with me in hot pursuit. As their taxi pulled away I said to the next driver in line, 'Do you speak English?'

His answer was not what I needed. 'Que?'

Oh, bollocks.

'Follow . . . that . . . taxi,' I said.

Eventually, hastened by a helpful '*arriba*', he seemed to get the message, and we took off.

After ten minutes he turned around and glared at me. 'Where we go? You have money?' He seemed to be able to turn on the English when he wanted to.

'Yes. I have money,' I lied.

Half an hour later the target's taxi turned down a dirt track. This did it for my driver. He stomped on the brakes. 'No more,' he shouted. I watched the headlights dip into the distance. Then the taxi stopped two hundred metres up the track and the target got out.

I was so relieved that I pacified my driver by handing him what money I had. We headed to the nearest town, where I got some more money from a hole in a wall. The taxi driver demanded £40 for his pains, and I was too knackered to argue. It was midnight, I'd been up at 5 a.m. for the past six days and I was in need of sleep. When he finally dropped me off I resisted the urge to lamp him, because it would have compromised the job. Instead I stood square, looked him in the eye and said, 'I'll be back,' in a parody of Arnold Schwarzenegger.

The hotel he'd driven me to was a dump. The room was freezing cold, and the mattress was sodden. The bath was plugless, so a soak was out. The shower didn't work and the toilet wouldn't flush. But what do you expect for £7.50? I slept in my clothes and shivered all night.

Next morning I phoned the client from the hotel kitchen,

surrounded by dead chickens lying in pools of blood. Before I left on a freedom flight home I video-ed the hotel, as I knew that without hard evidence no one would believe my description of the conditions. Glamour? Not this game.

I'm aware that I've inherited my toughness from our Mam. People might look at what I do and draw conclusions, but our Mam is a million times stronger than me. She's had to be. I don't know if I could have survived as well as her if I'd been on the emotional assault-course that's been her path through life. In comparison with hers, my journey seems straightforward. Yet she never let herself look back, however hard it got. She dealt with each day as it came, and I owe her a massive debt of gratitude for her example. We might not have had much money as kids, but we had the most important thing, plenty of love – although we sometimes found it hard to show it. But when I see Melissa, Katherine or Jane now I can't get enough of them. I hug my mother, too. Although she sometimes seems reserved, we're secure in the knowledge that we love each other.

As for me, I just get on with the job in hand. I've had to push camera-toting paparazzi away from my principal on many occasions, but so far no client of mine has ever been hit on. But that doesn't mean I can relax. You can never take what happened yesterday as evidence of what might happen tomorrow. That nutter is always lurking around the next corner. That kidnap attempt is just waiting to happen.

I remain on permanent standby. To paraphrase St Luke, I will continue to go out into the highways and hedges and compel them to come in.

GLOSSARY

AED	*Aircraft Engineering Department*
AEM	*Aircraft Engineering Mechanic*
APV, pig	*armoured personnel vehicle*
ASU	*active service unit*
AVGAS	*aviation gasoline*
basha	*shelter*
beastings	*hard physical training*
bergen	*large rucksack*
BFT	*basic fitness test*
BG	*bodyguard*
bleep	*electrician*
cam	*camouflage*
CFT	*combat fitness test*
CI	*Chief Instructor*
CQB	*close-quarter battle*
CTR	*close-target reconnaissance*
cuds	*countryside*
cut-offs	*secondary line of defence*
DCI	*Defence Council Instruction*
debussing	*exiting a vehicle*
DO	*Divisional Officer*
DPM	*disrupted pattern (camouflage) material*
DS	*Directing Staff*
DSM	*Detachment Sergeant Major*
E4A	*surveillance division of Special Branch*
FIBUA	*fighting in built-up areas*

FMB	*forward mounting base*
forward mounted	*in a temporary base*
foxtrot	*on foot*
FRV	*final rendezvous*
GOA	*ground observation apparatus*
GPMG	*general-purpose machine gun*
green army	*regular forces*
head shed	*Special Forces boss*
HME	*home-made explosives*
HMSU	*Headquarters Mobile Support Unit*
IA	*immediate action*
INLA	*Irish National Liberation Army*
IWB	*inside-the-waistband holster*
longs	*rifles*
LUP	*laying-up point*
M60	*5.56 calibre machine gun*
maggot	*sleeping bag*
MT	*Military Transport*
ND	*negligent discharge*
NIRTT	*Northern Ireland Reinforcement Training Team*
NITAT	*Northern Ireland Training and Advisory Team*
one up	*solo*
op	*an operator*
OP	*observation post*
ops room	*operations room*
out-of-bounds area	*an area temporarily off limits to any other agency than Special Forces*
player	*terrorist*
PTI	*physical training instructor*
PU	*pick-up*
PVCP	*permanent vehicle checkpoint*
RMTU	*Royal Marines Training Unit*
RTA	*road traffic accident*
RTB	*return to base*
R-to-I	*resistance to interrogation*
RTU	*return to unit*

GLOSSARY

RUC	*Royal Ulster Constabulary*
Rupert	*officer*
SB	*Special Branch*
shorts	*pistols*
SLR	*self-loading rifle*
SMG	*sub-machine gun*
SOCO	*scene of crime officer*
SP	*Special Projects*
spook	*Intelligence Corps analyst/collator*
TCG	*Tasking and Coordination Group*
TOG	*time on the ground*
tout	*informer, traitor*
UDA	*Ulster Defence Association*
UDR	*Ulster Defence Regiment*
UVF	*Ulster Volunteer Force*
VC	*voluntary contribution*
VRN	*vehicle registration number*
Walts	*(short for Walter Mittys) SAS nickname for Det operators*
WO	*Warrant Officer*
WRNS	*Women's Royal Naval Service (Wrens)*